# *Parametric Modeling*

# *with SolidWorks 2011*

**Randy H. Shih**
*Oregon Institute of Technology*

**Paul J. Schilling**
*University of New Orleans*

ISBN: 978-1-58503-633-2

**SDC**
**PUBLICATIONS**

Mission, Kansas

**Schroff Development Corporation**

P.O. Box 1334

Mission KS 66222

(913) 262-2664

www.SDCpublications.com

Publisher: Stephen Schroff

**Trademarks**

LEGO, MINDSTORMS and the Brick and Knob configurations are trademarks of the LEGO Group.
SolidWorks is a registered trademark of SolidWorks Corporation.
Microsoft Windows is a registered trademark of Microsoft Corporation.
All other trademarks are trademarks of their respective holders.

**Examination Copies:**

Books received as examination copies are for review purposes only and may not be made available for student use. Resale of examination copies is prohibited.

**Electronic Files:**

Any electronic files associated with this book are licensed to the original user only. These files may not be transferred to any other party.

Shih, Randy H. and Schilling, Paul J.
    Parametric Modeling with SolidWorks 2011
  Randy H. Shih and Paul J. Schilling

  ISBN 978-1-58503-633-2

The authors and publisher of this book have used their best efforts in preparing this book. These efforts include the development, research and testing of the material presented. The author and publisher shall not be liable in any event for incidental or consequential damages with, or arising out of, the furnishing, performance, or use of the material.

Printed and bound in the United States of America.

# Preface

The primary goal of **Parametric Modeling with SolidWorks 2011** is to introduce the aspects of designing with **Solid Modeling** and **Parametric Modeling**. This text is intended to be used as a practical training guide for students and professionals. This text uses *SolidWorks 2011* as the modeling tool and the chapters proceed in a pedagogical fashion to guide you from constructing basic solid models to building intelligent mechanical designs, creating multi-view drawings and assembly models. This text takes a hands-on, exercise-intensive approach to all the important *Parametric Modeling* techniques and concepts. This textbook contains a series of fifteen tutorial style lessons designed to introduce beginning CAD users to **SolidWorks**. This text is also helpful to *SolidWorks* users upgrading from a previous release of the software. The solid modeling techniques and concepts discussed in this text are also applicable to other parametric feature-based CAD packages. The basic premise of this book is that the more designs you create using *SolidWorks*, the better you learn the software. With this in mind, each lesson introduces a new set of commands and concepts, building on previous lessons. This book does not attempt to cover all of the *SolidWorks* features, only to provide an introduction to the software. It is intended to help you establish a good basis for exploring and growing in the exciting field of **Computer Aided Engineering**.

# Acknowledgments

This book would not have been possible without a great deal of support. The effort and support of the editorial and production staff of Schroff Development Corporation is gratefully acknowledged. I would especially like to thank Stephen Schroff and Mary Schmidt for their support and helpful suggestions during this project. Andy Bell and Tony Allen of LEGO® MINDSTORMS® Education also provided valuable assistance and help toward the project. Don Domes of ORTOP granting the use of their designs and resources are also appreciated. I am also very grateful that the Mechanical Engineering Technology Department of Oregon Institute of Technology has provided me with an excellent environment in which to pursue my interests in teaching and research.

Truly unbounded thanks are due to my wife Hsiu-Ling and daughter Casandra for their understanding and encouragement throughout this project.

Randy H. Shih, Spring, 2011

I would like to echo the appreciation for the support of Stephen Schroff, Mary Schmidt and the staff of Schroff Development Corporation.   In addition, the support of the Department of Mechanical Engineering at the University of New Orleans is gratefully acknowledged.

Paul J. Schilling, Spring, 2011

# Table of Contents

## Chapter 3
## Constructive Solid Geometry Concepts

## Chapter 4
## Feature Design Tree

## Chapter 5
## Geometric Relations Fundamentals

## Chapter 6
## Geometric Construction Tools

# Chapter 7
# Parent/Child Relationships and the BORN Technique

# Chapter 8
# Part Drawings and Associative Functionality

## Chapter 9
## Reference Geometry and Auxiliary Views

## Chapter 10
## Symmetrical Features in Designs

## Chapter 11
## Advanced 3D Construction Tools

## Chapter 12
## Assembly Modeling – Putting It All Together

## Chapter 13
## Design Library and Basic Motion Study

## Chapter 14
# Design Analysis with SimulationXpress

## Chapter 15
# CSWA Exam Preparation

## Chapter 16
# Assembly Modeling with the LEGO® MINDSTORMS® NXT Set

## Index

## Certified SolidWorks Associate (CSWA) Exam Overview

The Certified SolidWorks Associate (CSWA) Exam is a performance-based exam. The examination is comprised of 10 – 20 questions to be completed in three hours. The test items will require you to use the *SolidWorks* software to perform specific tasks and then answer questions about the tasks.

Performance-based testing is defined as *Testing by Doing*. This means you actually perform the given task then answer the questions regarding the task. Performance-based testing is widely accepted as a better way of insuring the user has the skills needed, rather than just recalling information.

The CSWA examination is designed to test specific performance tasks in the following areas:

### Sketch Entities – lines, rectangles, circles, arcs, ellipses, centerlines
Objectives: Creating Sketch Entities.

### Sketch Tools – offset, convert, trim
Objectives: Using Sketch Tools.

## Sketch Relations

Objectives: Using Geometric Relations.

| Certification Examination Performance Task | Covered in this book on Chapter – Page |
|---|---|

## Boss and Cut Features – Extrudes, Revolves, Sweeps, Lofts

Objectives: Creating Basic Swept Shapes.

| Certification Examination Performance Task | Covered in this book on Chapter – Page |
|---|---|

Certified Associate Reference Guide

## Fillets and Chamfers

Objectives: Creating Fillets and Chamfers.

| Certification Examination<br>Performance Task | Covered in this book on<br>Chapter – Page |
|---|---|

## Linear, Circular, and Fill Patterns

Objectives: Creating Patterned Features.

| Certification Examination<br>Performance Task | Covered in this book on<br>Chapter – Page |
|---|---|

## Dimensions

Objectives: Applying and Editing Smart Dimensions.

| Certification Examination<br>Performance Task | Covered in this book on<br>Chapter – Page |
|---|---|

## Feature Conditions – Start and End

Objectives: Controlling Feature Start and End Conditions.

## Mass Properties

Objectives: Obtaining Mass Properties for Parts and Assemblies.

## Materials

Objectives: Applying Material Selection to Parts.

## Inserting Components

Objectives: Inserting Components into an Assembly.

Certified Associate Reference Guide

## Standard Mates – Coincident, Parallel, Perpendicular, Tangent, Concentric, Distance, Angle

Objectives: Applying Standard Mates to Constrain Assemblies.

## Reference Geometry – Planes, Axis, Mate References

Objectives: Creating Reference Planes, Axes, and Mate References

## Drawing Sheets and Views

Objectives: Creating and Setting Properties for Drawing Sheets; Inserting and Editing Standard Views.

## Annotations
Objectives: Creating Annotations.

## Tips about Taking the Certified SolidWorks Associate (CSWA) Examination

1. **Study:** The first step to maximize your potential on an exam is to sufficiently prepare for it. You need to be familiar with the *SolidWorks* package, and this can only be achieved by doing designs and exploring the different commands available. The Certified SolidWorks Associate (CSWA) exam is designed to measure your familiarity with the *SolidWorks* software. You must be able to perform the given task and answer the exam questions correctly and quickly.

2. **Make Notes**: Take notes of what you learn either while attending classroom sessions or going through study material. Use these notes as a review guide before taking the actual test.

3. **Time Management**: The examination has a time limit. Manage the time you spend on each question. Always remember you do not need to score 100% to pass the exam. Also, keep in mind that some questions are weighed more heavily and may take more time to answer. You can flip back and forth to view different problems during the test time by using the arrow buttons. If you encounter a question you cannot answer in a reasonable amount of time, use the *Save As* feature in *SolidWorks* to save a copy of the file, and move on to the next question. You can return to any question and enter or change the answer as long as you do not hit the [**I am done**] button.

4. **Use the *SolidWords Help System***: If you get confused and can't think of the answer, remember the *SolidWorks Help System* is a great tool to confirm your considerations. In preparing for the exam, familiarize yourself with the help utility organization (e.g., Contents, Index, Search options).

5. **Use Internet Search**: Use of an internet search utility is allowed during the test. If a test question requires general knowledge, for example definitions of engineering or drafting concepts (stress, yield strength, auxiliary view, etc.), remember the internet is available as a tool to assist in your considerations.

6. **Use Common Sense**: If you are unable to get the correct answer and unable to eliminate all distracters, then you need to select the best answer from the remaining selections. This may be a task of selecting the best answer from amongst several correct answers, or it may be selecting the least incorrect answer from amongst several poor answers.

7. **Be Cautious and Don't Act in Haste:** Devote some time to ponder and think of the correct answer. Ensure that you interpret all the options correctly before selecting from available choices. Don't go into panic mode while taking a test. Use the ***Arrow Buttons*** to review each question. When you are confident that you have answered all questions, end the examination using the [**I am done**] button to submit your answers for scoring. You will receive a score report once you have submitted your answers.

8. **Relax before Exam:** In order to avoid last minute stress, make sure that you arrive 10 to15 minutes early and relax before taking the exam.

# Chapter 1
# Introduction – Getting Started

## Learning Objectives

- ♦ **Development of Computer Geometric Modeling**
- ♦ **Feature-Based Parametric Modeling**
- ♦ **Startup Options and Units Setup**
- ♦ **SolidWorks Screen Layout**
- ♦ **User Interface & Mouse Buttons**
- ♦ **SolidWorks On-Line Help**

## Introduction

The rapid changes in the field of **Computer Aided Engineering** (CAE) have brought exciting advances in the engineering community. Recent advances have made the long-sought goal of **concurrent engineering** closer to a reality. CAE has become the core of concurrent engineering and is aimed at reducing design time, producing prototypes faster, and achieving higher product quality. *SolidWorks* is an integrated package of mechanical computer aided engineering software tools developed by *SolidWorks Corporation*. *SolidWorks* is a tool that facilitates a concurrent engineering approach to the design and stress-analysis of mechanical engineering products. The computer models can also be used by manufacturing equipment such as machining centers, lathes, mills, or rapid prototyping machines to manufacture the product. In this text, we will be dealing only with the solid modeling modules used for part design and part drawings.

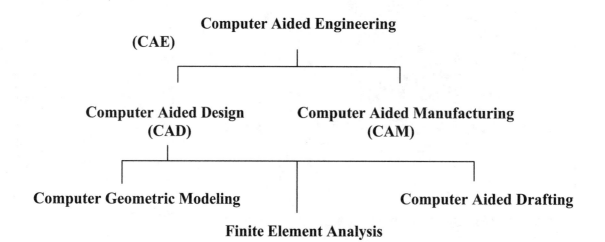

## Development of Computer Geometric Modeling

**Computer geometric modeling** is a relatively new technology, and its rapid expansion in the last fifty years is truly amazing. Computer-modeling technology has advanced along with the development of computer hardware. The first generation CAD programs, developed in the 1950s, were mostly non-interactive; CAD users were required to create program-codes to generate the desired two-dimensional (2D) geometric shapes. Initially, the development of CAD technology occurred mostly in academic research facilities. The Massachusetts Institute of Technology, Carnegie-Mellon University, and Cambridge University were the leading pioneers at that time. The interest in CAD technology spread quickly and several major industry companies, such as General Motors, Lockheed, McDonnell, IBM, and Ford Motor Co., participated in the development of interactive CAD programs in the 1960s. Usage of CAD systems was primarily in the automotive industry, aerospace industry, and government agencies that developed their own programs for their specific needs. The 1960s also marked the beginning of the development of finite element analysis methods for computer stress analysis and computer aided manufacturing for generating machine toolpaths.

The 1970s are generally viewed as the years of the most significant progress in the development of computer hardware, namely the invention and development of **microprocessors**. With the improvement in computing power, new types of 3D CAD programs that were user-friendly and interactive became reality. CAD technology quickly expanded from very simple **computer aided drafting** to very complex **computer aided design**. The use of 2D and 3D wireframe modelers was accepted as the leading edge technology that could increase productivity in industry. The developments of surface modeling and solid modeling technologies were taking shape by the late 1970s, but the high cost of computer hardware and programming slowed the development of such technology. During this period, the available CAD systems all required room-sized mainframe computers that were extremely expensive.

In the 1980s, improvements in computer hardware brought the power of mainframes to the desktop at less cost and with more accessibility to the general public. By the mid-1980s, CAD technology had become the main focus of a variety of manufacturing industries and was very competitive with traditional design/drafting methods. It was during this period of time that 3D solid modeling technology had major advancements, which boosted the usage of CAE technology in industry.

The introduction of the *feature-based parametric solid modeling* approach, at the end of the 1980s, elevated CAD/CAM/CAE technology to a new level. In the 1990s, CAD programs evolved into powerful design/manufacturing/management tools. CAD technology has come a long way, and during these years of development, modeling schemes progressed from two-dimensional (2D) wireframe to three-dimensional (3D) wireframe, to surface modeling, to solid modeling and, finally, to feature-based parametric solid modeling.

The first generation CAD packages were simply 2D **computer aided drafting** programs, basically the electronic equivalents of the drafting board. For typical models, the use of this type of program would require that several to many views of the objects be created individually as they would be on the drafting board. The 3D designs remained in the designer's mind, not in the computer database. Mental translations of 3D objects to 2D views are required throughout the use of these packages. Although such systems have some advantages over traditional board drafting, they are still tedious and labor intensive. The need for the development of 3D modelers came quite naturally, given the limitations of the 2D drafting packages.

The development of three-dimensional modeling schemes started with three-dimensional (3D) wireframes. Wireframe models are models consisting of points and edges, which are straight lines connecting between appropriate points. The edges of wireframe models are used, similar to lines in 2D drawings, to represent transitions of surfaces and features. The use of lines and points is also a very economical way to represent 3D designs.

The development of the 3D wireframe modeler was a major leap in the area of computer geometric modeling. The computer database in the 3D wireframe modeler contains the locations of all the points in space coordinates, and it is typically sufficient to create just one model rather than multiple views of the same model.  This single 3D model can then be viewed from any direction as needed.  Most 3D wireframe modelers allow the user to create projected lines/edges of 3D wireframe models. In comparison to other types of 3D modelers, the 3D wireframe modelers require very little computing power and generally can be used to achieve reasonably good representations of 3D models. However, because surface definition is not part of a wireframe model, all wireframe images have the inherent problem of ambiguity. Two examples of such ambiguity are illustrated.

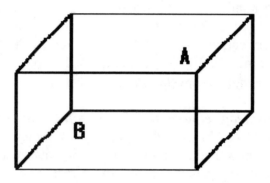

**Wireframe Ambiguity**: Which corner is in front, A or B?

**A non-realizable object**: Wireframe models contain no surface definitions.

Surface modeling is the logical development in computer geometry modeling to follow the 3D wireframe modeling scheme by organizing and grouping edges that define polygonal surfaces. Surface modeling describes the part's surfaces but not its interiors. Designers are still required to interactively examine surface models to insure that the various surfaces on a model are contiguous throughout. Many of the concepts used in 3D wireframe and surface modelers are incorporated in the solid modeling scheme, but it is solid modeling that offers the most advantages as a design tool.

In the solid modeling presentation scheme, the solid definitions include nodes, edges, and surfaces, and it is a complete and unambiguous mathematical representation of a precisely enclosed and filled volume. Unlike the surface modeling method, solid modelers start with a solid or use topology rules to guarantee that all of the surfaces are stitched together properly. Two predominant methods for representing solid models are **constructive solid geometry** (CSG) representation and **boundary representation** (B-rep).

The CSG representation method can be defined as the combination of 3D solid primitives. What constitutes a "primitive" varies somewhat with the software but typically includes a rectangular prism, a cylinder, a cone, a wedge, and a sphere. Most solid modelers also allow the user to define additional primitives, which are shapes typically formed by the basic shapes. The underlying concept of the CSG representation method is very straightforward; we simply **add** or **subtract** one primitive from another. The CSG approach is also known as the machinist's approach, as it can be used to simulate the manufacturing procedures for creating the 3D object.

In the B-rep representation method, objects are represented in terms of their spatial boundaries. This method defines the points, edges, and surfaces of a volume, and/or issues commands that sweep or rotate a defined face into a third dimension to form a solid. The object is then made up of the unions of these surfaces that completely and precisely enclose a volume.

By the 1980s, a new paradigm called *concurrent engineering* had emerged. With concurrent engineering, designers, design engineers, analysts, manufacturing engineers, and management engineers all work together closely right from the initial stages of the design. In this way, all aspects of the design can be evaluated and any potential problems can be identified right from the start and throughout the design process. Using the principles of concurrent engineering, a new type of computer modeling technique appeared. The technique is known as the *feature-based parametric modeling technique*. The key advantage of the *feature-based parametric modeling technique* is its capability to produce very flexible designs. Changes can be made easily and design alternatives can be evaluated with minimum effort. Various software packages offer different approaches to feature-based parametric modeling, yet the end result is a flexible design defined by its design variables and parametric features.

## Feature-Based Parametric Modeling

One of the key elements in the *SolidWorks* solid modeling software is its use of the **feature-based parametric modeling technique**. The feature-based parametric modeling approach has elevated solid modeling technology to the level of a very powerful design tool. Parametric modeling automates the design and revision procedures by the use of parametric features. Parametric features control the model geometry by the use of design variables. The word *parametric* means that the geometric definitions of the design, such as dimensions, can be varied at any time during the design process. Features are predefined parts or construction tools for which users define the key parameters. A part is described as a sequence of engineering features, which can be modified/changed at any time. The concept of parametric features makes modeling more closely match the actual design-manufacturing process than the mathematics of a solid modeling program. In parametric modeling, models and drawings are updated automatically when the design is refined.

Parametric modeling offers many benefits:

- **We begin with simple, conceptual models with minimal detail; this approach conforms to the design philosophy of "shape before size."**

- **Geometric relations, dimensional constraints, and relational parametric equations can be used to capture design intent.**

- **The ability to update an entire system, including parts, assemblies and drawings after changing one parameter of complex designs.**

- **We can quickly explore and evaluate different design variations and alternatives to determine the best design.**

- **Existing design data can be reused to create new designs.**

- **Quick design turn-around.**

## Getting Started with *SolidWorks*

[About SolidWorks dialog box image]

SolidWorks® Premium 2011 x64 Edition

SP0.0

Serial No.:

© 1995-2010 Dassault Systèmes
U.S. Patents 5,815,154; 6,219,049; 6,219,055; 6,611,725; 6,844,877; 6,898,560;
6,906,712; 7,079,990; 7,477,262; 7,558,705; 7,571,079; 7,590,497; 7,643,027;
7,672,822; 7,688,318; and 7,694,238; and certain foreign patents, including EP 1,116,190
and JP 3,517,643. Other patents pending.

Portions of this software © 1999, 2002-2010 ComponentOne.
Portions of this software © 2007-2010 DriveWorks Ltd.
Portions of this software © 1998-2010 Geometric Ltd.
Portions of this software © 1996-2010 Microsoft Corporation. All rights reserved.
Portions of this software © 1995-2010 Spatial Corporation.
Portions of this software © 2001-2010 Luxology, Inc. All rights reserved, patents pending.
Portions of this software © 1992-2010 The University of Tennessee. All rights

License Agreement...    Adobe Copyrights...

Click Connect to visit the SolidWorks web site and learn more about the Company and Product.    Connect...

- *SolidWorks* is composed of several application software modules (these modules are called *applications*), all sharing a common database. In this text, the main concentration is placed on the solid modeling modules used for part design. The general procedures required in creating solid models, engineering drawings, and assemblies are illustrated.

How to start *SolidWorks* depends on the type of workstation and the particular software configuration you are using. With most *Windows* systems, you may select **SolidWorks** on the *Start* menu or select the **SolidWorks** icon on the desktop. Consult your instructor or technical support personnel if you have difficulty starting the software. The program takes a while to load, so be patient.

The tutorials in this text are based on the assumption that you are using the *SolidWorks* default settings. If your system has been customized for other uses, contact your technical support personnel to restore the default software configuration.

Once the program is loaded into the memory, the *SolidWorks* program window appears. This screen contains the *Menu Bar* and the *Task Pane*. The *Menu Bar* contains a subset of commonly used tools from the *Standard* toolbar (**New**, **Open**, **Save**, etc.), the *SolidWorks* menus, the *SolidWorks Search* oval, and a flyout menu of *Help* options. By default, the *SolidWorks* menus are hidden.  To display them, move the cursor over or click the *SolidWorks* logo.

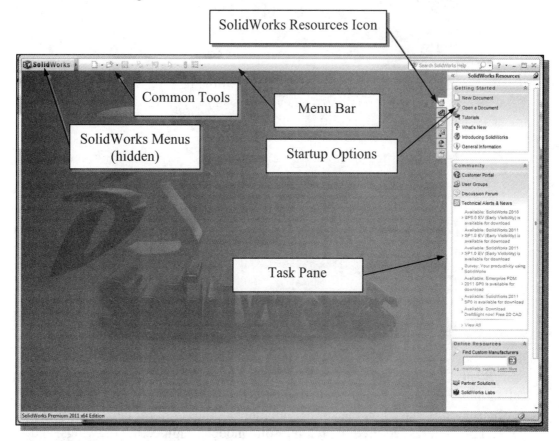

If the *Task Pane* does not appear to the right of the screen, right click on the *Menu Bar* to reveal a menu of toolbars and select the **Task Pane**, or select *View* from the *SolidWorks Menus* and select **Task Pane**.  Other options for the *Task Pane* are the *Design Library* and the *File Explorer*.  The icons for these options appear below the **SolidWorks Resources** icon.  To collapse the *Task Pane*, click anywhere in the main area of the *SolidWorks* window.  (**NOTE:**  If the *Task Pane* does not collapse upon clicking in the graphics area, it has been 'pinned' using the *Auto Show* button in the upper right corner. Simply left-click on the icon to unpin the *Task Pane* and allow it to collapse.)

The following two startup options are available: **New** and **Open**.  The **New** option allows us to start a new modeling task. The **Open** option allows us to open an existing model file.  These two commands can be executed in the *Getting Started* dialog box in the *SolidWorks Resources* task pane or on the *Menu Bar*.  The *Getting Started* dialog box also contains a **Tutorials** option which provides some quick helps that illustrate the features and general procedures of using *SolidWorks*.

➢ Select the **New** icon on the *Menu Bar* with a single click of the left-mouse-button.  The *New SolidWorks Document* dialog box appears.

➢ **NOTE:**  If the *Units and Dimensions Standard* dialog box appears, click **OK** to accept the default settings.

Three icons appear in the *New SolidWorks Document* dialog box. Selecting the appropriate icon will allow creation of a new **Part**, **Assembly**, or **Drawing** file. A part is a single three-dimensional (3D) solid model. Parts are the basic building blocks in modeling with *SolidWorks*. An assembly is a 3D arrangement of parts (components) and/or other assemblies (subassemblies). A drawing is a 2D representation of a part or assembly.

New SolidWorks Document

Part — a 3D representation of a single design component

Assembly — a 3D arrangement of parts and/or other assemblies

Drawing — a 2D engineering drawing, typically of a part or assembly

Advanced        OK        Cancel        Help

➢ Select the **Part** icon as shown.  Click **OK** in the *New SolidWorks Document* dialog box to open a new part file.

## Units Setup

When starting a new CAD file, the first thing we should do is to choose the units we would like to use.  We will use the English (feet and inches) setting for this example.

Part1

Options
Changes options settings for SolidWorks.

➢ Select the **Options** icon from the *Menu Bar* as shown to open the *Options* dialog box.  (The *Options* dialog box can also be opened from the *Tools* pull-down menu.)

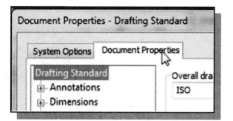

➢ When the *Options* dialog box opens, the **System Options** tab is active. The *Units* setup is located under the Document Properties tab. Select the **Document Properties** tab as shown.

➢ Select **Units** on the left menu as highlighted below. Select **IPS (inch, pound, second)** under the *Unit system* options. Select **.123** in the *Decimals* spin box for the *Length units* as shown to define the degree of accuracy with which the units will be displayed. Click **OK** at the bottom of the *Document Properties - Units* window to set the units.

Document Properties - Units

System Options | Document Properties

Drafting Standard
   ⊞ Annotations
   ⊞ Dimensions
      Virtual Sharps
   ⊞ Tables
Detailing
Grid/Snap
Units
Colors
Material Properties
Image Quality
Plane Display
DimXpert
   — Size Dimension
   — Location Dimension
   — Chain Dimension
   — Geometric Tolerance
   — Chamfer Controls
   — Display Options

Unit system
- ○ MKS (meter, kilogram, second)
- ○ CGS (centimeter, gram, second)
- ○ MMGS (millimeter, gram, second)
- ◉ IPS (inch, pound, second)
- ○ Custom

| Type | Unit | Decimals | Fractions | More |
|------|------|----------|-----------|------|
| **Basic Units** | | | | |
| Length | inches | .123 ▼ | | ... |
| Dual Dimension Length | inches | .12 ▲ | | ... |
| Angle | degrees | .123 | | |
| **Mass/Section Properties** | | .1234 | | |
| | | .12345 | | |
| Length | inches | .123456 | | |
| Mass | pounds | .1234567 | | |
| Per Unit Volume | inches^3 | .12345678 ▼ | | |
| **Motion Units** | | | | |
| Time | second | .12 | | |
| Force | pound-force | .12 | | |
| Power | watt | .12 | | |
| Energy | BTU | .12 | | |

OK        Cancel        Help

## *SolidWorks* Screen Layout

The default *SolidWorks* drawing screen contains the *Menu Bar*, the *Heads-up View* toolbar, the *FeatureManager Design Tree*, the *CommandManager* (below the *Menu Bar*), the *task pane* (collapsed to the right of the graphics area in the figure below), and the *Status Bar*. A line of quick text appears next to the icon as you move the *mouse cursor* over different icons. You may resize the *SolidWorks* drawing window by click and drag at the edges of the window, or relocate the window by click and drag at the *window title* area.

- **Menu Bar Toolbar**

In the default view of the *Menu Bar*, only the toolbar options are visible. The default *Menu Bar* toolbar consists of a subset of frequently used commands from the *Menu Bar* as shown above.

- **SolidWorks Pull-down Menus**

To display the *pull-down* menus, move the cursor over or click the *SolidWorks* logo. The *pull-down* menus contain operations that you can use for all modes of the system.

- **Heads-up View Toolbar**

The *Heads-up View* toolbar allows us quick access to frequently used view-related commands.  **NOTE:**  You can hide or customize the *Heads-up View* toolbar.

- **Features Toolbar**

When the *CommandManager* is used, the *Features* toolbar appears as shown above. When the *CommandManager* is turned *OFF*, the *Features* toolbar is displayed (by default) vertically at the left of the *SolidWorks* window.  The *Features* toolbar allows us quick access to frequently used features-related commands, such as **Extruded Boss/Base, Extruded Cut,** and **Revolved Boss/Base.**

- **Sketch Toolbar**

When the *CommandManager* is used, the *Sketch* toolbar appears as shown above. When the *CommandManager* is turned *OFF*, the *Sketch* toolbar is displayed (by default) vertically at the right of the *SolidWorks* window.  The *Sketch* toolbar provides tools for creating the basic geometry that can be used to create features and parts.

- **CommandManager**

The Solidworks *CommandManager* provides an alternate method for displaying the most commonly used toolbars. If the *CommandManager* is not visible, it can be turned *ON* by **right clicking** on any toolbar and selecting **Command-*Manager** from the top of the pop-up menu list of toolbars.

The *CommandManager* is a context-sensitive toolbar that dynamically updates based on the user's selection. When you click a tab below the *CommandManager*, it updates to display the corresponding toolbar. For example, if you click the *Sketches* tab, the *Sketch* toolbar appears. By default, the *CommandManager* has toolbars embedded in it based on the document type.

The display of the *CommandManager* is shown below, once with the *Features* toolbar selected, once with the *Sketch* toolbar selected. You will notice that when the *CommandManager* is used, the *Sketch* and *Features* toolbars do not appear on the left and right edges of the display window.

To turn *OFF* the *CommandManager* and use the standard display of toolbars, right click on the *CommandManager* (or any other toolbar) and toggle the *CommandManager* *OFF* by selecting it at the top of the pop-up menu.

**IMPORTANT NOTE:** The lessons in this text use the standard display of toolbars. If a user prefers to use the *CommandManager*, the only change is that it may be necessary to select the appropriate tab prior to selecting a command. For example, if the instruction is to "select the **Extruded Boss** command from the *Features* toolbar," it may be necessary to first select the **Features** tab on the *CommandManager* to display the *Features* toolbar.

- **Standard Display of Toolbars**

The default *SolidWorks* drawing screen using the standard display of toolbars, with the *CommandManager* turned *OFF*, is shown below.  The *Features* toolbar appears at the left of the window and the *Sketch* toolbar at the right.  This is the standard view used in the lessons in this text.

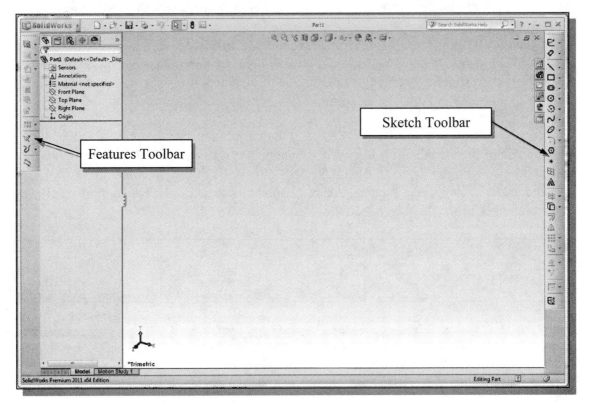

- **Mouse Gestures**

You can use a mouse gesture as a shortcut to execute some common commands. To activate a mouse gesture, move the cursor inside the graphics area, hold the right mouse button down and drag the mouse.  A gesture guide appears showing command mappings for the gesture directions.  Drag the mouse (while holding the right button down) across the appropriate button to execute the command.

There are separate gesture guides for drawings, assemblies, parts, and sketches.  The appropriate guide appears based on the current operation.  For example, in sketch mode a gesture guide with sketch commands appears as shown here. You can customize up to eight gestures for each guide.  To view or edit the current mouse gesture assignments, select **Customize** on the *Tools* pull-down menu, then select the **Mouse Gestures** tab.

- **FeatureManager Design Tree/PropertyManager/ConfigurationManager/ DimXpertManager/DisplayManager**

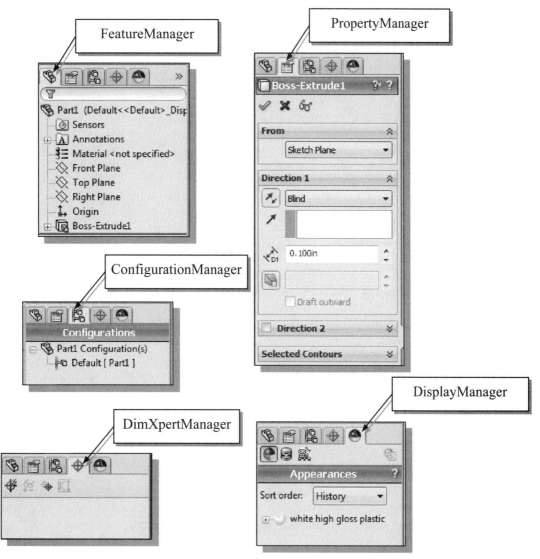

The left panel of the *SolidWorks* window is used to display the *FeatureManager Design Tree*, the *PropertyManager*, the *ConfigurationManager*, the *DimXpertManager* and the *DisplayManager*. These options can be chosen by selecting the appropriate tab at the top of the panel. The *FeatureManager Design Tree* provides an overview of the active part, drawing, or assembly in outline form. It can be used to show and hide selected features, filter contents, and manage access to features and editing. The *PropertyManager* opens automatically when commands are executed or entities are selected in the graphics window, and is used to make selections, enter values, and accept commands. The *Configuration Manager* is used to create, select, and view multiple configurations of parts and assemblies. The *DimXpertManager* lists the tolerance features defined using the SolidWorks 'DimXpert for parts' tools. The *DisplayManager* is used to control appearances, decals, scenes, lights, and cameras that are applied to the current model.

- **Graphics Area**

The graphics area is the area where models and drawings are displayed.

- **Reference Triad**

The *Reference Triad* appears in the graphics area of part and assembly documents. The triad is shown to help orient the user when viewing models and is for reference only.

- **Origin**

The *Origin* represents the (0,0,0) coordinate in a model or sketch. A model origin appears blue; a sketch origin appears red.

- **Confirmation Corner**

The *Confirmation Corner* offers an alternate way to accept features.

- **Graphics Cursor or Crosshairs**

The *graphics cursor* shows the location of the pointing device in the graphics window. During geometric construction, the coordinate of the cursor is displayed in the *Status Bar* area, located at the bottom of the screen. The cursor's appearance depends on the selected command or option.

- **Message and Status Bar**

The *Message and Status Bar* area displays a single-line description of a command when the cursor is on top of a command icon. This area also displays information pertinent to the active operation. In the figure above, the cursor coordinates are displayed while in the *Sketch* mode.

## Mouse Buttons

*SolidWorks* utilizes the mouse buttons extensively. In learning *SolidWorks'* interactive environment, it is important to understand the basic functions of the mouse buttons.

- **Left mouse button**
  The **left-mouse-button** is used for most operations, such as selecting menus and icons, or picking graphic entities. One click of the button is used to select icons, menus and form entries, and to pick graphic items.

- **Right mouse button**
  The **right-mouse-button** is used to bring up additional available options in a context-sensitive pop-up menu. These menus provide shortcuts to frequently used commands.

- **Middle mouse button/wheel**
  The middle mouse button/wheel can be used to Rotate (hold down the wheel button and drag the mouse), Pan (hold down the wheel button and drag the mouse while holding down the **Ctrl** key), or Zoom (hold down the wheel button and drag the mouse while holding down the **Shift** key) realtime. Spinning the wheel allows zooming to the position of the cursor.

Brings up additional available options.

Allows quick Pan, Zoom, and Rotate.

Picks icons, menus, and graphic entities.

## [Esc] – Canceling Commands

The [**Esc**] key is used to cancel a command in *SolidWorks*. The [**Esc**] key is located near the top-left corner of the keyboard. Sometimes, it may be necessary to press the [**Esc**] key twice to cancel a command; it depends on where we are in the command sequence. For some commands, the [**Esc**] key is used to exit the command.

## On-Line Help

❖ Several types of on-line help are available at any time during an *SolidWorks* session. *SolidWorks* provides many on-line help functions, such as:

• The **Help** menu: Click on the **Help** option in *Menu Bar* to access the *SolidWorks Help* menu system. (**NOTE:** Move the cursor over the *SolidWorks* logo in the *Menu Bar* to display the pull-down menu options.) The **SolidWorks Help** option provides general help information, such as command options and command references. The **SolidWorks Tutorials** option provides a collection of tutorials illustrating different *SolidWorks* operations.

• The SolidWorks Tutorials can also be accessed from the *SolidWorks Resources* task pane on the right side of the screen by selecting **Tutorials**.

• The **SolidWorks Help** option can also be accessed by clicking on the **Help** icon at the right end of the *Menu Bar*.

## Leaving *SolidWorks*

➢ To leave *SolidWorks*, use the left-mouse-button and click on **File** at the top of the *SolidWorks* screen window, then choose **Exit** from the pull-down menu. (**NOTE:** Move the cursor over the *SolidWorks* logo in the *Menu Bar* to display the pull-down menu options.)

## Creating a CAD Files Folder

It is a good practice to create a separate folder to store your CAD files. You should not save your CAD files in the same folder where the *SolidWorks* application is located. It is much easier to organize and backup your project files if they are in a separate folder. Making folders within this folder for different types of projects will help you organize your CAD files even further. When creating CAD files in *SolidWorks*, it is strongly recommended that you *save* your CAD files on the hard drive.

➢ To create a new folder in the *Windows* environment:

1. In *My Computer*, or start *Windows Explorer* under the *Start* menu, open the folder in which you want to create a new folder.

2. On the **File** menu, point to **New**, and then click **Folder**. The new folder appears with a temporary name.

3. Type a name for the new folder, and then press **ENTER**.

**NOTES:**

# Chapter 2
# Parametric Modeling Fundamentals

## Learning Objectives

- ♦ **Create Simple Extruded Solid Models**
- ♦ **Understand the Basic Parametric Modeling Procedure**
- ♦ **Create 2-D Sketches**
- ♦ **Understand the "Shape before Size" Approach**
- ♦ **Use the Dynamic Viewing Commands**
- ♦ **Create and Edit Parametric Dimensions**

Certified Associate Reference Guide

## Certified SolidWorks Associate Exam Objectives Coverage

### Sketch Entities – Lines, Rectangles, Circles, Arcs, Ellipses, Centerlines

Objectives: Creating Sketch Entities.

### Sketch Relations

Objectives: Using Geometric Relations.

### Boss and Cut Features – Extrudes, Revolves, Sweeps, Lofts

Objectives: Creating Basic Swept Features.

### Dimensions

Objectives: Applying and Editing Smart Dimensions.

### Feature Conditions – Start and End

Objectives: Controlling Feature Start and End Conditions.

# Introduction

The **feature-based parametric modeling** technique enables the designer to incorporate the original **design intent** into the construction of the model. The word ***parametric*** means the geometric definitions of the design, such as dimensions, can be varied at any time in the design process. Parametric modeling is accomplished by identifying and creating the key features of the design with the aid of computer software. The design variables, described in the sketches and described as parametric relations, can then be used to quickly modify/update the design.

In *SolidWorks*, the parametric part modeling process involves the following steps:

1.  **Create a rough two-dimensional sketch of the basic shape of the base feature of the design.**

2.  **Apply/modify geometric relations and dimensions to the two-dimensional sketch.**

3.  **Extrude, revolve, or sweep the parametric two-dimensional sketch to create the base solid feature of the design.**

4.  **Add additional parametric features by identifying feature relations and complete the design.**

5.  **Perform analyses on the computer model and refine the design as needed.**

6.  **Create the desired drawing views to document the design.**

The approach of creating two-dimensional sketches of the three-dimensional features is an effective way to construct solid models. Many designs are in fact the same shape in one direction. Computer input and output devices we use today are largely two-dimensional in nature, which makes this modeling technique quite practical. This method also conforms to the design process that helps the designer with conceptual design along with the capability to capture the ***design intent***. Most engineers and designers can relate to the experience of making rough sketches on restaurant napkins to convey conceptual design ideas. *SolidWorks* provides many powerful modeling and design-tools, and there are many different approaches to accomplishing modeling tasks. The basic principle of **feature-based modeling** is to build models by adding simple features one at a time. In this chapter, the general parametric part modeling procedure is illustrated; a very simple solid model with extruded features is used to introduce the *SolidWorks* user interface. The display viewing functions and the basic two-dimensional sketching tools are also demonstrated.

# The *Adjuster* Design

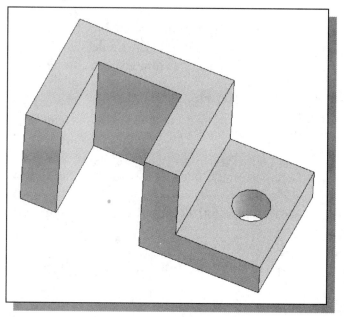

## Starting *SolidWorks*

1. Select the **SolidWorks** option on the *Start* menu or select the **SolidWorks** icon on the desktop to start *SolidWorks*. The *SolidWorks* main window will appear on the screen.

2. Select the **New** icon with a single click of the left-mouse-button on the *Menu Bar* toolbar.

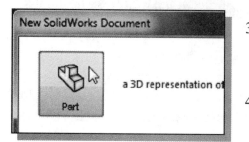

3. Select the **Part** icon with a single click of the left-mouse-button in the *New SolidWorks Document* dialog box.

4. Select **OK** in the *New SolidWorks Document* dialog box to open a new part document.

## *SolidWorks* Screen Layout

> The default *SolidWorks* drawing screen contains the *Menu Bar*, the *Heads-up View* toolbar, the *FeatureManager Design Tree*, the *Features* toolbar (at the left of the window by default), the *Sketch* toolbar (at the right of the window by default), the graphics area, the *task pane* (collapsed to the right of the graphics area in the figure below), and the *Status Bar*. A line of quick text appears next to the icon as you move the *mouse cursor* over different icons. You may resize the *SolidWorks* drawing window by click and drag at the edges of the window, or relocate the window by click and drag at the *window title* area.

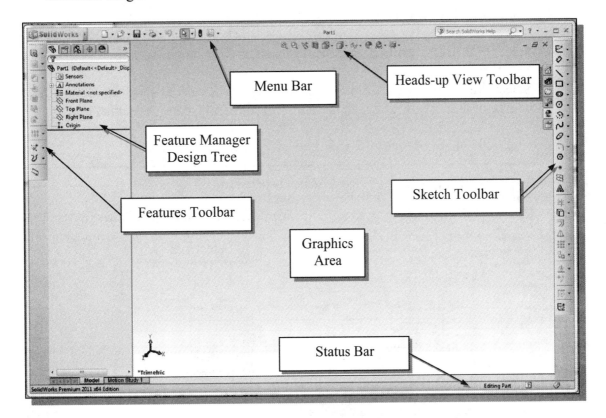

**IMPORTANT NOTE:** The Solidworks *CommandManager* provides an alternate method for displaying the most commonly used toolbars. If the *CommandManager* is active, the display will appear as shown on page 1-11. In this lesson, we will use the standard display of toolbars shown above. If a user prefers to use the *CommandManager*, the only change is that it may be necessary to select the appropriate tab prior to selecting a command. For example, if the instruction is to "select the Extruded Boss command from the *Features* toolbar," it may be necessary to first select the Features tab on the *CommandManager* to display the *Features* toolbar.

1. To turn **OFF** the *CommandManager* and use the standard display of toolbars, right click on the *CommandManager* (or any other toolbar) and toggle the *CommandManager OFF* by selecting it at the top of the pop-up menu.

## Units Setup

When starting a new CAD file, the first thing we should do is choose the units we would like to use. We will use the English setting (inches) for this example.

1. Select the **Options** icon from the *Menu Bar* toolbar to open the *Options* dialog box.

2. Select the **Document Properties** tab as shown below.

3. Click **Units** as shown below.

4. Select **IPS (inch, pound, second)** under the *Unit system* options.

5. Select **.123** in the *Decimals* spin box for the *Length units* as shown to define the degree of accuracy with which the units will be displayed to 3 decimal places.

6. Click **OK** in the *Options* dialog box to accept the selected settings

Document Properties - Units

System Options | Document Properties

**2. Document Properties**

Drafting Standard
  Annotations
  Dimensions
  Virtual Sharps
  Tables
Detailing
Grid/Snap
Units
Colors
Material Properties
Image Quality
Plane Display
DimXpert
  Size Dimension
  Location Dimension
  Chain Dimension
  Geometric Tolerance
  Chamfer Controls
  Display Options

**3. Units**

Unit system
  ○ MKS (meter, kilogram, second)
  ○ CGS (centimeter, gram, second)
  ○ MMGS (millimeter, gram, second)
  ● IPS (inch, pound, second)
  ○ Custom

**4. Select IPS**

| Type | Unit | Decimals | Fractions | More |
|------|------|----------|-----------|------|
| **Basic Units** | | | | |
| Length | inches | .123 | | ... |
| Dual Dimension Length | inches | .12 | | ... |
| Angle | degrees | .123 | | |
| | | .1234 | | |
| | | .12345 | | |
| **Mass/Section Properties** | | .123456 | | |
| Length | inches | .1234567 | | |
| Mass | pounds | .12345678 | | |
| Per Unit Volume | inches^3 | | | |
| **Motion Units** | | | | |
| Time | second | .12 | | |
| Force | pound-force | .12 | | |
| Power | watt | .12 | | |
| Energy | BTU | .12 | | |

**5. Decimals**

OK     Cancel     Help

## Creating Rough Sketches

Quite often during the early design stage, the shape of a design may not have any precise dimensions. Most conventional CAD systems require the user to input the precise lengths and locations of all geometric entities defining the design, which are not available during the early design stage. With *parametric modeling*, we can use the computer to elaborate and formulate the design idea further during the initial design stage. With *SolidWorks*, we can use the computer as an electronic sketchpad to help us concentrate on the formulation of forms and shapes for the design. This approach is the main advantage of *parametric modeling* over conventional solid-modeling techniques.

As the name implies, a ***rough sketch*** is not precise at all. When sketching, we simply sketch the geometry so that it closely resembles the desired shape. Precise scale or lengths are not needed. *SolidWorks* provides us with many tools to assist us in finalizing sketches. For example, geometric entities such as horizontal and vertical lines are set automatically. However, if the rough sketches are poor, it will require much more work to generate the desired parametric sketches. Here are some general guidelines for creating sketches in *SolidWorks*:

- **Create a sketch that is proportional to the desired shape.** Concentrate on the shapes and forms of the design.

- **Keep the sketches simple.** Leave out small geometry features such as fillets, rounds and chamfers. They can easily be placed using the Fillet and Chamfer commands after the parametric sketches have been established.

- **Exaggerate the geometric features of the desired shape.** For example, if the desired angle is 85 degrees, create an angle that is 50 or 60 degrees. Otherwise, *SolidWorks* might assume the intended angle to be a 90-degree angle.

- **Draw the geometry so that it does not overlap.** The geometry should eventually form a closed region. *Self-intersecting* geometry shapes are not allowed.

- **The sketched geometric entities should form a closed region.** To create a solid feature, such as an extruded solid, a closed region is required so that the extruded solid forms a 3D volume.

- ➢ **NOTE:** The concepts and principles involved in *parametric modeling* are very different from, and sometimes they are totally opposite to, those of conventional computer aided drafting. In order to understand and fully utilize *SolidWorks'* functionality, it will be helpful to take a *Zen* approach to learning the topics presented in this text: **Temporarily forget your knowledge and experiences of using conventional Computer Aided Drafting systems.**

## Step 1: Creating a Rough Sketch

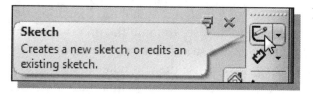

1. Select the **Sketch** button at the top of the *Sketch* toolbar to create a new sketch. Notice the left panel displays the *Edit Sketch PropertyManager* with the instruction "*Select a plane on which to create a sketch for the entity.*"

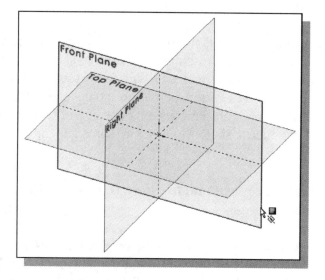

2. Move the cursor over the edge of the *Front Plane* in the graphics area. When the *Front Plane* is highlighted, click once with the **left-mouse-button** to select the *Front Plane* as the sketch plane for the new sketch.

3. Select the **Line** icon on the *Sketch* toolbar by clicking once with the **left-mouse-button**; this will activate the **Line** command. The *Line Properties PropertyManager* is displayed in the left panel.

## Graphics Cursors

Notice the cursor changes from an arrow to a pencil when a sketch entity is active.

4. Left-click a starting point for the shape, roughly near the lower center of the graphics window.

5. As you move the graphics cursor, you will see a digital readout next to the cursor. This readout gives you the line length. In the *Status Bar* area at the bottom of the window, the readout gives you the cursor location. Move the cursor around and you will notice different symbols appear at different locations.

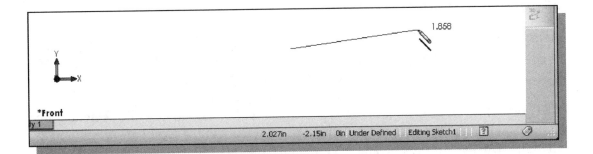

6. Move the graphics cursor toward the right side of the graphics window to create a horizontal line as shown below. Notice the geometric relation symbol displayed. When the **Horizontal** relation symbol is displayed, left-click to select **Point 2**.

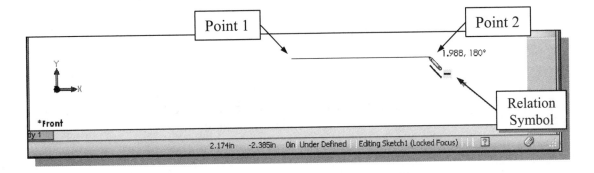

7. Complete the sketch as shown below, creating a closed region **ending at the starting point** (Point 1.) Do not be overly concerned with the actual size of the sketch. Note that all line segments are sketched horizontally or vertically.

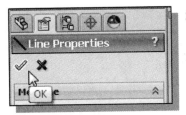

8. Click the **OK** icon (green check mark) in the *PropertyManager* to end editing of the current line, then click the **OK** icon again to end the Sketch Line command, or hit the [**Esc**] key once to end the Sketch Line command.

# Geometric Relation Symbols

*SolidWorks* displays different visual clues, or symbols, to show you alignments, perpendicularities, tangencies, etc. These relations are used to capture the *design intent* by creating relations where they are recognized. *SolidWorks* displays the governing geometric rules as models are built. To prevent relations from forming, hold down the [**Ctrl**] key while creating an individual sketch curve. For example, while sketching line segments with the Line command, endpoints are joined with a *Coincident relation*, but when the [**Ctrl**] key is pressed and held, the inferred relation will not be created.

| | | |
|---|---|---|
| 1.182, 90° | **Vertical** | indicates a line is vertical |
| 1.863, 180° | **Horizontal** | indicates a line is horizontal |
| 0.641 | **Dashed line** | indicates the alignment is to the center point or endpoint of an entity |
| 51.83 | **Parallel** | indicates a line is parallel to other entities |
| 0.338 | **Perpendicular** | indicates a line is perpendicular to other entities |
| 5.151 | **Coincident** | indicates the endpoint will be coincident with another entity |
| | **Concentric** | indicates the cursor is at the center of an entity |
| 0.689 | **Tangent** | indicates the cursor is at tangency points to curves |

## Step 2: Apply/Modify Relations and Dimensions

➢ As the sketch is made, *SolidWorks* automatically applies some of the geometric relations (such as **Horizontal**, **Parallel**, and **Perpendicular**) to the sketched geometry. We can continue to modify the geometry, apply additional relations, and/or define the size of the existing geometry. In this example, we will illustrate adding dimensions to describe the sketched entities.

1. Move the cursor on top of the **Smart Dimension** icon on the *Sketch* toolbar. The **Smart Dimension** command allows us to quickly create and modify dimensions. Left-click once on the icon to activate the **Smart Dimension** command.

2. The message "*Select one or two edges/vertices and then a text location*" is displayed in the *Status Bar* area at the bottom of the *SolidWorks* window. Select the bottom horizontal line by left-clicking once on the line.

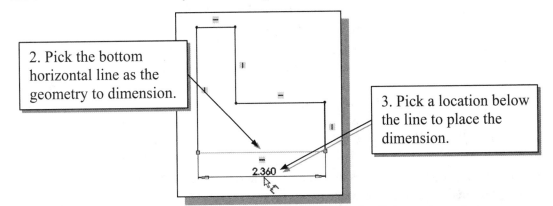

2. Pick the bottom horizontal line as the geometry to dimension.

3. Pick a location below the line to place the dimension.

3. Move the graphics cursor below the selected line and left-click to place the dimension. (Note that the value displayed on your screen might be different than what is shown in the figure above.)

4. Enter **2.0** in the *Modify* dialog box.

5. Left click the **OK** (green check mark) in the *Modify* dialog box to save the current value and exit the dialog.

6. Select the lower right-vertical line.

7. Pick a location toward the right of the sketch to place the dimension.

8. Enter **0.75** in the *Modify* dialog box.

9. Click **OK** in the *Modify* dialog box.

❖ The **Smart Dimension** command will create a length dimension if a single line is selected.

10. Select the top-horizontal line as shown below.

11. Select the bottom-horizontal line as shown below.

10. Pick the top line as the 1st geometry to dimension.

11. Pick the bottom line as the 2nd geometry to dimension.

12. Place the dimension next to the sketch.

12. Pick a location to the left of the sketch to place the dimension.

13. Enter **2.0** in the *Modify* dialog box.

14. Click **OK** in the *Modify* dialog box.

❖ When two parallel lines are selected, the **Smart Dimension** command will create a dimension measuring the distance between them.

15. On your own, repeat the above steps and create an additional dimension for the top line. Make the dimension **0.75**.

16. Click the **OK** icon in the *PropertyManager* as shown, or hit the **[Esc]** key once, to end the **Smart Dimension** command.

## Changing the Dimension Standard

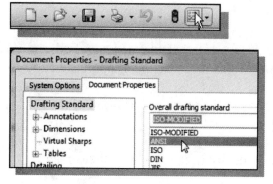

1. Select the **Options** icon from the *Menu Bar* to open the *Options* dialog box.

2. Select the **Document Properties** tab, then select **Drafting Standard** at the left.

3. Select **ANSI** in the pull-down selection window under the *Overall drafting standard* panel as shown.

4. Left-click **OK** in the *Options* dialog box to accept the settings.

The sketch should now look as shown below. Notice the change in appearance of the dimensions.

## Viewing Functions – *Zoom* and *Pan*

- *SolidWorks* provides a special user interface that enables convenient viewing of the entities in the graphics window. There are many ways to perform the **Zoom** and **Pan** operations.

1. Hold the **Ctrl** function key down. While holding the **Ctrl** function key down, press the mouse wheel down and drag the mouse to **pan** the display. This allows you to reposition the display while maintaining the same scale factor of the display.

2. Hold the **Shift** function key down. While holding the **Shift** function key down, press the mouse wheel down and drag the mouse to **zoom** the display. Moving downward will reduce the scale of the display, making the entities display smaller on the screen. Moving upward will magnify the scale of the display.

3. Turning the mouse wheel can also adjust the scale of the display. Turn the mouse wheel forward. Notice the scale of the display is reduced, making the entities display smaller on the screen.

4. Turn the mouse wheel backward. Notice scale of the display is magnified. (**NOTE:** Turning the mouse wheel allows zooming to the position of the cursor.)

5. On your own, use the options above to change the scale and position of the display.

6. Press the **F** key on the keyboard to automatically fit the model to the screen.

## Modifying the Dimensions of the Sketch

1.  Select the dimension that is to the bottom of the sketch by **double-clicking** with the **left-mouse-button** on the dimension text.

1. Select this dimension to modify.

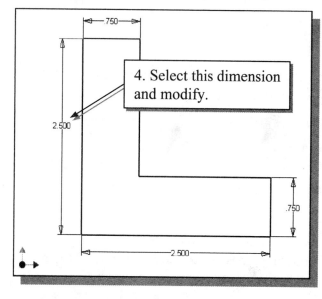

2.  In the *Modify* window, the current length of the line is displayed. Enter **2.5** to reset the length of the line.

3.  Click on the **OK** icon to accept the entered value.

➢ *SolidWorks* will now update the profile with the new dimension value.

4. Select this dimension and modify.

4.  On your own, repeat the above steps and adjust the left vertical dimension to **2.5** so that the sketch appears as shown.

5.  Press the [**Esc**] key once to exit the Dimension command.

6.  Click once with the **left-mouse-button** on the **Sketch** icon on the *Sketch* toolbar to exit the sketch.

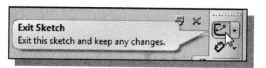

Exit Sketch
Exit this sketch and keep any changes.

➢ Notice the newly created sketch is listed on the *Feature-Manager Design Tree* as **Sketch1**. Also notice that **Sketch1** is highlighted in the *Design Tree*, indicating that the sketch is currently 'selected'.

## Step 3: Completing the Base Solid Feature

Now that the 2D sketch is completed, we will proceed to the next step: creating a 3D part from the 2D profile. Extruding a 2D profile is one of the common methods that can be used to create 3D parts. We can extrude planar faces along a path. We can also specify a height value and a tapered angle.

1. In the *Features* toolbar (located at the left of the window), select the **Extruded Boss/Base** command by clicking once with the left-mouse-button on the icon. The *Boss Extrude Property-Manager* is displayed in the left panel.

2. In the *Boss Extrude PropertyManager* panel, enter **2.5** as the extrusion distance. Notice that the sketch region is automatically selected as the extrusion profile.

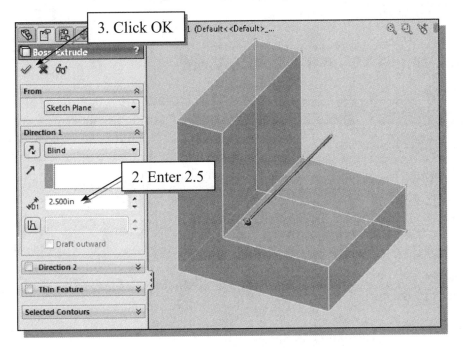

3. Click on the **OK** button to proceed with creating the 3D part.


➤ Note that all dimensions disappeared from the screen. All parametric definitions are stored in the **SolidWorks database** and any of the parametric definitions can be displayed and edited at any time.

## Isometric View

❖ *SolidWorks* provides many ways to display views of the three-dimensional design. We will first orient the model to display in the *isometric view*, by using the *View Orientation* pull-down menu on the *Heads-up View* toolbar.

1.  Select the **View Orientation** button on the *Heads-up View* toolbar by clicking once with the left-mouse-button.

2.  Select the **Isometric** icon in the *View Orientation* pull-down menu.

❖ Notice the other view-related commands that are available under the pull-down menu.

## Rotation of the 3D Model – *Rotate View*

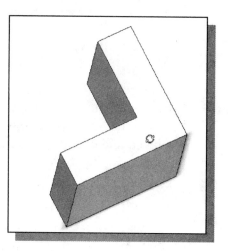

The **Rotate View** command allows us to rotate a part or assembly in the graphics window. Rotation can be around the center mark, free in all directions, or around a selected entity (vertex, edge, or face) on the model.

1.  Move the cursor over the SolidWorks logo to display the pull-down menus. Select **View →Modify → Rotate** from the pull-down menu as shown.

2.  Move the cursor inside the graphics area. Press down the left-mouse-button and drag in an arbitrary direction; the **Rotate View** command allows us to freely rotate the solid model.

•   The model will rotate about an axis normal to the direction of cursor movement. For example, drag the cursor horizontally across the screen and the model will rotate about a vertical axis.

3.  Press the [**Esc**] key once to exit the **Rotate View** command.

4. Select the **Isometric** icon in the *View Orientation* pull-down menu (see steps 1 and 2 in the previous section) to reset the display to the isometric view.

5. Execute the **Rotate View** option from the *View* pull-down menu (see step 1).

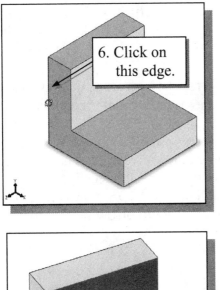

6. Click on this edge.

6. Move the cursor over the left edge of the solid model as shown. When the edge is highlighted, click the **left-mouse-button** once to select the edge.

7. Press down the left-mouse-button and drag. The model will rotate about this edge.

8. Left-click in the graphics area, outside the model, to unselect the edge.

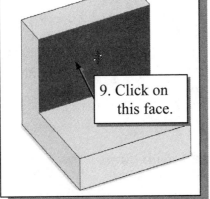

9. Click on this face.

9. Move the cursor over the upper front face of the solid model as shown. When the face is highlighted, click the **left-mouse-button** once to select the face.

10. Press down the left-mouse-button and drag. The model will rotate about the direction normal to this face.

11. Left-click in the graphics area, outside the model, to unselect the face.

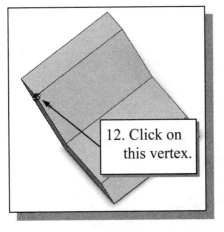

12. Click on this vertex.

12. Move the cursor over the upper front vertex as shown. When the vertex is highlighted, click the left-mouse-button once to select the vertex.

13. Press down the left-mouse-button and drag. The model will rotate about the vertex.

14. Left-click in the graphics area, outside the model, to unselect the vertex.

15. Press the [**Esc**] key once to exit the Rotate View command.

16. On your own, reset the display to the isometric view.

# Rotation and Panning – *Arrow Keys*

*SolidWorks* allows us to easily rotate a part or assembly in the graphics window using the arrow keys on the keyboard.

- Use the **arrow** keys to rotate the view horizontally or vertically. The **left-right** arrow keys rotate the model about a vertical axis. The **up-down** keys rotate the model about a horizontal axis.

- Hold down the Alt key and use the **left-right arrow** keys to rotate the model about an axis normal to the screen, i.e., to rotate clockwise and counter-clockwise.

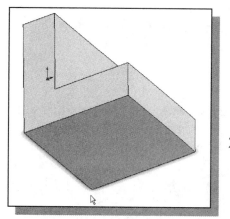

1.  Hit the **left arrow** key. The model view rotates by a pre-determined increment. The default increment is 15°. (This increment can be set in the *Options* dialog box.) On your own use the **left-right** and **up-down arrow** keys to rotate the view.

2.  Hold down the [**Alt**] key and hit the **left arrow** key. The model view rotates in the clockwise direction. On your own use the **left-right** and **up-down arrow** keys, and the Alt key plus the **left-right arrow** keys, to rotate the view.

3.  Reset the display to the Isometric view.

- Hold down the [**Shift**] key and use the **left-right** and **up-down arrow** keys to rotate the model in 90° increments.

4.  Hold down the [**Shift**] key and hit the **right arrow** key. The view will rotate by 90°. On your own use the [**Shift**] key plus the **left-right arrow** keys to rotate the view.

5.  Select the **Front** icon in the *View Orientation* pull-down menu as shown to display the **Front** view of the model.

6. Hold down the [**Shift**] key and hit the **left arrow** key.  The view rotates to the Right side view.

7. Hold down the [**Shift**] key and hit the **down arrow** key.  The view rotates to the Top view.

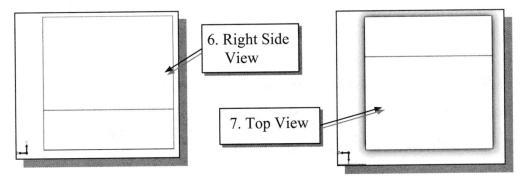

6. Right Side View

7. Top View

8. Reset the display to the **Isometric** view.

• Hold down the [**Ctrl**] key and use the left-right and up-down arrow keys to pan the model in increments.

9. Hold down the [**Ctrl**] key and hit the **left arrow** key.  The view pans, moving the model toward the left side of the screen.  On your own use [**Ctrl**] key plus the left-right and up-down arrow keys to pan the view.

## Viewing – Quick Keys

We can also use the function keys on the keyboard and the mouse to access the *Viewing* functions.

❖ **Panning –**

### (1) Hold Ctrl key, press and drag the mouse wheel

Hold the [**Ctrl**] function key down, and press and drag with the mouse wheel to pan the display. This allows you to reposition the display while maintaining the same scale factor of the display.

**Pan**          Ctrl   **+**

**Press and drag the mouse wheel**

### (2) Hold Ctrl key, use arrow keys

### ❖ Zooming –

### (1) Hold Shift key, press and drag the mouse wheel

Hold the [**Shift**] function key down, and press and drag with the mouse wheel to zoom the display. Moving downward will reduce the scale of the display, making the entities display smaller on the screen. Moving upward will magnify the scale of the display.

**Zoom**      | Shift | +

Press and drag the mouse wheel

### (2) Turning the mouse wheel

Turning the mouse wheel can also adjust the scale of the display. Turning forward will reduce the scale of the display, making the entities display smaller on the screen. Turning backward will magnify the scale of the display.

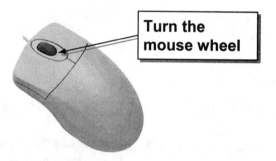

- Turning the mouse wheel allows zooming to the position of the cursor.

- If the cursor is outside the graphics area, the wheel will allow zooming to the center of the graphics area.

Turn the mouse wheel

### (3) Z key or Shift + Z key

Pressing the [**Z**] key on the keyboard will zoom out. Holding the [**Shift**] function key and pressing the [**Z**] key will zoom in.

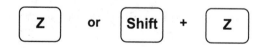

❖ **3D Rotation –**

### (1) Press and drag the mouse wheel

Press and drag with the mouse wheel to rotate the display.

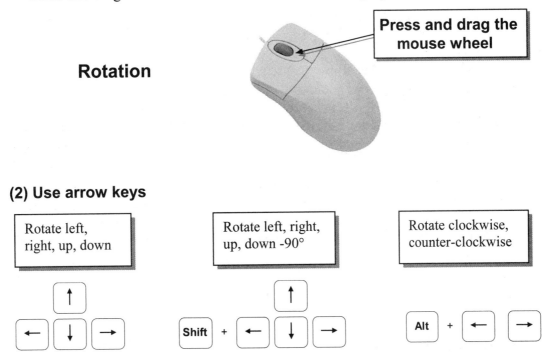

### (2) Use arrow keys

## Viewing Tools – Heads-up View Toolbar

The *Heads-up View* toolbar is a transparent toolbar which appears in each viewport and provides easy access to commonly used tools for manipulating the view. The default toolbar is described below.

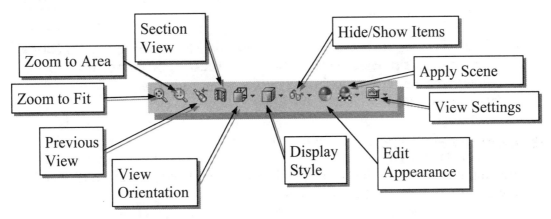

**Zoom to Fit** – Adjusts the view so that all items on the screen fit inside the graphics window.

**Zoom to Area** – Use the cursor to define a region for the view; the defined region is zoomed to fill the graphics window.

**Previous View** – Returns to the previous view.

**Section View** – Displays a cutaway of a part or assembly using one or more section planes

**View Orientation** – This allows you to change the current view orientation or number of viewports.

**Display Style** – This can be used to changes the display style (shaded, wireframe, etc.) for the active view.

**Hide/Show Items** – The pull-down menu is used to control the visibility of items (axes, sketches, relations, etc.) in the graphics area.

**Edit Appearance** – Edits the appearance of entities (e.g., parts, faces, features) in the model.

**Apply Scene** – Cycles through or applies a specific scene.

**View Settings** – Allows you to toggle various view settings (e.g., shadows, perspective).

## View Orientation

Click on the **View Orientation** icon on the *Heads-up View* toolbar to reveal the view orientation and number of viewports options.

Standard view orientation options – **Front, Back, Left, Right, Top, Bottom, Isometric, Trimetric, or Dimetric** – icons can be selected to display the corresponding standard view. In the figure to the left, the *Isometric* view is selected.

**Normal to** – In a part or assembly, zooms and rotates the model to display the selected plane or face. You can select the element either before or after clicking the Normal to icon.

The icons across the bottom of the pull-down menu allow you to display a single viewport (the default) or multiple viewports.

## Display Style

Click on the **Display Style** icon on the *Heads-up View* toolbar to reveal the display style options.

**Shaded with Edges** – Allows the display of a shaded view of a 3D model with its edges.

**Shaded** – Allows the display of a shaded view of a 3D model.

**Hidden Lines Removed** – Allows the display of the 3D objects using the basic wireframe representation scheme. Only those edges which are visible in the current view are displayed.

**Hidden Lines Visible** – Allows the display of the 3D objects using the basic wireframe representation scheme in which all the edges of the model are displayed, but edges that are hidden in the current view are displayed as dashed lines (or in a different color).

**Wireframe** – Allows the display of the 3D objects using the basic wireframe representation scheme in which all the edges of the model are displayed.

## Orthographic vs. Perspective

Besides the basic display modes, we can also choose orthographic view or perspective view of the display. Clicking on the View Settings icon on the *Heads-up View* toolbar will reveal the Perspective icon. Clicking on the Perspective icon toggles the perspective view *ON* and *OFF*.

➢ On your own, use the different options described in the above sections to familiarize yourself with the 3D viewing/display commands. Reset the display to the standard **isometric view** before continuing to the next section.

## Sketch Plane

Design modeling software is becoming more powerful and user friendly, yet the system still does only what the user tells it to do. When using a geometric modeler, we therefore need to have a good understanding of what its inherent limitations are. We should also have a good understanding of what we want to do and what to expect, as the results are based on what is available.

In most 3D geometric modelers, 3D objects are located and defined in what is usually called **world space** or **global space**. Although a number of different coordinate systems can be used to create and manipulate objects in a 3D modeling system, the objects are typically defined and stored using the world space. The world space is usually a **3D Cartesian coordinate system** that the user cannot change or manipulate.

In most engineering designs, models can be very complex, and it would be tedious and confusing if only the world coordinate system were available. Practical 3D modeling systems allow the user to define **Local Coordinate Systems** relative to the world coordinate system. Once a local coordinate system is defined, we can then create geometry in terms of this more convenient system.

Although objects are created and stored in 3D space coordinates, most of the geometry entities can be referenced using 2D Cartesian coordinate systems. Typical input devices such as a mouse or digitizers are two-dimensional by nature; the movement of the input device is interpreted by the system in a planar sense. The same limitation is true of common output devices, such as screen displays and plotters. The modeling software performs a series of three-dimensional to two-dimensional transformations to correctly project 3D objects onto a 2D picture plane.

The *SolidWorks* **sketch plane** is a special construction tool that enables the planar nature of 2D input devices to be directly mapped into the 3D coordinate system. The *sketch plane* is a local coordinate system that can be aligned to the world coordinate system, an existing face of a part, or a reference plane. By default, the *sketch plane* is aligned to the world coordinate system.

Think of a sketch plane as the surface on which we can sketch the 2D profiles of the parts. It is similar to a piece of paper, a white board, or a chalkboard that can be attached to any planar surface. The first profile we create is usually drawn on a sketch plane attached to a coordinate system such as the Front (XY), Top (XZ), and Right (YZ) sketch planes. Subsequent profiles can then be drawn on sketch planes that are defined on **planar faces of a part**, **work planes attached to part geometry**, or **sketch planes attached to a coordinate system**. The model we have created so far used the *SolidWorks* **Front Plane**, which is aligned to the XY plane of the world coordinate system.

1. Select the **Sketch** button at the top of the *Sketch* toolbar to create a new sketch.

2. In the *Edit Sketch PropertyManager*, the message "*Select: 1) a plane, a planar face, or an edge on which to create a sketch for the entity*" is displayed. *SolidWorks* expects us to identify a planar surface where the 2D sketch of the next feature is to be created. Move the graphics cursor on the 3D part and notice that *SolidWorks* will automatically highlight feasible planes and surfaces as the cursor is on top of the different surfaces. Pick the top horizontal face of the 3D solid object.

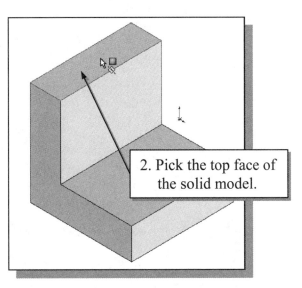

2. Pick the top face of the solid model.

➢ Note that the sketch plane is aligned to the selected face. *SolidWorks* automatically establishes a local coordinate system, and records its location with respect to the part on which it was created.

## Step 4-1: Adding an Extruded Boss Feature

- Next, we will create and profile another sketch, a rectangle, which will be used to create another extrusion feature that will be added to the existing solid object.

1. Select the **Line** command by clicking once with the **left-mouse-button** on the icon in the *Sketch* toolbar.

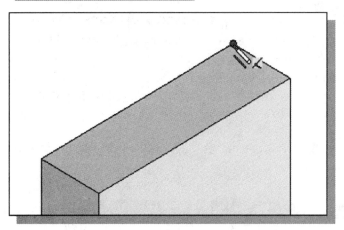

2. Move the cursor over the rear top vertex of the model. When the Coincident relation symbol appears as shown, click once with the **left-mouse-button**. This will start the first line, constraining its endpoint to be coincident with the vertex.

3. Create a sketch with segments perpendicular/parallel to the existing edges of the solid model as shown below. **Close the sketch by ending at Point 1. NOTE:** Use the Pan and Zoom options discussed earlier to control the view as needed.

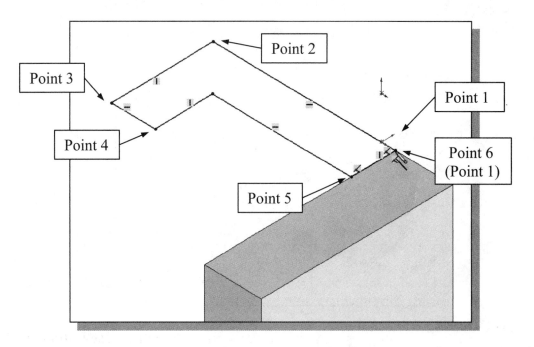

4. Click the **OK** icon (green check mark) in the *PropertyManager* twice, or hit the [**Esc**] key once, to end the Sketch Line command.

➢ We will hide the *Sketch Relation* icons in the sketch. The visibility of these and other items is controlled using the *Hide/Show Items* option on the *Heads-up View* toolbar.

5. Click on the **Hide/Show Items** icon on the *Heads-up View* toolbar to reveal the pull-down menu.

6. Click on the **View Sketch Relations** icon on the pull-down menu to toggle the sketch relation icon visibility *OFF*.

7. Click away from the pull-down menu to accept the settings.

8. Select the **Smart Dimension** command in the *Sketch* toolbar. The Smart Dimension command allows us to quickly create and modify dimensions. Left-click once on the icon to activate the Smart Dimension command.

9. The message "*Select one or two edges/vertices and then a text location*" is displayed in the *Status Bar* area, at the bottom of the *SolidWorks* window. Create the four dimensions to describe the size of the sketch as shown in the figure, entering the values shown (**2.5**, **2.5**, **0.75** and **0.75**).

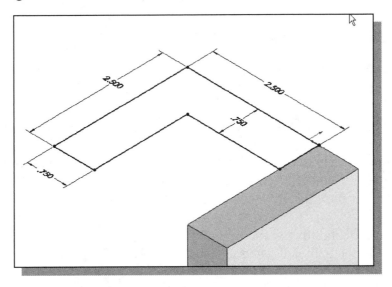

10. Click the **OK** icon in the *PropertyManager* as shown, or hit the [**Esc**] key once, to end the Smart Dimension command.

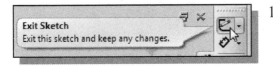

11. Click once with the **left-mouse-button** on the **Sketch** icon on the *Sketch* toolbar to exit the sketch.

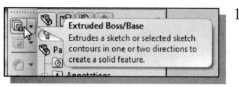

12. In the *Features* toolbar (located at the left of the window), select the **Extruded Boss/Base** command by clicking once with the left-mouse-button on the icon.

13. In the *Boss Extrude PropertyManager* panel, enter **2.5** as the extrusion distance. Notice that the sketch region is automatically selected as the extrusion profile.

14. Click the **Reverse Direction** button in the *PropertyManager* as shown. The extrude preview should appear as shown above.

15. Make sure the **Merge Result** option is selected (check box is checked).

❖ With the Merge Result option selected, the resultant body is merged into the existing body (if possible). If the Merge Result option is not selected, the *Extruded Boss/Base* feature creates a distinct solid body.

16. Click on the **OK** button to proceed with creating the extruded feature.

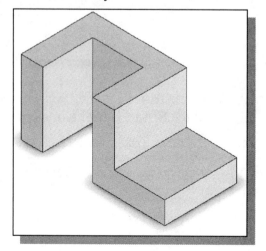

## Step 4-2: Adding an Extruded Cut Feature

- Next, we will create and profile a circle, which will be used to create a **cut** feature that will be added to the existing solid object.

    1. Click in the graphics area, away from the model, to ensure no items are selected.

    2. Select the **Sketch** button at the top of the *Sketch* toolbar to create a new sketch.

    3. In the *Edit Sketch PropertyManager*, the message "*Select: 1) a plane, a planar face, or an edge on which to create a sketch for the entity*" is displayed. *SolidWorks* expects us to identify a planar surface where the 2D sketch of the next feature is to be created. Move the graphics cursor on the 3D part and notice that *SolidWorks* will automatically highlight feasible planes and surfaces as the cursor is on top of the different surfaces. **Pick the horizontal face of the 3D solid object.**

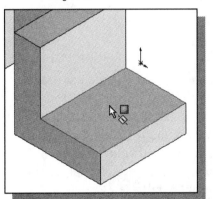

> Note that the sketch plane is aligned to the selected face.

**Circle**
Sketches a circle. Select the center of the circle, then drag to set its radius.

    4. Select the **Circle** command by clicking once with the **left-mouse-button** on the icon in the *Sketch* toolbar.

    5. Create a circle of arbitrary size on the top face of the solid model as shown. Click once with the left-mouse-button to select the center of the circle, move and click again to set the radius. Press the [**Esc**] key once to end the Circle command.

6.  On your own, create and modify the dimensions of the sketch as shown in the figure. **NOTE:** Select the center of the circle, then the appropriate edge to apply the linear dimensions. Select any point on the circle to apply the diameter dimension.

7.  Click the **OK** icon in the *PropertyManager*, or hit the [**Esc**] key once, to end the Smart Dimension command.

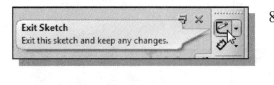

8.  Click once with the **left-mouse-button** on the **Sketch** icon on the *Sketch* toolbar to exit the sketch.

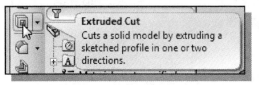

9.  In the *Features* toolbar (located at the left of the window), select the **Extruded Cut** command by clicking once with the left-mouse-button on the icon. The *Extrude PropertyManager* is displayed in the left panel. Notice that the sketch region (the circle) is automatically selected as the extrusion profile.

10. In the *Cut-Extrude PropertyManager* panel, click the arrow to reveal the pull-down options for the *End Condition* (the default end condition is 'Blind"), and select **Through All** as shown.

11. Click the **OK** button (green check mark) in the *Cut-Extrude PropertyManager* panel.

12. Click in the graphics area, away from the model, to ensure no items are selected.

13. Press the **F** key on the keyboard to fit the model to the screen.

## Save the Part File

1. Select **Save** in the *Menu Bar* pull-down menu, or you can also use the "**Ctrl-S**" combination (hold down the "Ctrl" key and hit the "S" key once) to save the part.

2. In the popup window, select the directory to store the model in and enter ***Adjuster*** as the name of the file.

3. Click on the **Save** button to save the file.

❖ You should form a habit of saving your work periodically, just in case something might go wrong while you are working on it. In general, one should save one's work at an interval of every 15 to 20 minutes. One should also save before making any major modifications to the model.

## Questions:

1. What is the first thing we should set up in *SolidWorks* when creating a new model?

2. Describe the general *parametric modeling* procedure.

3. What is the main difference between a rough sketch and a *profile*?

4. List two of the geometric relation symbols used by *SolidWorks*.

5. What was the first feature we created in this lesson?

6. Describe the steps required to define the orientation of the sketching plane?

7. Identify the following commands:

(a)

(b)

(c)

(d)

## Exercises: (All dimensions are in inches.)

1.   Plate Thickness: **.25**

2.   Plate Thickness: **.5**

3.

4.

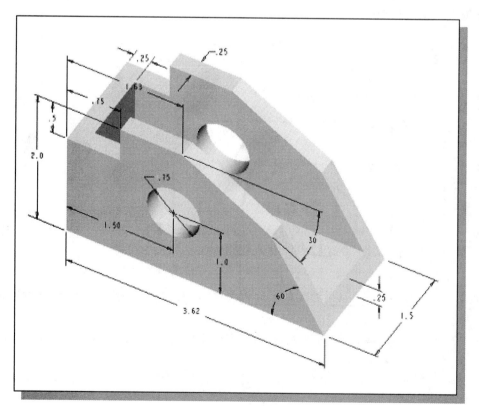

# Chapter 3
# Constructive Solid Geometry Concepts

## Learning Objectives

♦ **Understand Constructive Solid Geometry Concepts**

♦ **Create a Binary Tree**

♦ **Understand the Basic Boolean Operations**

♦ **Use the SolidWorks CommandManager User Interface**

♦ **Setup GRID and SNAP Intervals**

♦ **Understand the Importance of Order of Features**

♦ **Use the Different Extrusion Options**

## Certified SolidWorks Associate Exam Objectives Coverage

### Sketch Entities – Lines, Rectangles, Circles, Arcs, Ellipses, Centerlines
Objectives:  Creating Sketch Entities.

### Boss and Cut Features – Extrudes, Revolves, Sweeps, Lofts
Objectives:  Creating Basic Swept Features.

### Dimensions
Objectives: Applying and Editing Smart Dimensions.

### Feature Conditions – Start and End
Objectives: Controlling Feature Start and End Conditions.

## Introduction

In the 1980s, one of the main advancements in **solid modeling** was the development of the **Constructive Solid Geometry** (CSG) method. CSG describes the solid model as combinations of basic three-dimensional shapes (**primitive solids**). The basic primitive solid set typically includes: Rectangular-prism (Block), Cylinder, Cone, Sphere, and Torus (Tube). Two solid objects can be combined into one object in various ways using operations known as **Boolean operations**. There are three basic Boolean operations: **JOIN (Union)**, **CUT (Difference)**, and **INTERSECT**. The *JOIN* operation combines the two volumes included in the different solids into a single solid. The *CUT* operation subtracts the volume of one solid object from the other solid object. The *INTERSECT* operation keeps only the volume common to both solid objects. The CSG method is also known as the **Machinist's Approach**, as the method is parallel to machine shop practices.

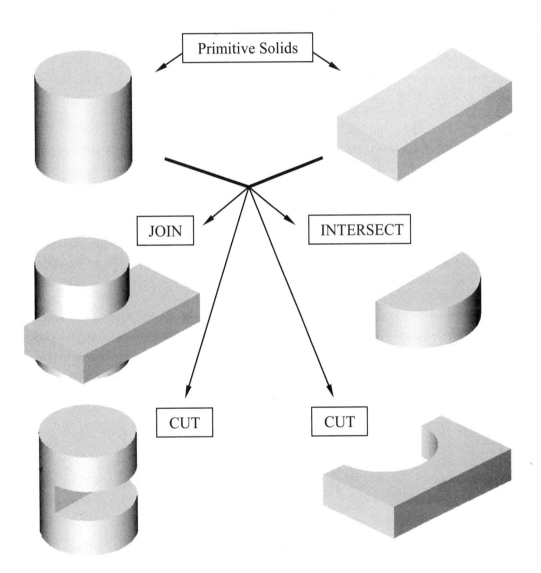

## Binary Tree

The CSG is also referred to as the method used to store a solid model in the database. The resulting solid can be easily represented by what is called a **binary tree**. In a binary tree, the terminal branches (leaves) are the various primitives that are linked together to make the final solid object (the root). The binary tree is an effective way to keep track of the *history* of the resulting solid. By keeping track of the history, the solid model can be re-built by re-linking through the binary tree. This provides a convenient way to modify the model. We can make modifications at the appropriate links in the binary tree and re-link the rest of the history tree without building a new model.

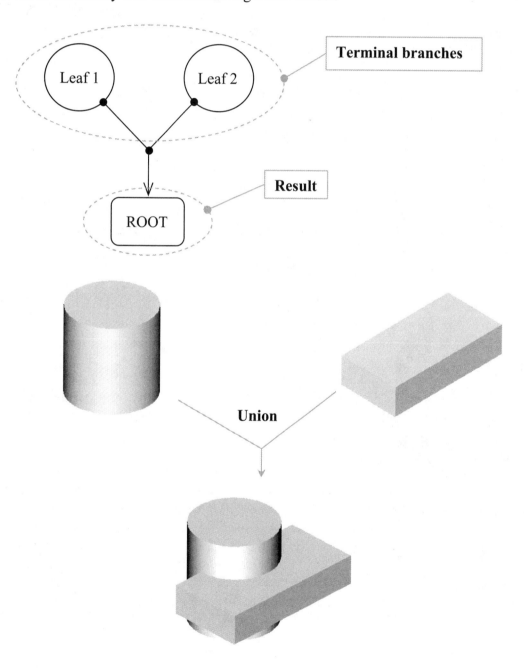

## The *Locator* Design

The CSG concept is one of the important building blocks for feature-based modeling. In *SolidWorks*, the CSG concept can be used as a planning tool to determine the number of features that are needed to construct the model. It is also a good practice to create features that are parallel to the manufacturing process required for the design. With parametric modeling, we are no longer limited to using only the predefined basic solid shapes. In fact, any solid features we create in *SolidWorks* are used as primitive solids; parametric modeling allows us to maintain full control of the design variables that are used to describe the features. In this lesson, a more in-depth look at the parametric modeling procedure is presented. The equivalent CSG operation for each feature is also illustrated.

> ➤ Before going through the tutorial, on your own, make a sketch of a CSG binary tree of the ***Locator*** design using only two basic types of primitive solids: cylinder and rectangular prism. In your sketch, how many *Boolean operations* will be required to create the model? What is your choice of the first primitive solid to use, and why? Take a few minutes to consider these questions and do the preliminary planning by sketching on a piece of paper. Compare the sketch you make to the CSG binary tree steps shown on page 3-5. Note that there are many different possibilities in combining the basic primitive solids to form the solid model. Even for the simplest design, it is possible to take several different approaches to creating the same solid model.

# Modeling Strategy – CSG Binary Tree

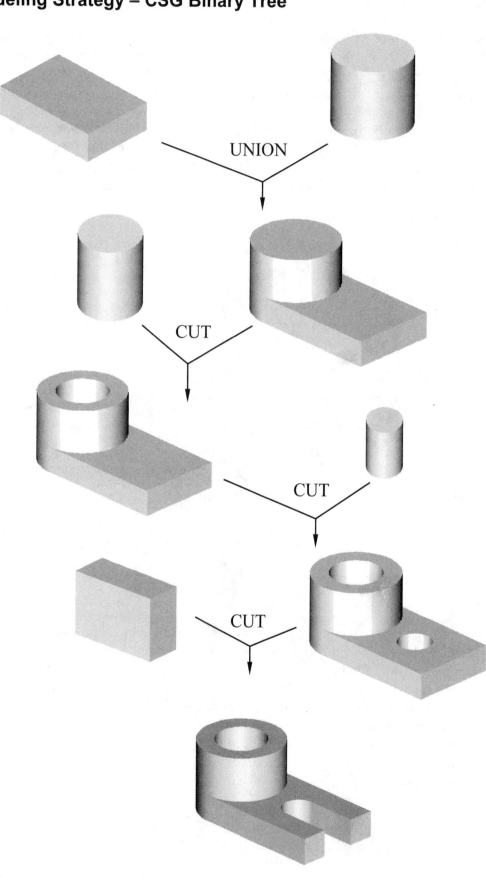

## Starting SolidWorks and Activating the CommandManager

1. Select the **SolidWorks** option on the *Start* menu or select the **SolidWorks** icon on the desktop to start *SolidWorks*. The *SolidWorks* main window will appear.

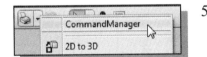

2. Select the **New** icon with a single click of the left-mouse-button on the *Menu Bar* toolbar.

3. Select the **Part** icon with a single click of the left-mouse-button in the *New SolidWorks Document* dialog box.

4. Select **OK** in the *New SolidWorks Document* dialog box to open a new part document.

**IMPORTANT NOTE:** The Solidworks *CommandManager* provides an alternate method for displaying the most commonly used toolbars (see page 1-13 for a more complete description). We will use the *CommandManager* in this lesson.

5. To turn *ON* the *CommandManager*, right click on any toolbar and toggle the *CommandManager ON* by selecting it at the top of the pop-up menu.

❖ Notice the *Features* and *Sketch* toolbars no longer appear at the edge of the window. These toolbars appear on the *Ribbon* display of the *CommandManager*.

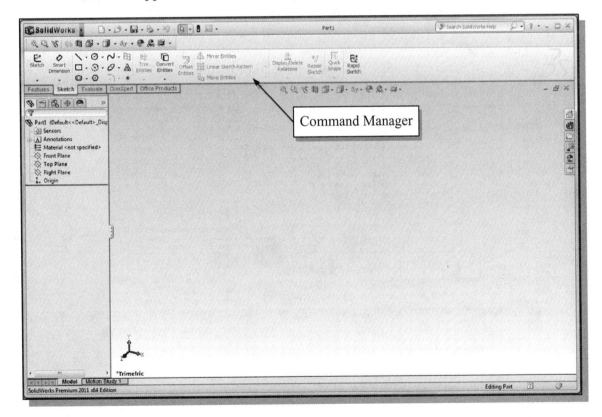

❖ Every object we construct in a CAD system is measured in units. We should determine the value of the units within the CAD system before creating the first geometric entities. For example, in one model, a unit might equal one millimeter of the real-world object; in another model, a unit might equal an inch. In most CAD systems, setting the model units does not always set units for dimensions. We generally set model units and dimension units to the same type and precision.

6. Select the **Options** icon from the *Menu Bar* toolbar to open the *Options* dialog box.

7. Select the **Document Properties** tab and the **Drafting Standard** option at the left of the *Document Properties* panel.

8. Select **ANSI** in the pull-down selection window under the *Overall drafting standard* panel as shown.

| Document Properties - Drafting Standard | |
|---|---|
| System Options    Document Properties | |
| Drafting Standard | Overall drafting standard |
| ⊞ Annotations | ANSI      Rename    Copy    Delete |
| ⊞ Dimensions | |
| Virtual Sharps | Load From External File... |
| ⊞ Tables | Save to External File... |
| Detailing | |

9. Click **Units** as shown below. We will use the default **MMGS (millimeter, gram, second)** unit system.

10. Select **.123** in the *Decimals* spin box for the *Length units* as shown to define the degree of accuracy with which the units will be displayed to 3 decimal places.

Document Properties - Units

System Options    Document Properties

Drafting Standard
⊞ Annotations
⊞ Dimensions
Virtual Sharps
⊞ Tables
Detailing
Grid/Snap
Units
Colors
Material Properties
Image Quality
Plane Display
DimXpert

Unit system
- ○ MKS (meter, kilogram, second)
- ○ CGS (centimeter, gram, second)
- ● MMGS (millimeter, gram, second)
- ○ IPS (inch, pound, second)
- ○ Custom

**10. Decimals**

**9. Units**

| Type | Unit | Decimals | Fractions | More |
|---|---|---|---|---|
| | millimeters | .123 | | |
| Dual Dimension Length | inches | .12 | | |
| | | .123 | | |
| Angle | degrees | .1234 | | |

Overall drafting standard has been changed to "ANSI-MODIFIED"

## *GRID* and *SNAP* Intervals Setup

1. Click **Grid/Snap** as shown below. We will use the default MMGS (millimeter, gram, second) unit system.

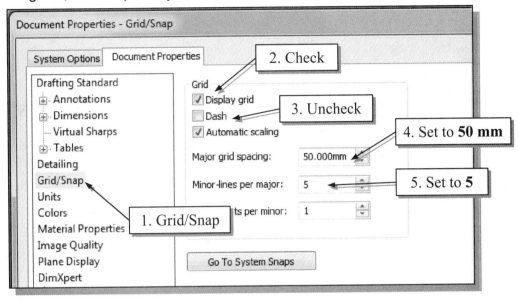

2. Check the Display grid checkbox under the *Grid* options.

3. Uncheck the Dash checkbox under the *Grid* options.

4. Set the Major grid spacing to **50 mm** under the *Grid* options.

5. Set the Minor-lines per major to **5** under the *Grid* options.

6. Click **OK** in the *Options* dialog box to accept the selected settings.

➢ Note that the above settings set the grid spacing in *SolidWorks*. Although the **Snap to grid** option is also available in *SolidWorks*, its usage in parametric modeling is not recommended.

## Base Feature

In *parametric modeling*, the first solid feature is called the **base feature,** which usually is the primary shape of the model. Depending upon the design intent, additional features are added to the base feature.

Some of the considerations involved in selecting the base feature are:

• **Design intent** – Determine the functionality of the design; identify the feature that is central to the design.

- **Order of features** – Choose the feature that is the logical base in terms of the order of features in the design.

- **Ease of making modifications** – Select a base feature that is more stable and is less likely to be changed.

➤ A rectangular block will be created first as the base feature of the **Locator** design.

1.  If necessary, select the **Sketch** tab on the *CommandManager* to display the *Sketch* toolbar.

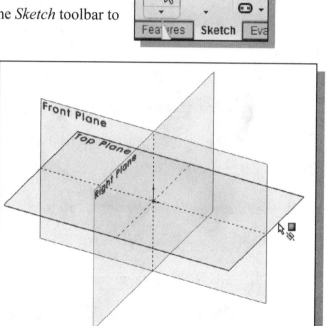

2.  Select the **Sketch** button on the *Sketch* toolbar to create a new sketch.

3.  Move the cursor over the edge of the Top Plane in the graphics area. When the Top Plane is highlighted, click once with the **left-mouse-button** to select the Top Plane (XZ Plane) as the sketch plane for the new sketch.

4.  Select the **Corner Rectangle** command by clicking once with the **left-mouse-button** on the icon in the *Sketch* toolbar.

5.  Create a rectangle of arbitrary size by selecting two locations on the screen as shown below.

6. Inside the graphics window, click once with the right-mouse-button to bring up the option menu.

7. Select **Select** to end the Rectangle command.

8. Select the **Smart Dimension** command by clicking once with the **left-mouse-button** on the icon in the *Sketch* toolbar.

9. The message "*Select one or two edges/vertices and then a text location*" is displayed in the *Status Bar* area at the bottom of the *SolidWorks* window. Select the bottom horizontal line by left-clicking once on the line.

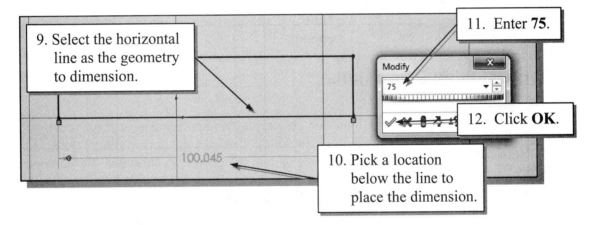

9. Select the horizontal line as the geometry to dimension.

11. Enter **75**.

12. Click **OK**.

10. Pick a location below the line to place the dimension.

10. Move the graphics cursor below the selected line and left-click to place the dimension. (Note that the value displayed on your screen might be different than what is shown in the figure above.)

11. Enter **75** in the *Modify* dialog box.

12. Click **OK** in the *Modify* dialog box.

13. On your own, create the vertical size dimension of the sketched rectangle as shown.

14. Click the **OK** icon in the *PropertyManager*, or hit the [**Esc**] key once, to end the Smart Dimension command.

## Modifying the Dimensions of the Sketch

1. Select the dimension that is to the right side of the sketch by *double-clicking* with the left-mouse-button on the dimension text.

1. Select the dimension to modify.

2. In the *Modify* window, the current length of the line is displayed. Enter **50** to reset the length of the line.

3. Click on the **OK** icon to accept the entered value.

4. Hit the [**Esc**] key once to end the Dimension command.

## Repositioning Dimensions

1. Move the cursor near the vertical dimension; note that the dimension is highlighted. Move the cursor slowly until a small marker appears next to the cursor, as shown in the figure.

2. Drag with the left-mouse-button to reposition the selected dimension.

3. Repeat the above steps to reposition the horizontal dimension.

4. Click once with the **left-mouse-button** on the **Exit Sketch** icon on the *Sketch* toolbar to end the Sketch option.

## Completing the Base Solid Feature

1. Make sure that the sketch you created is highlighted in the *FeatureManager Design Tree* as shown. This indicates that the sketch is currently selected and will automatically be used when we execute the Extruded Boss/Base command. If the sketch is not selected, click on Sketch1 once to select it.

2.  Select the **Features** tab on the *CommandManager* to display the *Features* toolbar.

3.  Select the **Extruded Boss/Base** button on the *Features* toolbar to create a new extruded feature.

➢ Notice the pre-selected sketch is automatically used for the creation of the *Extruded Boss Feature*.

4.  In the *Extrude PropertyManager* panel, enter **15** as the extrusion distance. Notice that the sketch region is automatically selected as the extrusion profile.

5.  Click on the **OK** button to proceed with creating the 3D part.

6.  Use the *Viewing* options to view the created part. On the *Heads-up View* toolbar, select **View Orientation** (to open the *View Orientation* pull-down menu) and select the **Isometric** icon to reset the display to the Isometric view before going to the next section.

## Creating the Next Solid Feature

1. Click the left-mouse-button in the graphics area, away from the model, to ensure that no features are selected.

2. Select the **Sketch** tab on the *CommandManager* to display the *Sketch* toolbar.

3. Select the **Sketch** button on the *Sketch* toolbar to create a new sketch.

4. In the *Edit Sketch PropertyManager* panel, the message "*Select a plane on which to create a sketch for the entity*" is displayed. *SolidWorks* expects us to identify a planar surface where the 2D sketch of the next feature is to be created. Move the graphics cursor on the 3D part and notice that *SolidWorks* will automatically highlight feasible planes and surfaces as the cursor is on top of the different surfaces.

5. Rotate the view using the **up arrow** key to display the bottom face of the solid model as shown below.

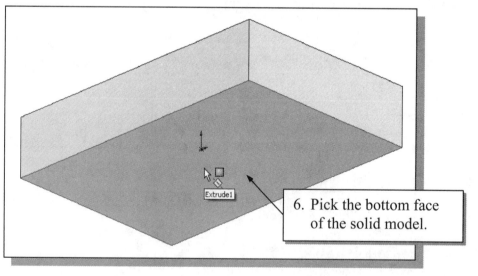

Extrude1

6. Pick the bottom face of the solid model.

6. Pick the bottom face of the 3D model as the sketching plane.

Circle
Sketches a circle. Select the center of the circle, then drag to set its radius.

➢ Note that the sketching plane is aligned to the selected face.

7. Select the **Circle** command by clicking once with the left-mouse-button on the icon in the *Sketch* toolbar.

➢ We will align the center of the circle to the midpoint of the base feature.

8. Move the cursor along the shorter edge of the base feature and select the **midpoint** when it is highlighted and the Midpoint sketch relation icon appears.

8. Midpoint sketch relation icon.

9. Select the corner of the base feature to create a circle, as shown below.

10. Press the [**Esc**] key once to end the Circle command.

11. Click once with the **left-mouse-button** on the **Exit Sketch** icon on the *Sketch* toolbar to exit the Sketch option.

12. Select the **Isometric** icon in the *Standard Views* pull-down menu to reset the display to the isometric view.

13. Notice the new sketch – **Sketch2** – is highlighted in the *Design Tree*, indicating that the sketch is currently 'selected'.

14. Select the **Features** tab on the *CommandManager* to display the *Features* toolbar.

15. Select the **Extruded Boss/Base** command on the *Features* toolbar.

➢ Notice that the sketch region is automatically selected as the extrusion profile.

16. In the *Extrude PropertyManager* panel, enter **40** as the extrusion distance as shown below. Confirm the **Merge result** checkbox is checked.

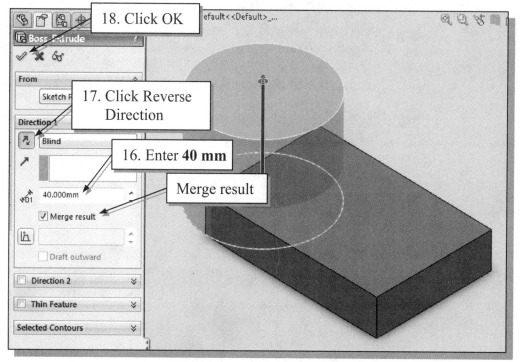

17. Click the **Reverse Direction** button in the *PropertyManager* as shown. The extrude preview should appear as shown above.

18. Click on the **OK** button to proceed with creating the extruded feature.

- The two features are joined together into one solid part; the *CSG-Union* operation was performed. This is the effect of the *Merge result* option.

## Creating an Extruded Cut Feature

- We will create a circular cut as the next solid feature of the design. We will align the sketch plane to the top of the last cylinder feature.

1. Select the **Sketch** tab on the *CommandManager* to display the *Sketch* toolbar.

2. Select the **Sketch** button on the *Sketch* toolbar to create a new sketch.

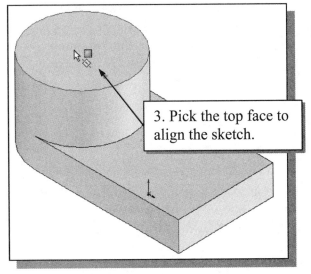

3. Pick the top face of the cylinder as shown.

3. Pick the top face to align the sketch.

4. Select the **Circle** command by clicking once with the left-mouse-button on the icon in the *Sketch* toolbar.

Circle
Sketches a circle. Select the center of the circle, then drag to set its radius.

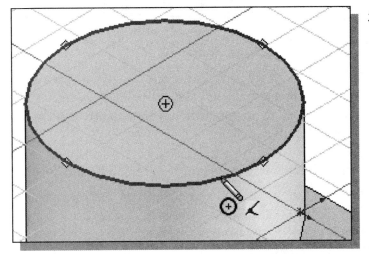

5. Move the cursor over the circular edge of the top face as shown. (Do not click.) Notice the center and quadrant marks appear on the circle.

6. Select Center

7. Draw Circle

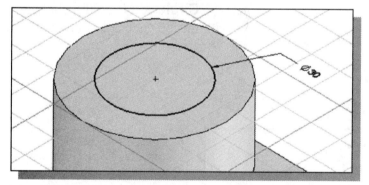

6. Select the **Center** point of the top face of the 3D model by left-clicking once on the icon as shown.

7. Sketch a circle of arbitrary size inside the top face of the cylinder as shown.

8. Use the right-mouse-button to display the option menu and select **Select** in the popup menu to end the Circle command.

9. Inside the graphics window, click once with the right-mouse-button to display the option menu. Select the **Smart Dimension** option in the popup menu.

10. Create a dimension to describe the size of the circle and set it to **30mm**.

11. Inside the graphics window, click once with the right-mouse-button to display the option menu. Select **Select** in the popup menu to end the Smart Dimension command.

12. Click once with the **left-mouse-button** on the **Exit Sketch** icon on the *Sketch* toolbar to exit the Sketch option.

13. Select the **Features** tab on the *CommandManager*.

14. In the *Features* toolbar, select the **Extruded Cut** command by clicking once with the left-mouse-button on the icon.

➢ The *Cut-Extrude PropertyManager* is displayed in the left panel.  Notice that the sketch region (the circle) is automatically selected as the extrusion profile.

15. In the *Cut-Extrude PropertyManager* panel, click the arrow to reveal the pull-down options for the *End Condition* (the default end condition is 'Blind') and select **Through All** as shown.

16. Click the **OK** button (green check mark) in the *Cut-Extrude PropertyManager* panel.

- The circular volume is removed from the solid model; the *CSG-Cut* operation resulted in a single solid.

## Creating a Hole with the *Hole Wizard*

- The last cut feature we created is a *sketched feature*, where we created a rough sketch and performed an extrusion operation. We can also create a hole using the *SolidWorks* Hole Wizard. With the Hole Wizard, the hole feature does not need a sketch and can be created automatically. Holes, fillets, chamfers, and shells are all examples of features that do not require a sketch.

1. In the *Features* toolbar, select the **Hole Wizard** command by clicking once with the left-mouse-button on the icon as shown.

2. In the *Hole Specification PropertyManager*, select the **Positions** panel by clicking once with the left-mouse-button on the **Positions** tab as shown. The Positions tab allows you to locate the hole on a planar or non-planar face.

3. Move the cursor over the horizontal surface of the base feature. Notice that the surface is highlighted. Click the **left mouse button** to select a location inside the horizontal surface as the position for the hole.

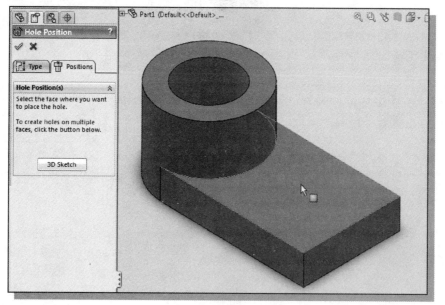

➢ Notice the *Sketch* toolbar is active and the **Point** button is selected. The Point command has been automatically executed to insert a point to serve as the center for the hole. We will use dimensions to locate the point.

4.  Select the **Smart Dimension** command by clicking once with the **left-mouse-button** on the icon in the *Sketch* toolbar.

5.  Pick the center point by clicking once with the left-mouse-button as shown.

6.  Pick the right-edge of the top face of the base feature by clicking once with the left-mouse-button as shown.

7.  Select a location for the dimension by clicking once with the left-mouse-button as shown.

8.  Enter **30** in the *Modify* dialog box, and select **OK**.

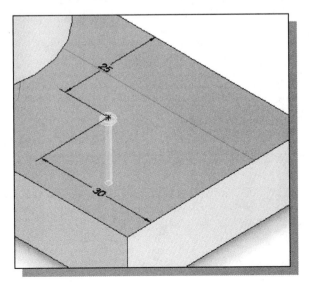

9.  On your own, enter the additional dimension as shown (the dimension is **25** mm).

10. Press the [**Esc**] key once to end the **Smart Dimension** command.

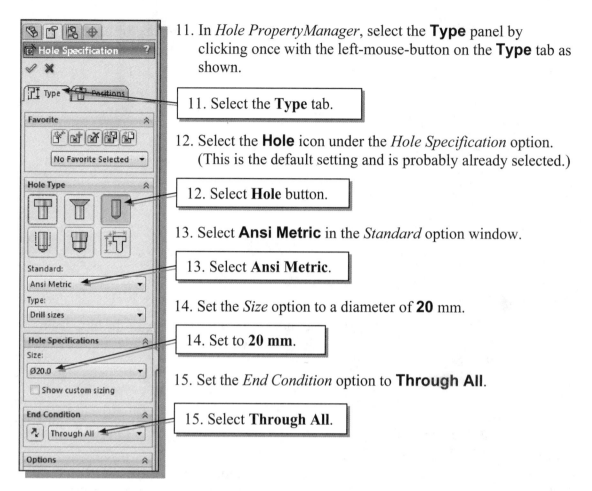

11. In *Hole PropertyManager*, select the **Type** panel by clicking once with the left-mouse-button on the **Type** tab as shown.

> 11. Select the **Type** tab.

12. Select the **Hole** icon under the *Hole Specification* option. (This is the default setting and is probably already selected.)

> 12. Select **Hole** button.

13. Select **Ansi Metric** in the *Standard* option window.

> 13. Select **Ansi Metric**.

14. Set the *Size* option to a diameter of **20** mm.

> 14. Set to **20 mm**.

15. Set the *End Condition* option to **Through All**.

> 15. Select **Through All**.

16. Click the **OK** button (green check mark) in the *Hole PropertyManager* to proceed with the *Hole* feature.

- The circular volume is removed from the solid model; the *CSG-Cut* operation resulted in a single solid.

## Creating a Rectangular Extruded Cut Feature

- Next create a rectangular cut as the last solid feature of the **Locator**.

1. Select the **Sketch** tab on the *CommandManager* to display the *Sketch* toolbar.

2. Select the **Sketch** button on the *Sketch* toolbar to create a new sketch.

3. Pick the right face of the base feature as shown.

4. Select the **Corner Rectangle** command by clicking once with the left-mouse-button on the icon in the *Sketch* toolbar.

5. Create a rectangle that is aligned to the top and bottom edges of the base feature as shown.

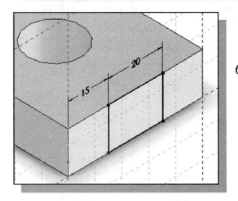

6. On your own, create and modify the two dimensions as shown. The dimensions are **15** mm and **20** mm.

7. Click once with the **left-mouse-button** on the **Exit Sketch** icon on the *Sketch* toolbar to exit Sketch option.

8. Notice the sketch is selected. (It is highlighted in the *FeatureManager Design Tree* and in the graphics area).

9. Press the **Esc** key once to unselect the sketch. Notice the color of the sketch changes to grey.

10. Select the **Features** tab on the *CommandManager*.

11. In the *Features* toolbar, select the **Extruded Cut** command by clicking once with the left-mouse-button on the icon.

➤ Notice that in the *PropertyManager* and on the *Status Bar* you are prompted to select a plane, face, etc. This is because no plane or sketch was pre-selected when the Extrude-Cut command was executed.

➤ When creating an extruded feature, *SolidWorks* allows the user to pre-select a sketch prior to executing the *Extrude* command or to first execute the *Extrude* command and then select the sketch.

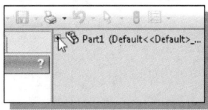

12. We will select the sketch using the *Design Tree* inside the graphics area. Move the cursor over the cross next to the **Part** icon at the upper left corner of the graphics area. Click once with the **left-mouse-button** to expand the *Design Tree*.

13. In the *Design Tree*, select the **Sketch** by clicking once with the **left-mouse-button** as shown.

➤ Notice that the sketch is selected for use in the *Cut-Extrude* feature and the sketch region (the rectangle) is automatically selected as the extrusion profile.

14. In the *Extrude PropertyManager* panel, click the arrow to reveal the pull-down options for the *End Condition* (the default end condition is Blind) and select **Up To Next** as shown.

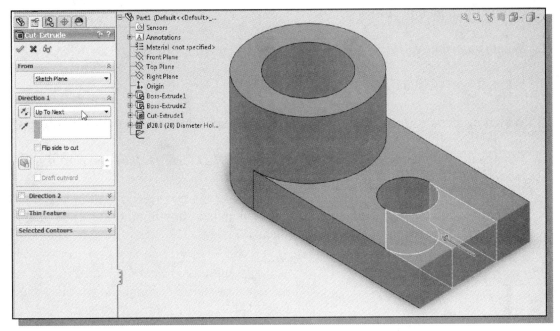

15. Click the **OK** button (green check mark) in the *Cut-Extrude PropertyManager* panel.

16. Save the model with the name *Locator*.

## Questions:

1. List and describe three basic *Boolean operations* commonly used in computer geometric modeling software?

2. What is a *primitive solid*?

3. What does *CSG* stand for?

4. Which *Boolean operation* keeps only the volume common to the two solid objects?

5. What is the main difference between an *EXTRUDED CUT feature* and a *HOLE feature* in *SolidWorks*?

6. Using the CSG concepts, create *Binary Tree* sketches showing the steps you plan to use to create the two models shown on the next page:

Ex.1)

Ex.2)

**Exercises:** (All dimensions are in inches.)

1.

2.

3.

4.

**NOTES:**

## Chapter 4
# Feature Design Tree

## Learning Objectives

- ♦ **Understand Feature Interactions**
- ♦ **Use the FeatureManager Design Tree**
- ♦ **Modify and Update Feature Dimensions**
- ♦ **Perform History-Based Part Modifications**
- ♦ **Change the Names of Created Features**
- ♦ **Implement Basic Design Changes**

## Certified SolidWorks Associate Exam Objectives Coverage

### Sketch Entities – Lines, Rectangles, Circles, Arcs, Ellipses, Centerlines

Objectives: Creating Sketch Entities.

### Boss and Cut Features – Extrudes, Revolves, Sweeps, Lofts

Objectives: Creating Basic Swept Features.

### Dimensions

Objectives: Applying and Editing Smart Dimensions.

### Feature Conditions – Start and End

Objectives: Controlling Feature Start and End Conditions.

## Introduction

In *SolidWorks*, the **design intents** are embedded into features in the **FeatureManager Design Tree**. The structure of the design tree resembles that of a **CSG binary tree**. A CSG binary tree contains only *Boolean relations*, while the **SolidWorks design tree** contains all features, including *Boolean relations*. A design tree is a sequential record of the features used to create the part. This design tree contains the construction steps, plus the rules defining the design intent of each construction operation. In a design tree, each time a new modeling event is created previously defined features can be used to define information such as size, location, and orientation. It is therefore important to think about your modeling strategy before you start creating anything. It is important, but also difficult, to plan ahead for all possible design changes that might occur. This approach in modeling is a major difference of **FEATURE-BASED CAD SOFTWARE**, such as *SolidWorks*, from previous generation CAD systems.

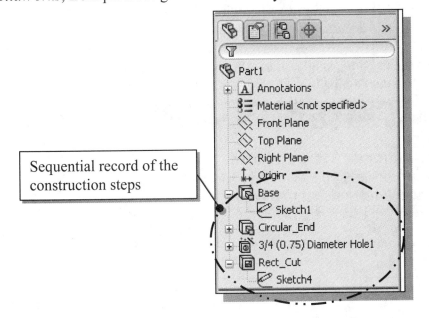

Sequential record of the construction steps

Feature-based parametric modeling is a cumulative process. Every time a new feature is added, a new result is created and the feature is also added to the design tree. The database also includes parameters of features that were used to define them. All of this happens automatically as features are created and manipulated. At this point, it is important to understand that all of this information is retained, and modifications are done based on the same input information.

In *SolidWorks*, the design tree gives information about modeling order and other information about the feature. Part modifications can be accomplished by accessing the features in the design tree. It is therefore important to understand and utilize the feature design tree to modify designs. *SolidWorks* remembers the history of a part, including all the rules that were used to create it, so that changes can be made to any operation that was performed to create the part. In *SolidWorks*, to modify a feature, we access the feature by selecting the feature in the *FeatureManager Design Tree* window.

## Starting *SolidWorks*

1. Select the **SolidWorks** option on the *Start* menu or select the **SolidWorks** icon on the desktop to start *SolidWorks*. The *SolidWorks* main window will appear.

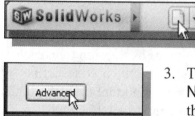

2. Select the **New** icon with a single click of the left-mouse-button on the *Menu Bar*.

3. The *New SolidWorks Document* dialog window appears in Novice mode. Click once with the left-mouse-button on the **Advanced** button to switch to Advanced mode.

❖ In Advanced mode, the *New SolidWorks Document* dialog box offers the same three options as in Novice mode. These options allow starting a new document using the default templates for a Part, Assembly, or Drawing. However, the Advanced mode will allow us to start new documents with user-defined templates.

4. Select the **Part** icon with a single click of the left-mouse-button in the *New SolidWorks Document* dialog box.

5. Select **OK** in the *New SolidWorks Document* dialog box to open a new part document.

**IMPORTANT NOTE:** In this lesson and following lessons, we will use the standard display of toolbars. If a user prefers to use the *CommandManager*, the only change that may be necessary is to select the appropriate tab prior to selecting a command. For example, if the instruction is to "select the **Extruded Boss** command from the *Features* toolbar," it may be necessary to first select the Features tab on the *CommandManager* to display the *Features* toolbar.

6. To turn **OFF** the *CommandManager* and use the standard display of toolbars, right click on the *CommandManager* (or any other toolbar) and toggle the *CommandManager OFF* by selecting it at the top of the pop-up menu.

## Creating a User-Defined Part Template

❖ We will create a part template which includes setting for the use of ANSI standards for dimensions and English (inch, pound, second) units. In the future, using this template will eliminate the need to adjust these document settings each time a new part is started.

1. Select the **Options** icon from the *Menu Bar* to open the *Options* dialog box.

2. Select the **Document Properties** tab.

3. Select **ANSI** in the pull-down selection window under the *Overall drafting standard* panel as shown.

4. Click **Units** as shown below.

5. Select **IPS (inch, pound, second)** under the *Unit system* options.

6. Select **.123** in the *Decimals* spin box for the *Length units* as shown to define the degree of accuracy with which the units will be displayed to 3 decimal places.

7. Click **OK** in the *Options* dialog box to accept the selected settings.

8. Click the arrow next to the **Save** icon in the *Menu Bar* to reveal the save options and select **Save As**.

9.  We will create a new folder for the user-defined templates. Decide where you want to locate this new folder and use the browser in the *Save As* dialog box to select the location. It may be necessary to expand the browser by clicking the **Browse Folders** button as shown. (**NOTE:** In the figure below, the **C:** folder is chosen.)

10. In the *Save As* dialog box, select the **New Folder** option by clicking once with the left-mouse-button on the icon as shown.

11. The new folder appears with the default name *New Folder*. Type the filename **Tutorial_Templates** for the new folder. (**NOTE:** This folder could also be created using Windows Explorer, etc.)

12. Left click on the **Hide Folders** button to hide the browser.

13. Under *Save as type*, select **Part Templates (\*.prtdot)**. Notice the browser automatically goes to the default *templates* folder.

14. Use the *Save in* browser to select the **Tutorial_Templates** folder you created.

15. Enter the *File name* **Part_IPS_ANSI**.

14. Select the **Tutorial_Templates** folder.

15. Enter **Part_IPS_ANSI**.

13. Select **Part Templates**.

16. Click **Save** to save the new part template file.

17. Select **Close** in the *File* pull-down menu to close the document. (**NOTE:** You may have to move the mouse over the SolidWorks icon to reveal the pull-down menus.)

➢ We will now open a new part document using the template we just saved.

18. Select the **New** icon with a single click of the left-mouse-button on the *Menu Bar*. The *New SolidWorks Document* dialog box appears in Advanced mode.

19. Notice that the new template does not appear as an option. Click **Cancel** in the *New SolidWorks Document* dialog box.

20. Select the **Options** icon from the *Menu Bar* to open the *Options* dialog box.

21. Select **File Locations** under the *System Options* tab as shown.

22. Make sure **Document Templates** is selected as the *Show folders for:* option.

23. Click the **Add** button to add the directory with the user-defined templates to the list of folders containing document templates.

**System Options - File Locations**

System Options

General
Drawings
    Display Style
    Area Hatch/Fill
Colors
Sketch
    Relations/Snaps
Display/Selection
Performance
Assemblies
External References
Default Templates
File Locations
FeatureManager

Show folders for:

Document Templates

Folders:

C:\ProgramData\SolidWorks\SolidWorks 2010\templates\
C:\Program Files\SolidWorks Corp\SolidWorks\lang\english\Tutorial

Add...
Delete
Move Up
Move Down

22. Document Templates

23. Add

21. File Locations

**Browse For Folder**

Tutorial_Templates
▷ Users
▷ Windows
▷ FACTORY_IMAGE (D:)
▷ DVD RW Drive (E:)
▷ Network
▷ Control Panel
Recycle Bin
▷ Downloads

Folder:    Tutorial_Templates

Make New Folder    OK    Cancel

24. Locate and select the **Tutorial_Templates** folder using the browser, and click **OK** in the *Browse For Folder* dialog box.

25. Select **OK** in the *Options* dialog box.

**SolidWorks**

⚠ Would you like to make the following changes to your search paths?

Add:
    C:\Tutorial_Templates\

Yes    No

26. If a pop-up window appears with the question "*Would you like to make the following changes to your search paths?*" click **Yes**.

27. Select the **New** icon with a single click of the left-mouse-button on the *Menu Bar*. Notice the Tutorial_Templates folder now appears as a tab in the *New SolidWorks Document* dialog box.

28. Select the **Tutorial_Templates** tab.

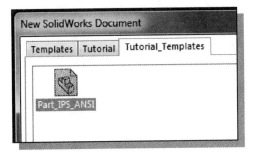

29. Notice the Part_IPS_ANSI template appears. Select the **Part_IPS_ANSI** template as shown.

30. Click on the **OK** button to open a new document.

## The *Saddle Bracket* Design

❖ Based on your knowledge of *SolidWorks* so far, how many features would you use to create the design? Which feature would you choose as the **BASE FEATURE**, the first solid feature, of the model? What is your choice in arranging the order of the features? Would you organize the features differently if additional fillets were to be added in the design? Take a few minutes to consider these questions and do preliminary planning by sketching on a piece of paper. You are also encouraged to create the model on your own prior to following through the tutorial.

## Modeling Strategy

## The *SolidWorks FeatureManager Design Tree*

- In the *SolidWorks* screen layout, the **FeatureManager Design Tree** is located to the left of the graphics window. *SolidWorks* can be used for part modeling, assembly modeling, part drawings, and assembly presentation. The *FeatureManager Design Tree* window provides a visual structure of the features, relations, and attributes that are used to create the part, assembly, or scene. The *FeatureManager Design Tree* also provides right-click menu access for tasks associated specifically with the part or feature, and it is the primary focus for executing many of the *SolidWorks* commands.

➢ The first item displayed in the *FeatureManager Design Tree* is the name of the part, which is also the filename. By default, the name "*Part1*" is used when we first started *SolidWorks*. The *FeatureManager Design Tree* can also be used to modify parts and assemblies by moving, deleting, or renaming items within the hierarchy. Any

changes made in the *FeatureManager Design Tree* directly affect the part or assembly and the results of the modifications are displayed on screen instantly. The *FeatureManager Design Tree* also reports any problems and conflicts during the modification and updating procedure.

## Creating the Base Feature

1. Move the graphics cursor to the **Front Plane** icon in the *FeatureManager Design Tree*. Notice the *Front Plane* icon is highlighted in the design tree and the *Front Plane* outline appears in the graphics area. Click once with the **left-mouse-button** to select the Front Plane.

2. In the *Sketch* toolbar, select the **Sketch** command by left-clicking once on the icon. Notice the Front Plane automatically becomes the sketch plane because it was pre-selected.

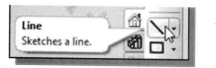

3. Select the **Line** icon on the *Sketch* toolbar by clicking once with the **left-mouse-button**; this will activate the Line command.

4. On your own, create and adjust the geometry by adding and modifying dimensions as shown below.

5. Click once with the **left-mouse-button** on the **Sketch** icon on the *Sketch* toolbar to exit the Sketch option.

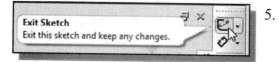

6. Select the **View Orientation** button on the *Heads-up View* toolbar by clicking

7. Select the **Isometric** icon in the *View Orientation* pull-down menu.

8. Make sure the sketch – Sketch1 – is selected in the *FeatureManager Design Tree*.

9. In the *Features* toolbar, select the **Extruded Boss/Base** command by clicking once with the left-mouse-button on the icon.

10. In the *Extrude PropertyManager* panel, click the drop down arrow to reveal the options for the *End Condition* (the default end condition is Blind) and select **Mid Plane** as shown.

11. In the *Extrude PropertyManager* panel, enter **2.5** as the extrusion distance. Notice that the sketch region is automatically selected as the extrusion profile.

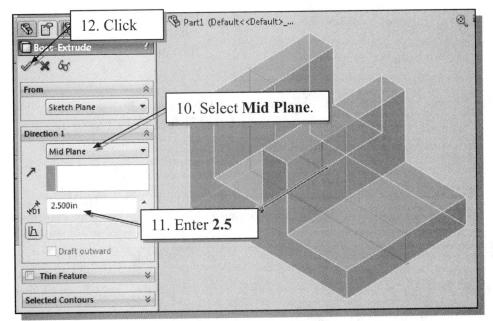

12. Click on the **OK** button to accept the settings and create the base feature.

➢ On your own, use the *Viewing* functions to view the 3D model. Also notice the **Boss-Extrude** feature is added to the *Model Tree* in the *FeatureManager Design Tree* area.

## Adding the Second Solid Feature

1.  In the *Sketch* toolbar, select the **Sketch** command by left-clicking once on the icon.

Move the cursor near the center of the top horizontal face. (Do **not** left-click).

2.  Notice the left panel displays the *Edit Sketch PropertyManager* with the instruction "*Select a plane on which to create a sketch for the entity.*" Move the graphics cursor on the 3D part and notice that *SolidWorks* will automatically highlight feasible planes and surfaces as the cursor is on top of the different surfaces. Move the cursor inside the upper horizontal face of the 3D object as shown.

3.  Click once with the **right-mouse-button** to bring up the option menu and select **Select Other** to switch to the next feasible choice.

4.  The *Select Other* pop-up dialog box appears. On your own, move the cursor over the options (e.g., Face) in the box to examine all possible surface selections.

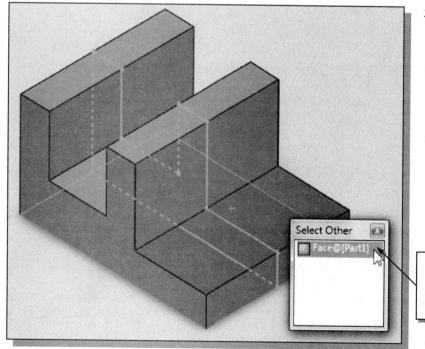

5.  Click on the **Face** selection in the *Select Other* dialog box to select the **bottom horizontal face** of the solid model when it is highlighted as shown in the figure.

Accept the bottom surface to align the sketching plane.

## Creating a 2D Sketch

1. Select the **Circle** command by clicking once with the left-mouse-button on the icon in the *Sketch* toolbar.

➤ We will align the center of the circle to the midpoint of the base feature.

2. Move the cursor along the shorter edge of the base feature and pick the midpoint of the edge when the **Midpoint** is highlighted as shown in the figure.

3. Select the front corner of the base feature to create a circle as shown below.

R = 1.25

4. Inside the graphics window, click once with the right-mouse-button to display the option menu. Select **Select** in the popup menu to end the Circle option.

5. Click once with the **left-mouse-button** on the **Sketch** icon on the *Sketch* toolbar to exit the Sketch option.

6. Make sure the sketch – **Sketch2** – is selected in the *FeatureManager Design Tree*.

7. In the *Features* toolbar, select the **Extruded Boss/Base** command by clicking once with the left-mouse-button on the icon.

8. Click the **Reverse Direction** button in the *PropertyManager* as shown. The extrude preview should appear as shown below.

9. In the *Extrude PropertyManager* panel, click the drop down arrow to reveal the pull options for the *End Condition* (the default end condition is **Blind**) and select **Up To Surface**.

10. Select the top face of the base feature as the termination surface for the extrusion. Notice **Face<1>** appears in the surface selection window in the *Extrude PropertyManager*.

11. Confirm the **Merge result** checkbox is checked.

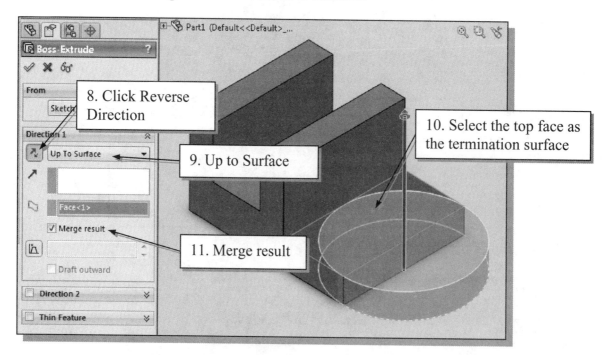

12. Click on the **OK** button to proceed with the **Join** operation.

## Renaming the Part Features

♦ Currently, our model contains two extruded features. The feature is highlighted in the display area when we select the feature in the *FeatureManager Design Tree* window. Each time a new feature is created, the feature is also displayed in the *Design Tree* window. By default, *SolidWorks* will use generic names for part features. However, when we begin to deal with parts with a large number of features, it will be much easier to identify the features using more meaningful names. Two methods can be used to rename the features: 1. **clicking** twice on the name of the feature; and 2. using the **Properties** option. In this example, the use of the first method is illustrated.

1. Select the first extruded feature in the *Model Browser* area by left-clicking once on the name of the feature, **Extrude1**. Notice the selected feature is highlighted in the graphics window.

2. Left-mouse-click on the feature name again to enter the Edit mode as shown.

3. Type **Base** as the new name for the first extruded feature and press the [**Enter**] key.

4. On your own, rename the second extruded feature to **Circular_End**.

## Adjusting the Width of the Base Feature

❖ One of the main advantages of parametric modeling is the ease of performing part modifications at any time in the design process. Part modifications can be done through accessing the features in the design tree. *SolidWorks* remembers the history of a part, including all the rules that were used to create it, so that changes can be made to any operation that was performed to create the part. For our *Saddle Bracket* design, we will reduce the size of the base feature from 3.25 inches to 3.0 inches, and the extrusion distance to 2.0 inches.

1. Inside the *FeatureManager Design Tree* area, **right-mouse-click** on **Annotations** to bring up the option menu and select the **Show Feature Dimensions** option in the pop-up menu. This option will allow us to view and edit dimensions by moving the cursor over the corresponding feature on the model.

2. Move the cursor over the model to reveal the dimension indicating the **3.25** overall width of the **Base** feature.

3. Select the overall width of the **Base** feature, the **3.25** dimension value, by double-clicking on the dimension text, as shown.

4. Enter **3.0** in the *Modify* window and click the **OK** button.

5. Hit the [**Esc**] key to exit the Dimension command.

6. On your own, repeat the above steps and modify the extruded distance from **2.5** to **2.0**.

7. Click **Rebuild** in the *Menu Bar*.

➢ Note that *SolidWorks* updates the model by re-linking all elements used to create the model. Any problems or conflicts that occur will also be displayed during the updating process.

8. **Right-mouse-click** on **Annotations** to bring up the option menu and de-select the **Show Feature Dimensions** option in the pop-up menu.

## Adding a Hole

1. Select the **Sketch** button on the *Sketch* toolbar to create a new sketch.

2. Pick the upper horizontal face as shown.

3. Select the **Circle** command by clicking once with the left-mouse-button on the icon in the *Sketch* toolbar.

4. Move the cursor over the circular edge of the face as shown. (Do not click.) Notice the center and quadrant marks appear on the circle.

5. Select the **Center** point of the top face of the 3D model by left-clicking once on the icon as shown.

6. Sketch a circle of arbitrary size inside the top face of the cylinder as shown.

7. Use the right-mouse-button to display the option menu and select **Select** in the popup menu to end the Circle command.

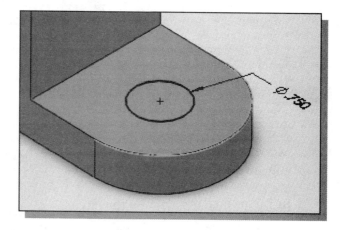

8. Inside the graphics window, click once with the right-mouse-button to display the option menu. Select the **Smart Dimension** option in the popup menu.

9. Create a dimension to describe the size of the circle and set it to **0.75 in**.

10. Inside the graphics window, click once with the right-mouse-button to display the option menu. Select **Select** in the popup menu to end the Smart Dimension command.

11. Click once with the **left-mouse-button** on the **Sketch** icon on the *Sketch* toolbar to exit the Sketch option.

12. In the *Features* toolbar, select the **Extruded Cut** command by clicking once with the left-mouse-button on the icon.

➤ The *Cut-Extrude PropertyManager* is displayed in the left panel. Notice that the sketch region (the circle) is automatically selected as the extrusion profile.

13. In the *Cut-Extrude PropertyManager* panel, click the arrow to reveal the pull-down options for the *end condition* (the default end condition is Blind) and select **Through All** as shown.

14. Click the **OK** button (green check mark) in the *Cut-Extrude PropertyManager* panel.

15. On your own, rename the feature as **3/4″ Hole** in the *FeatureManager Design Tree*.

## Creating a Rectangular Extruded Cut Feature

1. Move the cursor into the graphics area, away from the model, and click once with the left-mouse-button to ensure that no features are selected.

2. Select the **Sketch** button on the *Sketch* toolbar to create a new sketch.

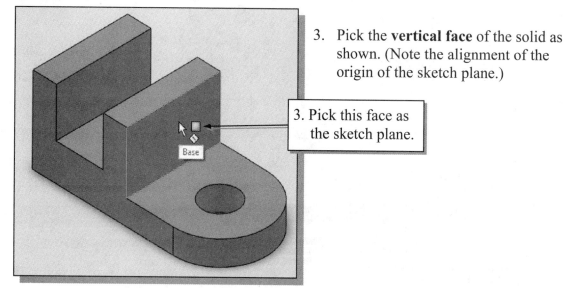

3. Pick the **vertical face** of the solid as shown. (Note the alignment of the origin of the sketch plane.)

> 3. Pick this face as the sketch plane.

4. On your own, create a rectangular (**1.0″ W x 0.75″ H**) **Extruded Cut** feature as shown. The rectangle is offset **0.5″** from the edge. Use the **Up To Next** option for the *End Condition* and change the name of the feature to **Rect_Cut**.

# History-Based Part Modifications

- *SolidWorks* uses the *history-based part modification* approach, which enables us to make modifications to the appropriate features and re-link the rest of the history tree without having to reconstruct the model from scratch. We can think of it as going back in time and modifying some aspects of the modeling steps used to create the part. We can modify any feature that we have created. As an example, we will adjust the depth of the rectangular cutout.

1. In the *FeatureManager Design Tree* window, select the last cut feature, **Rect_Cut**, by left-clicking once on the name of the feature.

2. In the *FeatureManager Design Tree* window, right-mouse-click once on the **Rect_Cut** feature.

3. Select the **Edit Feature** button in the pop-up menu. Notice the *Extrude PropertyManager* appears on the screen.

4. In the *Extrude PropertyManager*, set the termination *End Condition* to the **Through All** option.

5. Click on the **OK** button to accept the settings.

- As can been seen, the history-based modification approach is very straightforward and it only took a few seconds to adjust the cut feature to the **Through All** option.

## A Design Change

❖ Engineering designs usually go through many revisions and changes. *SolidWorks* provides an assortment of tools to handle design changes quickly and effectively. We will demonstrate some of the tools available by changing the **Base** feature of the design.

1. In the *FeatureManager Design Tree* window, select the **Base** feature by left-clicking once on the name of the feature.

2. Pick the **Edit Sketch** button in the pop-up menu.

❖ *SolidWorks* will now display the original 2D sketch of the selected feature in the graphics window. We have literally gone back in time to the point where we first created the 2D sketch. Notice the feature being modified is also highlighted in the desktop *FeatureManager Design Tree*.

3. Click on the **Normal To** icon in the *View Orientation* pull-down menu on the *Heads-up View* toolbar.

• The **Normal To** command automatically aligns the *sketch plane* of a selected entity to the screen. We have literally gone back in time to the point where we first created the 2D sketch.

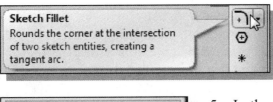

4. Select the **Sketch Fillet** command in the *Sketch* toolbar.

5. In the *Sketch Fillet PropertyManager*, enter **0.25** as the new radius of the fillet. (**NOTE:** If the *Fillet Parameters* panel is minimized, click on the double arrows to expand the panel.)

6. Select the two edges as shown to create the fillet.

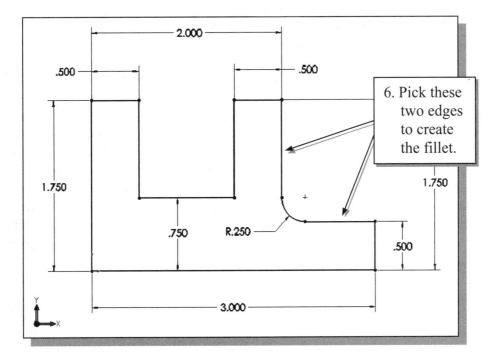

- Note that the fillet is created automatically with the dimension attached. The attached dimension can also be modified through the history tree.

7. Click the **OK** icon (green check mark) in the *PropertyManager*, or hit the [**Esc**] key once, to end the Sketch Fillet command.

8. Click on the **Rebuild** icon in the *Menu Bar*.

9. Save the part with the filename **Saddle_Bracket**. **NOTE:** Do **not** save the part file in the Tutorial_Templates folder.

❖ In a typical design process, the initial design will undergo many analyses, testing, and reviews. The *history-based part modification* approach is an extremely powerful tool that enables us to quickly update the design. At the same time, it is quite clear that PLANNING AHEAD is also important in doing feature-based modeling.

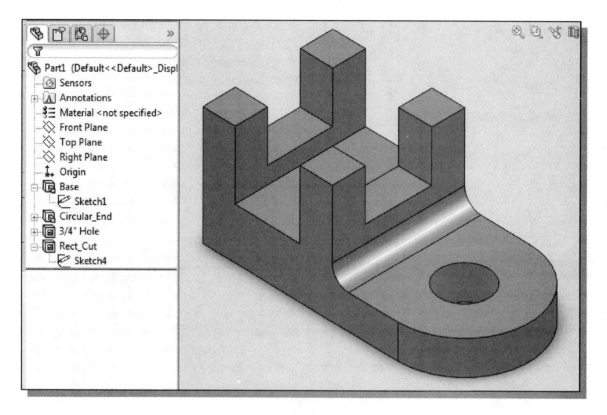

## Questions:

1.  What are stored in the *SolidWorks FeatureManager Design Tree*?

2.  When extruding, what is the difference between Blind and Through All?

3.  Describe the *history-based part modification* approach.

4.  What determines how a model reacts when other features in the model change?

5.  Describe the steps to rename existing features.

6.  Describe two methods available in *SolidWorks* to *modify the dimension values* of parametric sketches.

7.  Create *Design Tree sketches* showing the steps you plan to use to create the two models shown on the next page:

Ex.1)

Ex.2)

## Exercises: (Dimensions are in inches.)

1.  Base plate thickness: **0.25** inches. Boss height **0.5** inches.

2.

3.

4.

**NOTES:**

# Chapter 5
# Geometric Relations Fundamentals

## Learning Objectives

- ◆ **Create Geometric Relations**
- ◆ **Use Dimensional Variables**
- ◆ **Display, Add, and Delete Geometric Relations**
- ◆ **Understand and Apply Different Geometric Relations**
- ◆ **Display and Modify Parametric Relations**
- ◆ **Create Fully Defined Sketches**

Certified Associate Reference Guide

## Certified SolidWorks Associate Exam Objectives Coverage

### Sketch Relations
Objectives: Using Geometric Relations.

### Dimensions
Objectives: Applying and Editing Smart Dimensions.

## DIMENSIONS and RELATIONS

A primary and essential difference between parametric modeling and previous generation computer modeling is that parametric modeling captures the *design intent*. In the previous lessons, we have seen that the design philosophy of *"shape before size"* is implemented through the use of *SolidWorks'* Smart Dimension commands. In performing geometric constructions, dimensional values are necessary to describe the **SIZE** and **LOCATION** of constructed geometric entities. Besides using dimensions to define the geometry, we can also apply geometric rules to control geometric entities. More importantly, *SolidWorks* can capture design intent through the use of **geometric relations**, **dimensional constraints** and **parametric relations**. **Geometric relations** are geometric restrictions that can be applied to geometric entities; for example, *horizontal*, *parallel*, *perpendicular*, and *tangent* are commonly used *geometric relations* in parametric modeling. For part modeling in *SolidWorks*, relations are applied to *2D sketches*. They can be added automatically as the sketch is created or by using the **Add Relation** command. **Dimensional constraints** are used to describe the SIZE and LOCATION of individual geometric shapes. They are added using the *SolidWorks* **Smart Dimension** command. One should also realize that depending upon the way the geometric relations and dimensional constraints are applied, the same results can be accomplished by applying different constraints to the geometric entities. In *SolidWorks*, **parametric relations** can be applied using **Links** and **Equations**. Links are used when multiple dimensions have the same value. The dimension value is linked through the use of a named variable. *SolidWorks* Equations are user-defined mathematical relations between model dimensions, using dimension names as variables. In parametric modeling, features are made of geometric entities with dimensional, geometric, and parametric constraints describing individual design intent. In this lesson, we will discuss the fundamentals of geometric relations and parametric links and equations.

## Create a *Simple Triangular Plate* Design

➢  In parametric modeling, **geometric properties** such as *horizontal*, *parallel*, *perpendicular*, and *tangent* can be applied to geometric entities automatically or manually. By carefully applying proper **geometric relations**, very intelligent models can be created. This concept is illustrated by the following example.

## Fully Defined Geometry

In *SolidWorks*, as we create 2D sketches, geometric relations such as *horizontal* and *parallel* are automatically added to the sketched geometry. In most cases, additional relations and dimensions are needed to fully describe the sketched geometry beyond the geometric relations added by the system. Although we can use *SolidWorks* to build partially constrained or totally unconstrained solid models, the models may behave unpredictably as changes are made. In most cases, it is important to consider the design intent, develop a modeling strategy, and add proper constraints to geometric entities. In the following sections, a simple triangle is used to illustrate the different tools that are available in *SolidWorks* to create/modify geometric relations and dimensional constraints.

## Starting SolidWorks

1. Select the **SolidWorks** option on the *Start* menu or select the **SolidWorks** icon on the desktop to start *SolidWorks*. The *SolidWorks* main window will appear on the screen.

2. Select the **New** icon with a single click of the left-mouse-button on the *Menu Bar*. The *New SolidWorks Document* dialog box should appear in **Advanced** mode. If it appears in **Novice** mode, click once with the left-mouse-button on the **Advanced** icon.

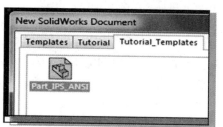

3. Select the **Tutorial_Templates** tab. (**NOTE:** You added this tab in Chapter 4.)

4. Select the **Part_IPS_ANSI** template as shown.

5. Click on the **OK** button to open a new document using the Part_IPS_ANSI template. The *Dimensioning Standard* will automatically be ANSI and the units will be set to inch, pound, second (IPS) as defined in the template.

6. Move the graphics cursor to the **Front Plane** icon in the *FeatureManager Design Tree*. Notice the **Front Plane** icon is highlighted in the design tree and the *Front Plane* outline appears in the graphics area. Click once with the **left-mouse-button** to select the **Front Plane** as the sketch plane.

7. In the *Sketch* toolbar, select the **Sketch** command by left-clicking once on the icon.

8. Select the **Line** icon on the *Sketch* toolbar by clicking once with the **left-mouse-button**.

9.  Create a triangle of arbitrary size positioned near the center of the screen as shown below. (Note that the base of the triangle is horizontal.)

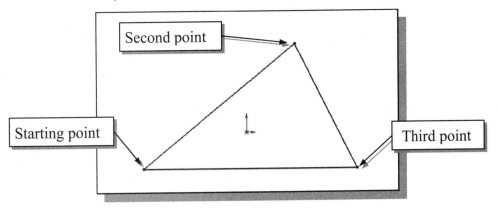

10. Press the [**Esc**] key to exit the Line command.

## Displaying Existing Relations

1.  Select the **Hide/Show Items** icon on the *Heads-up View* toolbar to reveal the pull-down menu. In the pull-down menu, left-click once on the **View Sketch Relations** button. This allows us to display relations that are already applied to the 2D profile. This button toggles the visibility of the *Sketch Relations* symbols *ON* and *OFF*.

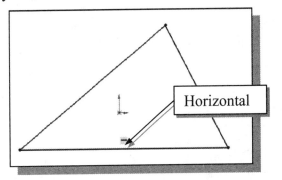

➢  In *SolidWorks*, relations are applied as geometric entities are created. *SolidWorks* will attempt to add proper relations to the geometric entities based on the way the entities were created. Relations are displayed as symbols next to the entities as they are created. The current profile consists of three line entities: three straight lines. The horizontal line has a **Horizontal** *relation* applied to it.

2.  Move the cursor on top of the **Horizontal** icon and notice the line to which this relation is applied is highlighted.

3.  On your own, toggle the visibility of the *Sketch Relations* symbols *OFF*.

# Applying Geometric Relations/Dimensional Constraints

- *SolidWorks* relations for 2D sketches are summarized below.

| Icon | Relation | Entities Selected | Effect |
|---|---|---|---|
| ⊥ | Perpendicular | Two lines | Causes selected lines to lie at right angles to one another. |
| ∥ | Parallel | Two or more lines | Causes selected lines to lie parallel to one another. |
| ∂ | Tangent | An arc, spline, or ellipse and a line or arc | Constrains two curves to be tangent to one another. |
| ⋋ | Coincident | A point and a line, arc, or ellipse | Constrains a point to a curve. |
| ╱ | Midpoint | Two lines or a point and a line | Causes a point to remain at the midpoint of a line. |
| ◎ | Concentric | Two or more arcs, or a point and an arc | Constrains selected items to the same center point. |
| ╱ | Colinear | Two or more lines | Causes selected lines to lie along the same line. |
| — | Horizontal | One or more lines or two or more points | Causes selected items to lie parallel to the X-axis of the sketch coordinate system. |
| │ | Vertical | One or more lines or two or more points | Causes selected items to lie parallel to the Y-axis of the sketch coordinate system. |
| = | Equal | Two or more lines or two or more arcs | Constrains selected arcs/circles to the same radius or selected lines to the same length. |
| ⱴ | Fix | Any entity | Constrains selected entities to a fixed location relative to the sketch coordinate system. However, endpoints of a fixed line, arc, or elliptical segment are free to move along the underlying fixed curve. |
| ⊡ | Symmetric | A centerline and two points, lines, arcs or ellipses | Causes items to remain equidistant from the centerline, on a line perpendicular to the centerline. |
| ◗ | Coradial | Two or more arcs | Causes the selected arcs to share the same centerpoint and radius. |
| X | Intersection | Two lines and one point | Causes the point to remain at the intersection of the two lines. |
| ⋋ | Merge Points | Two points (sketchpoints or endpoints) | Causes the two points to be merged into a single point. |

1. Select the **Smart Dimension** command by clicking once with the **left-mouse-button** on the icon in the *Sketch* toolbar.

2. On your own, create the dimension as shown in the figure below.

3. Press the [**Esc**] key once to exit the Smart Dimension command.

4. **Left click** on the arrow next to the **Display/Delete Relations** button on the *Sketch* toolbar to reveal additional sketch relation commands.

5. Select the **Add Relation** command from the pop-up menu. Notice the *Add Relations PropertyManager* appears. The *Selected Entities* window in the *Add Relations PropertyManager* is blank because no entities are selected.

6. Select the lower right corner of the triangle by clicking once with the **left-mouse-button**.

> Look at the *Add Relations PropertyManager*. In the *Selected Entities* window '**Point3**' is now displayed. '**Distance1**' appears in the *Existing Relations* window. This refers to the dimension on the horizontal line for which Point3 is an endpoint. In the *Add Relations* menu, the **Fix** relation is displayed. This represents the only relation which can be added for the selected entity.

7. Click once with the left-mouse-button on the **Fix** icon in the *Add Relations PropertyManager* as shown. This activates the **Fix** relation.

8. Click the **OK** icon in the *PropertyManager*, or hit the [**Esc**] key once, to end the Add Relations command.

9. On your own, turn *ON* the sketch relations visibility to confirm the Fix constraint is properly applied, then turn the visibility *OFF* again.

> Geometric constraints can be used to control the direction in which changes can occur. For example, in the current design we are adding a horizontal dimension to control the length of the horizontal line. If the length of the line is modified to a greater value, *SolidWorks* will lengthen the line toward the left side. This is due to the fact that the Fix constraint will restrict any horizontal movement of the horizontal line toward the right side

10. Double-click with the left-mouse-button on the dimension text in the graphics area to open the *Modify* dialog box.

11. Enter a value that is greater than the displayed value to observe the effects of the modification. (For example, the dimension value is 3.75; so enter **4.5** in the text box area.) Click the **OK** button in the *Modify* dialog box.

12. On your own, use the **Undo** command to reset the dimension value to the previous value.

13. **Left click** on the arrow next to the **Display/Delete Relations** button on the *Sketch* toolbar to reveal additional sketch relation commands.

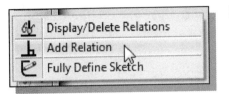

14. Select the **Add Relation** command from the pop-up menu. Notice the *Add Relations PropertyManager* appears. The *Selected Entities* window in the *Add Relations PropertyManager* is blank because no entities are selected.

15. Select the inclined line on the right by clicking once with the **left-mouse-button** as shown in the figure below.

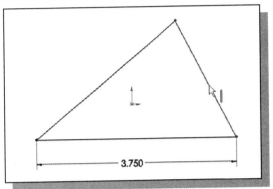

➢ Look at the *Add Relations PropertyManager*. In the *Selected Entities* text box '**Line2**' is now displayed. There are no relations in the *Existing Relations* text box. In the *Add Relations* panel, the **Horizontal**, **Vertical**, and **Fix** relations are displayed. These are the relations which can be added for the selected entity.

16. Click once with the left-mouse-button on the **Vertical** icon in the *Add Relations PropertyManager* as shown. This activates the **Vertical** relation.

17. Click the **OK** icon in the *PropertyManager*, or hit the [**Esc**] key once, to end the **Add Relations** command.

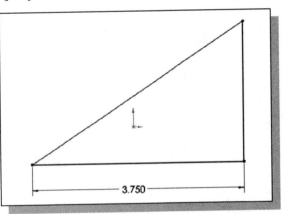

➢ One should think of the relations and dimensions as defining elements of the geometric entities. How many more relations or dimensions will be necessary to fully constrain the sketched geometry? Which relations or dimensions would you use to fully define the sketched geometry?

18. Select the **Hide/Show Items** icon on the *Heads-up View* toolbar to reveal the pull-down menu. In the pull-down menu, left-click once on the **View Sketch Relations** button.

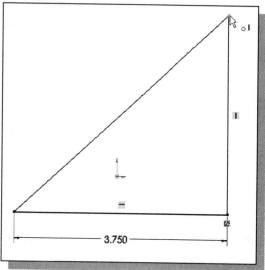

19. Move the cursor on top of the top corner of the triangle.

20. Click and drag the top corner of the triangle and note that the corner can be moved to a new location. Release the mouse button at a new location and notice the corner is adjusted only in an upward or downward direction. Note that the two adjacent lines are automatically adjusted to the new location.

21. On your own, experiment with dragging the other corners to new locations.

- The relations and dimensions that are applied to the geometry provide a full description for the location of the two lower corners of the triangle. The **Vertical** relation, along with the **Fix** relation at the lower right corner, does not fully describe the location of the top corner of the triangle. We will need to add additional information, such as the length of the vertical line or an angle dimension.

22. Select the **Smart Dimension** command by clicking once with the **left-mouse-button** on the icon in the *Sketch* toolbar.

23. Select the *inclined line*.

24. Select the *horizontal line*. Selecting the two lines automatically executes an angle dimension.

25. Select a location for the dimension as shown

26. Enter **45°** in the *Modify* dialog box and select **OK**.

27. Press the [**Esc**] key once to exit the Smart Dimension command.

- The geometry is fully defined with the added dimension.

# Over-Defining and Driven Dimensions

- We can use *SolidWorks* to build partially defined solid models. In most cases, these types of models may behave unpredictably as changes are made. However, *SolidWorks* will not let us over-define a sketch; additional dimensions can still be added to the sketch, but they are used as references only. These additional dimensions are called ***driven dimensions***. *Driven dimensions* do not constrain the sketch; they only reflect the values of the dimensioned geometry. They are shaded differently (grey by default) to distinguish them from normal (parametric) dimensions. A *driven dimension* can be converted to a normal dimension only if another dimension or geometric relation is removed.

1. Select the **Smart Dimension** command in the *Sketch* toolbar.

2. Select the ***vertical line***.

3. Pick a location that is to the right side of the triangle to place the dimension text.

4. A *warning* dialog box appears on the screen stating that the dimension we are trying to create will over-define the sketch. Click on the **OK** button to proceed with the creation of a driven dimension.

5. Press the [**Esc**] key once to exit the Smart Dimension command.

6. On your own, modify the angle dimension to **35°** and observe the changes of the 2D sketch and the driven dimension.

7. Press the [**Esc**] key to ensure that no objects are selected.

## Deleting Existing Relations

1. On your own, make sure the visibility of the *Sketch Relations* is turned *ON*. (**HINT:** See Step 1 on page 5-5.)

2. Move the cursor on top of the **Fixed** relation icon and right-mouse-click once to bring up the option menu.

3. Select **Delete** to remove the Fixed relation that is applied to the lower right corner of the triangle.

4. Move the cursor on top of the top corner of the triangle.

5. Drag the top corner of the triangle and note that the entire triangle is free to move in all directions. Drag the corner toward the top right corner of the graphics window as shown in the figure. Release the mouse button to move the triangle to the new location.

6. On your own, experiment with dragging the other corners and/or the three line segments to new locations on the screen.

❖ **Dimensional constraints** are used to describe the SIZE and LOCATION of individual geometric shapes. **Geometric relations** are **geometric restrictions** that can be applied to geometric entities. The constraints applied to the triangle are sufficient to maintain its size and shape, but the geometry can be moved around; its location definition isn't complete.

7. On your own, reapply the **Fixed** relation to the lower right corner of the triangle.

8. On your own, **delete** the reference dimension.

9. Confirm the same relations and dimensions are applied on your sketch as shown.

10. On your own, turn *OFF* the visibility of the *Sketch Relations*.

❖ Note that the sketch is fully defined and Fully Defined is displayed in the *Status Bar* at the bottom of the screen.

| Fully Defined | Editing Sketch1 | 🔒 | ❓ |

## Using the Fully Define Sketch Tool

➢ In *SolidWorks*, the **Fully Define Sketch** tool can be used to calculate which dimensions and relations are required to fully define an under defined sketch. Fully defined sketches can be updated more predictably as design changes are implemented. One general procedure for applying dimensions to sketches is to use the **Smart Dimension** command to add the desired dimensions, and then use the **Fully Define Sketch** tool to fully constrain the sketch. It is also important to realize that different dimensions and geometric relations can be applied to the same sketch to accomplish a fully defined geometry.

1. **Right click** once on the **3.750** linear dimension and select **Delete** in the option menu. Notice Under Defined is now displayed in the *Status Bar*.

2. **Left click** on the arrow next to the **Display/Delete Relations** button on the *Sketch* toolbar to reveal additional sketch relation commands.

3. Select the **Fully Define Sketch** command from the pop-up menu.

4. The *Fully Define Sketch PropertyManager* appears. **If necessary**, click once with the **left-mouse-button** on the arrows to reveal the Dimensions option panel as shown.

5. Notice that under the *Horizontal Dimensions Scheme* option, Baseline is selected. The origin is selected as the default baseline datum and appears in the datum selection window as Point1@Origin.

6. Click once with the **left-mouse-button** in the *Datum* selection text box to select a different datum to serve as the baseline.

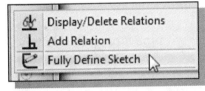

4. Left-click (if necessary)

6. Select

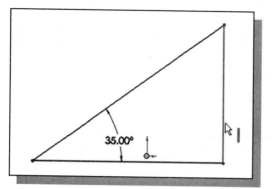

7. In the graphics window select the vertical line. Notice Line2 is now displayed in the *Datum* selection window as the *Horizontal Dimensions* baseline.

8. On your own, select an appropriate baseline datum for the vertical dimensions.

9. Select **Calculate** in the *PropertyManager* to continue with the Fully Define Sketch command.

**Entities to Fully Define**
- ⦿ All entities in sketch
- ○ Selected entities

Calculate

❖ Note that *SolidWorks* automatically applies the horizontal dimension, using the vertical line as the baseline. Since this is the only dimension necessary to fully define the sketch, it is the only dimension added. Notice that Fully Defined is now displayed in the *Status Bar*.

10. Click the **OK** button accept the results and exit the Fully Define Sketch tool.

## Adding Additional Geometry

1. Select the **Circle** command by clicking once with the left-mouse-button on the icon in the *Sketch* toolbar.

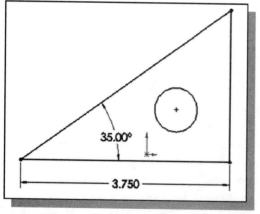

2. On your own, create a circle of arbitrary size inside the triangle as shown below.

3. Press the [**Esc**] key to ensure that no objects are selected.

❖ Notice that Under Defined is now displayed in the *Status Bar*.

Display/Delete Relations
Add Relation
Fully Define Sketch

4. Select **Add Relation** from the pop-up menu on the *Sketch* toolbar.

5. Pick the circle by left-mouse-clicking once on the geometry.

6. Pick the inclined line.

➢ Look at the *Add Relations PropertyManager*. In the *Selected Entities* text box **Arc1** and **Line1** are now displayed. There are no relations in the *Existing Relations* window. In the *Add Relations* menu, the **Tangent** and **Fix** relations are displayed. These are the relations which can be added for the selected entities.

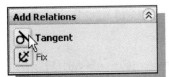

7. Click once with the left-mouse-button on the **Tangent** icon in the *Add Relations PropertyManager* as shown. This activates the Tangent relation.

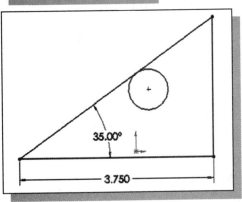

8. Click the **OK** icon in the *PropertyManager*, or hit the [**Esc**] key once, to end the Add Relations command.

• How many more relations or dimensions do you think will be necessary to fully define the circle? Which relations or dimensions would you use to fully define the geometry?

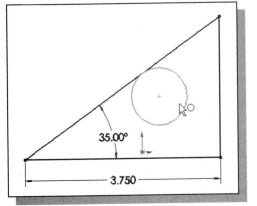

9. Move the cursor on top of the right side of the circle, and then drag the circle toward the right edge of the graphics window. Notice the size of the circle is adjusted while the system maintains the Tangent relation.

10. Drag the center of the circle toward the upper right direction. Notice the Tangent relation is always maintained by the system.

➢ On your own, experiment with adding additional relations and/or dimensions to fully define the sketched geometry. Use the **Undo** command to undo any changes before proceeding to the next section.

11. Press the [**Esc**] key to ensure that no objects are selected.

12. Inside the graphics window, click once with the **left-mouse-button** on the **center of the circle** to select the centerpoint.

13. Hold down the **[Ctrl]** key and click once with the **left-mouse-button** on the **vertical line**. Holding the [Ctrl] key allows selecting the vertical line while maintaining selection of the circle centerpoint. This is a method to select multiple entities.

- Notice the *Properties PropertyManager* for the selected entities is displayed. This provides an alternate way to control the relations for selected properties.

14. Click once with the left-mouse-button on the **Coincident** icon in the *Add Relations* panel in the *PropertyManager* as shown. This activates the Coincident relation.

15. Click the **OK** icon in the *PropertyManager*.

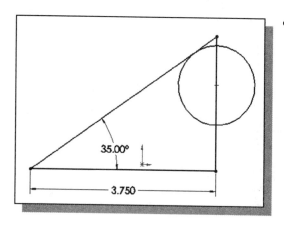

- Is the circle fully defined? (**HINT:** Drag the circle to see whether it is fully defined.)

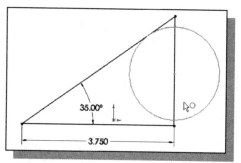

16. On your own, select the circle centerpoint <u>and</u> the vertical line in the graphics area. (**HINT:** Repeat steps 21 and 22.) Notice the *PropertyManager* appears.

17. In the *PropertyManager*, Coincident1 is listed under *Existing Relations*. Move the cursor over **Coincident1** and click once with the **right-mouse-button**.

18. Select **Delete** in the pop-up menu by clicking once with the **left-mouse-button**.

19. Click the **OK** icon in the *PropertyManager*.

20. On your own, add a Coincident relation between the center of the circle and the horizontal line.

- Which relations or dimensions would you use to fully define the geometry?

❖ The application of different relations affects the geometry differently. The design intent is maintained in the CAD model's database and thus allows us to create very intelligent CAD models that can be modified/revised fairly easily. On your own, experiment and observe the results of applying different relations to the triangle. For example: (1) adding another Fix constraint to the top corner of the triangle; (2) deleting the horizontal dimension and adding another Fix relation to the left corner of the triangle; and (3) adding another Tangent relation and adding the size dimension to the circle.

21. On your own, modify the 2D sketch as shown below.

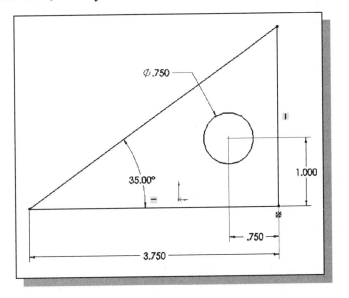

➢ On your own, use the **Extruded Boss/Base** command and create a 3D solid model with a plate thickness of **0.25**.

## Relations Settings

• Select **Options** in the *Menu Bar*. Click on **Relations/Snaps** under the **System Options** tab to display and/or modify the relation settings. On your own, adjust the settings and experiment with the effects of the different settings on sketching.

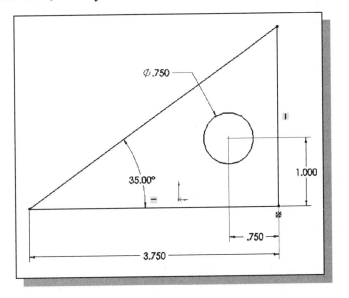

## Parametric Relations

- In parametric modeling, dimensions are design parameters that are used to control the sizes and locations of geometric features. Dimensions are more than just values; they can also be used as feature control variables. This concept is illustrated by the following example.

 1.  Select the **New** icon with a single click of the left-mouse-button on the *Menu Bar*. The *New SolidWorks Document* dialog box should appear in Advanced mode. If it appears in Novice mode, click once with the left-mouse-button on the **Advanced** icon.

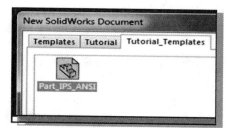

2.  Select the **Tutorial_Templates** tab. (**NOTE:** You added this tab in Chapter 4.)

3.  Select the **Part_IPS_ANSI** template as shown.

4.  Click on the **OK** button to open a new document using the Part_IPS_ANSI template.

- Another graphics window appears on the screen. We can switch between the two models using the *Window* pull-down menu.

5.  Click once with the **left-mouse-button** on the **Front Plane** icon in the *FeatureManager Design Tree* to pre-select the Front Plane as the sketch plane.

 6.  In the *Sketch* toolbar, select the **Sketch** command by left-clicking once on the icon.

7.  Select the **Corner Rectangle** command by clicking once with the **left-mouse-button** on the icon in the *Sketch* toolbar.

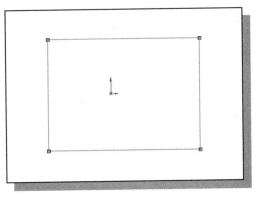

8.  Create a rectangle of arbitrary size positioned near the center of the screen.

 9.  Select the **Circle** command by clicking once with the left-mouse-button on the icon in the *Sketch* toolbar.

10. Create a **circle** of arbitrary size inside the rectangle as shown.

11. On your own, adjust the geometry by adding dimensions as shown below. (**NOTE:** Create and modify the overall width of the rectangle first and the overall height of the rectangle second. These two dimensions will be used as the control variables for the rest of the dimensions.)

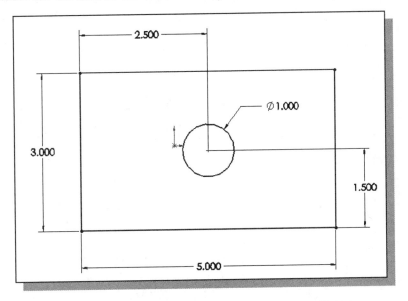

•  On your own, change the overall width of the rectangle to **6.0** and the overall height of the rectangle to **3.6** and observe the location of the circle in relation to the edges of the rectangle. Adjust the dimensions back to **5.0** and **3.0** as shown in the above figure before continuing.

## Dimensional Values and Dimensional Variables

Initially in *SolidWorks*, dimension values are used to create different geometric entities. The text created by the Smart Dimension command also reflects the actual location or size of the entity. Each dimension is also assigned a name that allows the dimension to be used as a control variable. The default format is "Dxx," where the "xx" is a number that *SolidWorks* increments automatically each time a new dimension is added.  The full name has the form "Dxx@yyyyy", where the "yyyyy" is the entity in which the dimension is applied.  For example "D2@Sketch1" is the full name for the second dimension applied in Sketch 1.

Let us look at our current design, which represents a plate with a hole at the center. The dimensional values describe the size and/or location of the plate and the hole. If a modification is required to change the width of the plate, the location of the hole will remain the same as described by the two location dimensional values. This is okay if that is the design intent. On the other hand, the *design intent* may require (1) keeping the hole at the center of the plate and (2) maintaining the size of the hole to be one-third of the height of the plate. We will establish a set of parametric relations using the dimensional variables to capture the design intent described in statements (1) and (2) above.

1.  Move the cursor over the **width dimension** of the rectangle to display the *Dimension Name* in the cursor pop-up box.

*   Notice the *variable name* **D1@Sketch1** is displayed in the cursor box.

## Parametric Equations

- Each time we add a dimension to a model, that value is established as a parameter for the model. We can use parameters in equations to set the values of other parameters.

  1. Double-click with the left-mouse-button on the **horizontal location dimension** of the circle to display the *Modify* window.

  2. Click on the drop down **arrow** next to **2.500in** in the *Modify* window to reveal the pull-down options menu.

  3. Select **Add Equation** in the menu.  The *Add Equation* window will appear.

  4. The start of the equation appears as follows:  "D3@Sketch1" =.  (**NOTE:** If you added the dimensions in a different order, this dimension may have a different number.)  Finish the equation to make this dimension equal to half the width as follows:  **"D3@Sketch1" = "D1@Sketch1"/2**.

| Add Equation | | | | | | | | |
|---|---|---|---|---|---|---|---|---|
| "D3@Sketch1" = "D1@Sketch1"/2 | | | | | | | | ⌃ |
| | | | | | | Comment | | |
| secant | arcsin | sin | abs | 1 | 2 | 3 | / | |
| cosec | arccos | cos | exp | 4 | 5 | 6 | * | |
| cotan | arcsec | tan | log | 7 | 8 | 9 | - | |
| arccosec | arccotan | atn | sqr | = | 0 | . | + | |
| | | sgn | int | pi | ( | ) | ^ | |
| OK | | Cancel | | Undo | | | ⌄ | |

5. Click on **OK**.  The *Equations Part 2* window will appear.

❖ The *Equations-Part2* window displays all equations. It is possible to add or edit equations directly in this window.

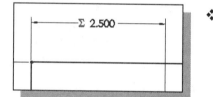

6. Notice the equation you entered appears. Notice the *Evaluates to* value of **2.5in.**

7. Click **OK**.

❖ Notice, the derived dimension values are displayed with **Σ** in front of the numbers. The parametric relations we entered are used to control the location of the circle; the location is based on the width of the rectangle.

## Viewing the Established Equations

1. On your own, move the cursor over each dimension and note the corresponding dimension name. We will use these names to create additional equations.

2. Move the cursor over the *SolidWorks* icon on the *Menu Bar* to reveal the pull-down menus, click once with the left-mouse-button on the **Tools** icon and select **Equations** in the pull-down menu as shown.

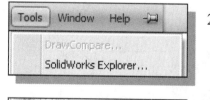

• The Equations command can be used to display all equations used to define the model. We can also edit equations, and create additional design variables and equations.

3. Click the **Add** icon in the *Equations-Part2* window. The *Add Equation* window is displayed.

• We will enter an equation to constrain the vertical location dimension for the circle equal to half the height of the rectangle.

4. Move the cursor to the graphics area and click once with the **left-mouse-button** on the vertical (1.500″) location dimension. (**NOTE:** You may have to reposition the *Add Equation* window to uncover the dimension in the graphics area.) Notice the dimension name automatically appears in the equation line of the *Add Equation* window.

5. In the *Add Equation* window, click on the **=** button.

6. Move the cursor to the graphics area and select the vertical dimension on the rectangle.

7. In the *Add Equation* window, click on the divide by (*/*) button.

8. In the *Add Equation* window, click on the **2** button. The equation should appear as shown below (although the dimension names may be different, depending on the order in which they were created).

9. Click the **OK** button in the *Add Equation* window to add the equation.

10. On your own, add an equation to constrain the diameter of the circle to be ⅓ the height of the plate.

11. Click **OK** in the *Equations-Part2* window to accept the equations.

12. On your own, change the dimensions of the rectangle to **6.0 x 3.6** and observe the changes to the location and size of the circle. (**HINT:** Double-click the dimension text to bring up the *Modify* window.)

❖ *SolidWorks* automatically adjusts the dimensions of the design, and the parametric relations we entered are also applied and maintained. The dimensional constraints are used to control the size and location of the hole. The design intent, previously expressed by statements (1) and (2) at the beginning of this section, is now embedded into the model.

## Adding Linked Dimensions

1. On your own, add two unconstrained circles as shown below.

2. Press the [**Esc**] key (twice, if necessary) to ensure no items are selected.

3.  Select **Add Relation** from the pop-up menu on the *Sketch* toolbar. Notice the *Selected Entities* window in the *Add Relations PropertyManager* is blank because no entities are selected.

4.  Select the centerpoints of the three circles.

5.  Click once with the left-mouse-button on the **Horizontal** icon in the *Add Relations PropertyManager* as shown. This activates the **Horizontal** relation. Notice the two new holes become aligned horizontally with the constrained central hole.

6.  On your own, add a **Smart Dimension** with a value of **1.75** between the centerpoints of the central circle and the circle to the left as shown.

7.  Double-click with the left-mouse-button on the **horizontal location dimension** between the circles to display the *Modify* window.

8.  Click on the drop down **arrow** next to 1.750in in the *Modify* window to reveal the pull-down options menu.

9.  Select **Link Value** in the menu.  The *Shared Values* window will appear.

10. In the *Shared Values* window, enter **Offset** for the Name and click **OK**.

11. Add a **Smart Dimension** between the centerpoints for the central circle and the circle to the right as shown.

12. Click on the drop down **arrow** next to the numerical dimension value in the *Modify* window to reveal the pull-down options menu.

13. Select **Link Value** in the menu. The *Shared Values* window will appear.

14. In the *Shared Values* window, click on the arrow to the right of the *Name* entry line to reveal the existing shared value names, select **Offset** for the Name, and click **OK**.

15. Notice the two linked dimensions both read 1.750. On your own, change the value of the dimension to the right to **1.5**. (**HINT:** Double-click on the dimension to open the *Modify* window.)

16. Change the offset dimension back to **1.75** by changing either of the linked dimensions.

17. On your own, add a linked dimension to constrain the two new holes to have the same diameter. Name the link **Dia2** and change the diameter value to **0.5**. The final sketch should look like the one below.

➤ On your own, use the **Extrude** command and create a 3D solid model with a plate thickness of **0.25**.

## Saving the Part File

1. Click the arrow next to the **Save** icon in the *Menu Bar* to reveal the save options and select **Save As**.

2. In the popup window, enter **Plate** as the name of the file.

3. Click on the **Save** button to save the file.

4. Move the cursor over the SolidWorks icon on the *Menu Bar* to reveal the pull-down menus and click on the **Window** pull-down menu.

5. Select the **Part1** option to switch to the model of the triangular plate from the first half of this lesson.

6. On your own, save the triangular plate with the filename **Triangle**.

## Questions:

1. What is the difference between *dimensional* constraints and *geometric* relations?

2. How can we confirm that a sketch is fully defined?

3. How do we distinguish between derived dimensions and parametric dimensions on the screen?

4. Describe the procedure to Display/Edit user-defined equations.

5. List and describe three different geometric relations available in *SolidWorks*.

6. Does *SolidWorks* allow us to build partially defined solid models? What are the advantages and disadvantages of building these types of models?

7. Identify and describe the following commands.

   (a)

   (b)

   (c)

   (d)

## Exercises:

(Create and establish three parametric relations for each of the following designs.)

1.  Dimensions are in millimeters. (Base thickness: 10 mm., Boss height: 20 mm.)

2.  Dimensions are in inches. Plate thickness: 0.25 inches.

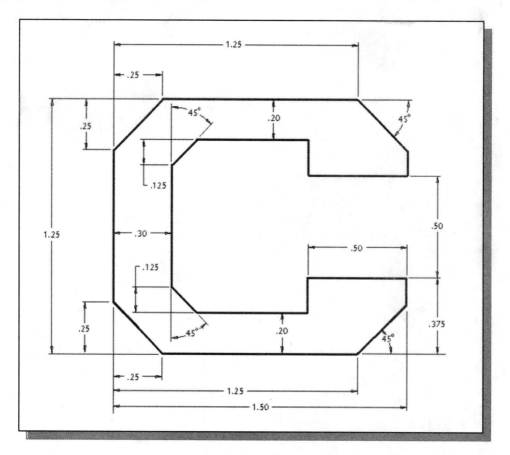

3. Dimensions are in inches

4. Dimensions are in inches.

**NOTES:**

# Chapter 6
# Geometric Construction Tools

## Learning Objectives

- ♦ **Apply Geometry Relations**
- ♦ **Use the Trim/Extend Command**
- ♦ **Use the Offset Command**
- ♦ **Understand the Profile Sketch Approach**
- ♦ **Use the Convert Entities Command**
- ♦ **Understand and Use Reference Geometry**
- ♦ **Edit with Click and Drag**
- ♦ **Use the Fully Define Sketch Tool**
- ♦ **Use the Selected Contours Option**

| **Certified SolidWorks Associate Exam Objectives Coverage** |
|---|

**Certified Associate Reference Guide**

## Introduction

The main characteristics of solid modeling are the accuracy and completeness of the geometric database of the three-dimensional objects. However, working in three-dimensional space using input and output devices that are largely two-dimensional in nature is potentially tedious and confusing. *SolidWorks* provides an assortment of two-dimensional construction tools to make the creation of wireframe geometry easier and more efficient. *SolidWorks* includes sketch tools to create basic geometric entities such as lines, arcs, etc. These entities are grouped to define a boundary or profile. A *profile* is a closed region and can contain other closed regions. Profiles are commonly used to create extruded and revolved features. An *invalid profile* consists of self-intersecting curves or open regions. In this lesson, the basic geometric construction tools, such as Trim and Extend, are used to create profiles. Mastering the geometric construction tools along with the application of proper geometric and parametric relations is the true essence of *parametric modeling*.

## The *Gasket* Design

❖ Based on your knowledge of *SolidWorks* so far, how would you create this design? What are the more difficult geometry involved in the design? Take a few minutes to consider a modeling strategy and do preliminary planning by sketching on a piece of paper. You are also encouraged to create the design on your own prior to following through the tutorial.

# Modeling Strategy

## Starting SolidWorks

1. Select the **SolidWorks** option on the *Start* menu or select the **SolidWorks** icon on the desktop to start *SolidWorks*. The *SolidWorks* main window will appear on the screen.

2. Select the **New** icon with a single click of the left-mouse-button on the *Menu Bar*.

3. Under the *Templates* tab of the *New SolidWorks Document* dialog box, select the **Part** icon with a single click of the left-mouse-button.

4. Select **OK** in the *New SolidWorks Document* dialog box to open a new part document.

5. Select the **Options** icon from the *Menu Bar* to open the *Options* dialog box.

6. Select the **Document Properties** tab.

7. Select **ANSI** in the pull-down selection window under the *Overall drafting standard* panel as shown.

8. Click **Units** as shown below. We will use the default MMGS (millimeter, gram, second) unit system.

9. Select **.123** in the *Decimals* spin box for the *Length units* as shown to define the degree of accuracy with which the units will be displayed to 3 decimal places.

## Creating a 2D Sketch

1. Click once with the **left-mouse-button** to select the **Front Plane** icon in the *FeatureManager Design Tree*. Notice the **Front Plane** icon is highlighted in the design tree and the *Front Plane* outline appears in the graphics area.

2. In the *Sketch* toolbar, select the **Sketch** command by left-clicking once on the icon. Notice the **Front Plane** automatically becomes the sketch plane because it was pre-selected.

3. Click on the **Line** icon in the *Sketch* toolbar.

4. Create a sketch as shown in the figure below. Start the sketch from the top right corner. The line segments are all parallel and/or perpendicular to each other. We will intentionally make the line segments of arbitrary length, as it is quite common during the design stage that not all of the values are determined.

5. Inside the graphics window, right-mouse-click to bring up the option menu and select **Select** to end the Line command.

6. Select the **Circle** command by clicking once with the left-mouse-button on the icon in the *2D Sketch Panel*.

7. Pick a location that is above the bottom horizontal line as the center location of the circle.

8. Move the cursor toward the right and create a circle of arbitrary size, by clicking once with the left-mouse-button.

9. Inside the graphics window, click once with the right-mouse-button to display the option menu. Select **Select** in the popup menu to end the Circle option.

10. Click on the **Line** icon in the *Sketch* toolbar.

11. Move the cursor near the upper portion of the circle and, when the **Coincident** constraint symbol is displayed, click once with the **left-mouse-button** to select the starting point for the line.

Coincident Symbol

12. For the other end of the line, select a location that is on the lower horizontal line and about one-third from the right endpoint. Notice the **Coincident** constraint symbol is displayed when the cursor is on the horizontal line.

13. Inside the graphics window, right-mouse-click to bring up the option menu.

14. In the option menu, select **Select** to end the Line command.

## Editing the Sketch by Dragging the Entities

❖   In *SolidWorks*, we can click and drag any under-defined curve or point in the sketch to change the size or shape of the sketched profile. As illustrated in the previous chapter, this option can be used to identify under-defined entities. This *editing by dragging* method is also an effective visual approach that allows designers to quickly make changes.

1.   Move the cursor on the lower left vertical edge of the sketch. Click and drag the edge to a new location that is toward the right side of the sketch.

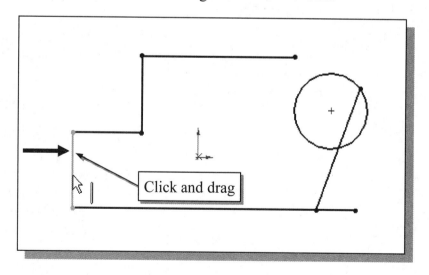

❖   Note that we can only drag the vertical edge horizontally; the connections to the two horizontal lines are maintained while we are moving the geometry.

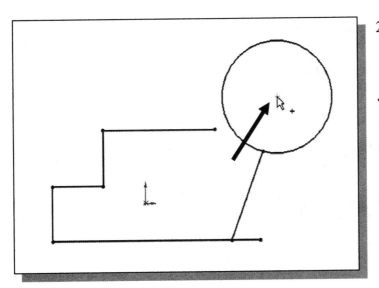

2.  Click and drag the center point of the circle to a new location.

❖  Note that as we adjust the size and the location of the circle, the connection to the inclined line is maintained.

3.  Click and drag the lower endpoint of the inclined line to a new location.

❖  Note that as we adjust the size and the location of the inclined line, the location of the bottom horizontal edge is also adjusted.

➢  Note that several changes occur as we adjust the size and the location of the inclined line. The location of the bottom horizontal line and the length of the vertical line are adjusted accordingly.

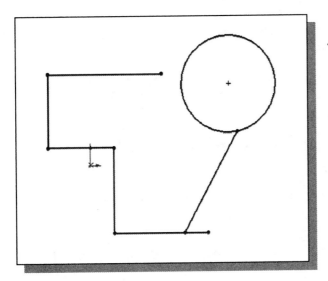

4.  On your own, adjust the sketch so that the shape of the sketch appears roughly as shown.

❖  The *editing by dragging* method is an effective approach that allows designers to explore and experiment with different design concepts.

## Adding Additional Relations

1.  Choose **Smart Dimension** in the *Sketch* toolbar.

2.  Add the horizontal location dimension, from the top left vertical edge to the center of the circle as shown. (Do not be overly concerned with the dimensional value; we are still working on creating a *rough sketch*.)

3.  Click the **OK** icon in the *PropertyManager*, or hit the [**Esc**] key once, to end the Smart Dimension command.

4.  Select the **Add Relation** command from the pop-up menu on the *Sketch* toolbar. Notice the *Selected Entities* window in the *Add Relations PropertyManager* is blank because no entities are selected.

5.  Pick the inclined line by left-mouse-clicking once on the geometry.

6.  Pick the circle.

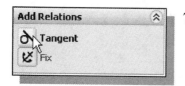

7.  Click once with the left-mouse-button on the **Tangent** icon in the *Add Relations PropertyManager* as shown. This activates the **Tangent** relation. The sketched geometry is adjusted as shown below.

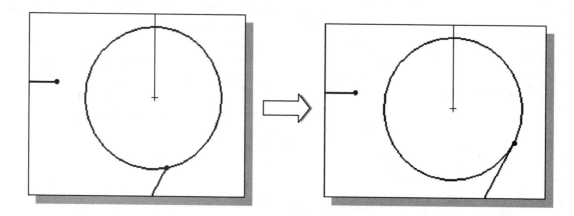

8.  Click the **OK** icon in the *PropertyManager*, or hit the [**Esc**] key once, to end the Add Relations command.

9.  Click and drag the circle to a new location.

❖  Note that the dimension we added now restricts the horizontal movement of the center of the circle. The Tangent relation to the inclined line is maintained.

## Using the Trim and Extend Commands

➢  In the following sections, we will illustrate using the Trim and Extend commands to complete the desired 2D profile.

❖  The **Trim** and **Extend** commands can be used to shorten/lengthen an object so that it ends precisely at a boundary. As a general rule, *SolidWorks* will try to clean up sketches by forming a closed region sketch.

1.  **Left-click** on the **arrow** next to the **Trim Entities** button on the *Sketch* toolbar to reveal additional commands.

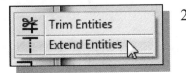

2.  Select the **Extend Entities** command from the pop-up menu.

3. We will first extend the top horizontal line to the circle. Move the cursor near the right hand endpoint of the top horizontal line. *SolidWorks* will automatically display the possible result of the selection. When the extended line appears, click once with the left-mouse-button.

4. Press the [**Esc**] key once to end the Extend command.

**Trim Entities**
Trims or extends a sketch entity to be coincident to another, or deletes a sketch entity.

5. We will next trim the bottom horizontal line to the inclined line. Select the **Trim Entities** icon on the *Sketch* toolbar.

**Options**

- Power trim
- Corner
- Trim away inside
- Trim away outside
- Trim to closest

6. Select the **Trim to closest** option in the *Trim PropertyManager*.

7. Move the cursor near the right hand endpoint of the bottom horizontal line. The portion of the line that will be trimmed is highlighted. Click once with the **left-mouse-button** to trim the line.

8. Click the **OK** icon in the *PropertyManager*, or hit the [**Esc**] key once, to end the Trim command.

Display/Delete Relations
Add Relation
Fully Define Sketch

9. Select the **Add Relation** command from the pop-up menu on the *Sketch* toolbar.

10. In the graphics area, select the **center point of the circle** and the **top horizontal line** as shown.

11. Click once with the left-mouse-button on the **Coincident** icon in the *Add Relations PropertyManager* as shown. This activates the Coincident relation.

12. Click the **OK** icon in the *PropertyManager*, or hit the [**Esc**] key once, to end the Add Relations command.

13. On your own, create the **height dimension** to the left of the sketch as shown.

14. On your own, **Trim** the circle as shown.

15. Hit the [**Esc**] key to end the Trim command.

16. Turn *ON* the visibility of the *Sketch Relations* (on the *Hide/Show Items* pull-down menu in the *Heads-up* toolbar) to examine the applied constraints. Confirm that the **Tangent** and **Coincident** relations are applied as shown.

17. Turn *OFF* the visibility of the *Sketch Relations*.

## Adding Dimensions with the Fully Define Sketch Tool

➢ In *SolidWorks*, the **Fully Define Sketch** tool can be used to calculate which dimensions and relations are required to fully define an under defined sketch. Fully defined sketches can be updated more predictably as design changes are implemented. The general procedure for applying dimensions to sketches is to use the **Smart Dimension** command to add the desired key dimensions, and then use the **Fully Define Sketch** tool as a quick way to calculate all other sketch dimensions necessary. *SolidWorks* remembers which dimensions were added by the user and which were calculated by the system, so that automatic dimensions do not replace the desired dimensions. In the following steps we will use the Fully Define Sketch tool to apply the dimensions necessary, but will disable the automatic application of sketch relations.

1. Select the **Fully Define Sketch** command from the pop-up menu on the *Sketch* toolbar.

2. The *Fully Define Sketch PropertyManager* appears. **Uncheck** the Relations box to disable the calculation of geometric relations.

3. Click once with the **left-mouse-button** on the arrows to reveal the Dimensions option panel, if necessary.

4. Notice that under the *Horizontal Dimensions Scheme* option, Baseline is selected. The origin is selected as the default baseline datum and appears in the datum selection window as Point1@Origin. Click once with the **left-mouse-button** in the *Datum* selection text box to select a different datum to serve as the baseline.

5. In the graphics window, select the vertical line as shown. Notice Line2 is now displayed in the *Datum* selection text box as the *Horizontal Dimensions* baseline.

6. In the *PropertyManager*, under the *Vertical Dimensions Scheme* option panel, click once with the **left-mouse-button** in the *Datum* selection text box.

7.  In the graphics window, select the horizontal line as shown. Notice **Line1** is now displayed in the *Datum* selection text box as the *Vertical Dimensions* baseline.

8.  Select **Calculate** in the *PropertyManager* to continue with the Fully Define Sketch command.

9.  A dialog box appears with the statement "*Fully Define Sketch is complete but the sketch is still under defined.*" This is because the sketch is not fixed to a location in the coordinate system. Select **OK** to close the dialog box.

**SolidWorks**

Fully Define Sketch is complete but the sketch is still under defined. To fully define the sketch, do one of the following:
o Dimension to model edges or vertices
o Dimension to the origin
o Right-click a point in the sketch and select to Fix it
o Select all the relations in the dialog if not selected and calculate

☐ Do not show this message again                        OK

10. Click **OK** in the *PropertyManager* to accept the results and exit the Fully Define Sketch command.

➢  The *Autodimension* results should appear as shown. (**NOTE:** Dimensional values will be different; this is only a rough sketch.)

11. On your own, change the dimensions to the desired values as shown below. (**HINT:** Change the larger values first.)

## Fully Defined Geometry

The sketch is under defined. The shape is now fully constrained, but the position is not fixed. On your own, left-click on any sketch feature and drag the mouse. Notice the sketch shape does not change, but the entire sketch is free to move.

1.  Press the [**Esc**] key to ensure no items are selected.

2.  Select the **Add Relation** command from the pop-up menu on the *Sketch* toolbar.

3.  Pick the centerpoint of the arc by left-mouse-clicking once on the geometry.

4.  Pick the sketch plane coordinate origin. (**NOTE:** If the origin symbol is not visible in the graphics area, turn *ON* the visibility by selecting Origins under the *View* toolbar.)

5.  Click once with the left-mouse-button on the **Coincident** icon in the *Add Relations PropertyManager* as shown.

6.  Click the **OK** icon in the *PropertyManager*, or hit the [**Esc**] key once, to end the Add Relations command.

7.  Press the [**F**] key to zoom the sketch to fit the graphics area. Note that the sketch is fully defined with the added relation. Fully Defined is displayed in the *Status Bar* at the bottom of the screen, and the color of the sketch features changes to black.

## Creating Fillets and Completing the Sketch

1. Click on the **Sketch Fillet** icon in the *Sketch* toolbar.

2. The *Sketch Fillet PropertyManager* appears. Enter **20 mm** for the fillet radius as shown.

3. Notice *"Select a sketch vertex or entities to fillet"* is displayed in the *Message* panel of the *PropertyManager*. Select the corner where the horizontal line meets the arc, as shown.

4. On your own, create the three additional fillets as shown in the figure below. Note that all the rounds and fillets are created with the same radius.

5. Click on the **OK** icon in the *PropertyManager* to end the Sketch Fillet command.

6. Click once with the **left-mouse-button** on the **Sketch** icon on the *Sketch* toolbar to exit the Sketch option.

## Profile Sketch

❖ In *SolidWorks*, **profiles** are closed regions that are defined from sketches. Profiles are used as cross sections to create solid features. For example, **Extrude**, **Revolve**, **Sweep**, **Loft**, and **Coil** operations all require the definition of at least a single profile. The sketches used to define a profile can contain additional geometry since the additional geometry entities are consumed when the feature is created. To create a profile we can create single or multiple closed regions, or we can select existing solid edges to form closed regions. A profile cannot contain self-intersecting geometry; regions selected in a single operation form a single profile. As a general rule, we should dimension and constrain profiles to prevent them from unpredictable size and shape changes. *SolidWorks* does allow us to create under-defined profiles; the dimensions and/or geometric relations can be added/edited later.

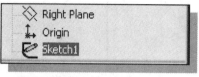

1. Make sure the sketch – Sketch1 – is selected in the *FeatureManager Design Tree*.

2. In the *Features* toolbar, select the **Extruded Boss/Base** command by clicking once with the left-mouse-button on the icon.

❖ *SolidWorks* automatically highlights the selected closed region and the defining geometry, which forms the profile required for the operation.

3. In the *Extrude PropertyManager*, enter **5 mm** as the extrusion distance.

4. Click on the **OK** button to accept the settings and create the base feature.

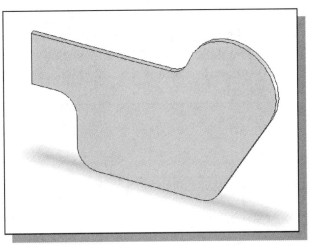

❖ Note that all the sketched geometry entities and dimensions are consumed and have disappeared from the screen when the feature is created.

## Redefining the Sketch and Profile using Contour Selection

- Engineering designs usually go through many revisions and changes. *SolidWorks* provides an assortment of tools to handle design changes quickly and effectively. We will demonstrate some of the tools available by changing the base feature of the design. The profile used to create the extrusion is selected from the sketched geometry entities. In *SolidWorks*, any profile can be edited and/or redefined at any time. It is this type of functionality in parametric solid modeling software that provides designers with greater flexibility and the ease to experiment with different design considerations.

- In the *SolidWorks PropertyManager* for features requiring definition of a profile, the **Selected Contours** selection window can be used to select sketch contours and model edges, and apply features to them. Contour Selection is a grouping mechanism that allows us to use a partial sketch to create features. It is a tool that helps maintain design intent by reducing the amount of trimming necessary to build the contour. In the previous section, the Boss-Extrude feature was created using a single continuous sketch contour to define the profile. In this section we will demonstrate the utility of the Contour Selection tool to generate a similar profile from a sketch containing self-intersecting geometry and multiple closed regions.

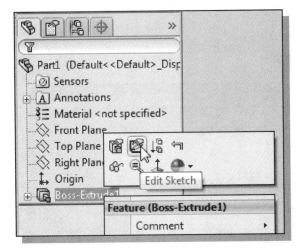

1. In the *FeatureManager Design Tree*, **right-mouse-click** once on the **Boss-Extrude1** feature to bring up the option menu; then pick the **Edit Sketch** icon in the pop-up menu as shown.

2. Select the **View Orientation** button on the *Heads-up View* toolbar, then select the **Normal to** icon to obtain a view normal to the sketch.

3.  On your own, create the rough sketch as shown in the figure below. We will intentionally under-define the new sketch to illustrate the flexibility of the system. The dimensions of the new sketch elements are not important. It is important that **tangent relations** are added where the circles meet tangent to lines or other circles.

4.  Select the **Sketch** icon on the *Sketch* toolbar to exit the Sketch option.

➤   The *SolidWorks* pop-up window may appear indicating an error will occur when *SolidWorks* attempts to rebuild the model. This is due to the multiple possible contours for extrusion now present in the sketch. We will next redefine the profile for the base feature using the **Selected Contours** tool.

**SolidWorks**

⚠ Cannot rebuild the feature using this sketch

The sketch has a problem that prevents its feature from rebuilding successfully.

➜ Show the problem using Check Sketch for Feature

➜ Exit the sketch and rebuild anyway
The feature will have an error.

[ Cancel ]

5.  If the *SolidWorks* pop-up window appears, select the option '**Exit the sketch and rebuild anyway**'.

6.  The *What's Wrong* window appears with an explanation of the error. Select the **Close** button to close this window.

**What's Wrong**

| Type | Feature | Preview | Help | Description |
|---|---|---|---|---|
| ⊗ Error | Boss-Extrude1 | | | The sketch cannot be used for a feature because an endpoint is wrongly shared by multiple entities. |

☑ Show errors   ☑ Show warnings   ☑ Display What's Wrong during rebuild      [ Close ]  [ Help ]

7. In the *FeatureManager Design Tree*, **right-mouse-click** once on the **Boss-Extrude1** feature to bring up the option menu; then pick the **Edit Feature** icon in the pop-up menu. (Notice the red **x** next to the icon indicating the error in the feature.)

❖ *SolidWorks* will now display the 2D sketch of the selected feature in the graphics window. We have literally gone back in time to the point where we define the extrusion feature. The original sketch and the new sketch we just created are wireframe entities recorded by the system as belonging to the same **SKETCH**; but only the **selected profile** entities are used to create the feature. We will now change the selected profile entities.

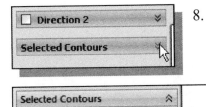

8. In the *Boss-Extrude1 PropertyManager*, click on the arrow to reveal the *Selected Contours* option panel as shown (if necessary).

9. If the *Selected Contours* panel is not blank, move the cursor over the panel and click once with the **right mouse button**. In the pop-up option menu, select **Clear Selections**.

➢ Sketch1 is displayed in the graphics area with no entities selected to define the profile for extrusion. The instruction *"Pick a sketch entity to define an open or closed contour. To define a region, pick inside an area bounded by sketch geometry"* appears in the *Status Bar*. The profile can be defined by either selecting sketch entities (lines, circles, etc.) to define a boundary, or by selecting bound areas for inclusion. We will use the latter option here.

10. Move the cursor inside the bound area shown in the figure. When the area is highlighted, click once with the **left-mouse-button** to select the area for inclusion in the profile. Notice **Sketch1-Region<1>** now appears in the *Selected Contours* panel on the *PropertyManager*.

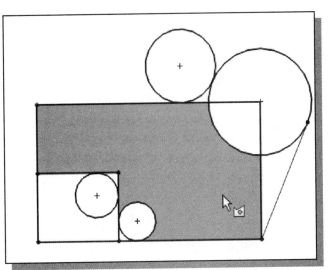

11. On your own, select additional areas for inclusion as shown. (If an incorrect area is selected, simply click on it again to unselect it. Be careful to click inside bound areas and not on the sketch entities. If difficulty is encountered, clear the selections and start over.)

12. In the *Boss-Extrude1 PropertyManager*, click on the **OK** button to accept the settings and update the solid feature.

- The feature is recreated using the newly sketched geometric entities, which are under defined and with no dimensions.

- The *Selected Contours* approach eliminates the need to trim the geometry manually. This approach encourages engineering content over drafting technique.

13. On your own, repeat the above steps and set the profile back to the **original profile**. The model should again look like the one shown at the top of page 6-19.

# Create an OFFSET Extruded Cut Feature

> To complete the design, we will create a cutout feature by using the **Offset** command. First we will set up the sketching plane to align with the front face of the 3D model.

1. In the *Sketch* toolbar, select the **Sketch** command by left-clicking once on the icon.

2. Notice the left panel displays the *Edit Sketch PropertyManager* with the instruction *"Select: a plane, planar face, ..."* **Select the front face** of the 3D model in the graphics window.

3. We will now convert the edge of the front face of the model into segments in the new sketch. **Select** the front face as shown.

**Convert Entities**
Converts selected model edges or sketch entities into sketch segments.

4. Select the **Convert Entities** icon in the *Sketch* toolbar.

> The Convert Entities command converts selected model features into sketch segments. Notice the edges of the selected surface have been converted to line and arc segments in the current sketch.

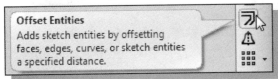

**Offset Entities**
Adds sketch entities by offsetting faces, edges, curves, or sketch entities a specified distance.

5. Select the **Offset Entities** icon in the *Sketch* toolbar.

6.  In the *Offset PropertyManager*, enter **5 mm** for the offset distance.

7.  In the *Offset PropertyManager*, select the options for *Add dimensions*, *Reverse*, and *Select chain* as shown.

8.  In the graphics area, select any segment of the face outline which was just converted.  Because the *Select chain* option is active, *SolidWorks* will automatically select all of the connecting geometry to form a closed region.

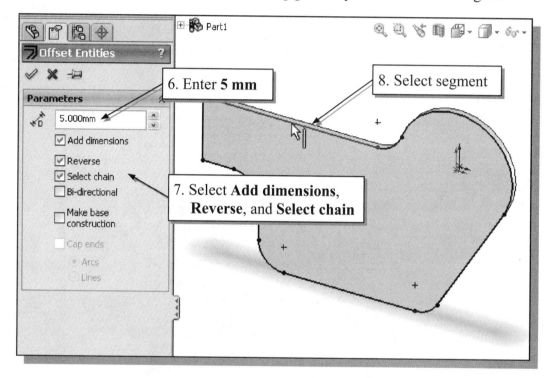

9.  Click on the **OK** button to accept the settings and create the offset feature.

10. On your own, modify the offset dimension to **15 mm** as shown in the figure.

11. Click once with the **left-mouse-button** on the **Sketch** icon on the *Sketch* toolbar to exit the Sketch option.

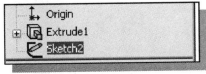

12. Make sure the sketch – Sketch2 – is selected in the *FeatureManager Design Tree*.

13. In the *Features* toolbar, select the **Extruded Cut** command by clicking once with the left-mouse-button on the icon. The *Cut-Extrude PropertyManager* is displayed in the left panel.

14. In the *Cut-Extrude PropertyManager* panel, click the arrow to reveal the pull-down options for the *End Condition* (the default end condition is Blind) and select **Through All** as shown.

15. In the *Cut-Extrude PropertyManager* panel, click on the arrow to reveal the *Selected Contours* option text box as shown. Notice there are no entries in the box.

16. In the graphics area, move the cursor over the interior of the offset contour as shown in the figure below. Click once with the **left-mouse-button** to select the profile. Notice Sketch2-Region<1> now appears in the *Selected Contours* box on the *PropertyManager*.

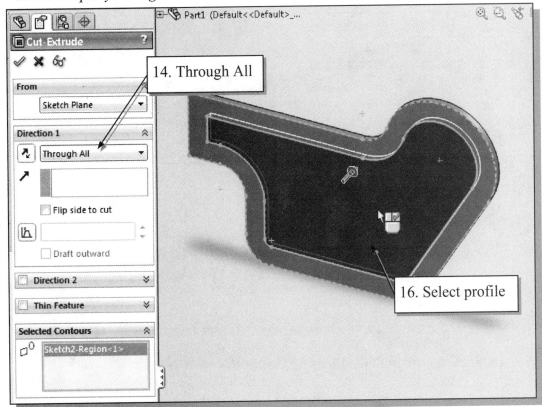

17. Click on the **OK** button to accept the settings and create the cut-extrude feature.

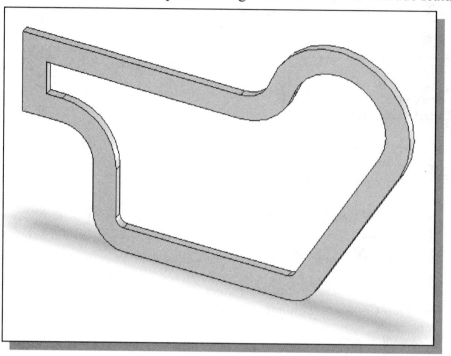

➤ The offset geometry is associated with the original geometry. On your own, adjust the overall height of the design to **150 millimeters** (i.e., change the 120 mm vertical dimension to 105 mm) and confirm that the offset geometry is adjusted accordingly.

18. Save the part with the filename *Gasket*.

## Alternate Construction Method – Thin Feature Option

➢ The **Thin Feature** option is a powerful tool in *SolidWorks*. It allows us to control the thickness (not the depth) of the extruded contour. Using this option, we can create the gasket by creating a single Extrude-Thin feature.

1. In the *Menu Bar*, select the **arrow** next to the Save icon and select the **Save As** option from the pull-down menu.

2. Save the part with the filename *Gasket2*.

3. In the *FeatureManager Design Tree*, **right-mouse-click** once on the **Cut-Extrude1** feature to bring up the option menu, then pick the **Delete** command in the pop-up menu as shown.

4. The *Confirm Delete* pop-up window appears. Check the **Also delete absorbed features** option box.

5. Notice Sketch2 appears in the *And all dependent items:* panel.

6. Select **Yes** to delete the Cut-Extrude1 feature and Sketch2.

**Confirm Delete**

Do you really want to delete this:

Cut-Extrude1 ( Feature )

And all dependent items:

Sketch2 ( Sketch )

Yes

Yes to All

No

Cancel

Help

☑ Also delete absorbed features
☑ Also delete all child feature
☐ Don't ask me again

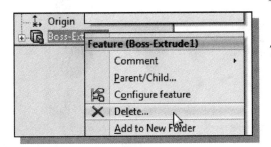

7. In the *FeatureManager Design Tree*, **right-mouse-click** once on the **Boss-Extrude1** feature to bring up the option menu; then pick the **Delete** command in the pop-up menu as shown.

8.  The *Confirm Delete* pop-up window appears. **Do not check** the Also delete absorbed features option box.

**Confirm Delete**

Do you really want to delete this:

> Boss-Extrude1 ( Feature )

And all dependent items:

☐ Also delete absorbed features
☑ Also delete all child feature
☐ Don't ask me again

Yes
Yes to All
No
Cancel
Help

9.  Select **Yes** to delete the Boss-Extrude1 feature. (Do not include the dependent sketch.)

➢ Sketch1 is now the only sketch or feature in the *FeatureManager Design Tree*.

◇ Front Plane
◇ Top Plane
◇ Right Plane
⭶ Origin
⮢ (-) Sketch1

10. Select **Sketch1** in the *FeatureManager Design Tree*.

**Extruded Boss/Base**
Extrudes a sketch or selected sketch contours in one or two directions to create a solid feature.

11. In the *Features* toolbar, select the **Extruded Boss/Base** command by clicking once with the left-mouse-button on the icon.

➢ Notice that no contours are automatically selected due to the complexity of the sketch. The *Selected Contours* panel is active.

12. Select the original gasket sketch contour in the graphics area as shown.

☐ Draft outward

☐ **Direction 2**

☐ **Thin Feature**

**Selected Contours**

13. Verify that the **Blind** *end condition* and **5 mm** *depth* are still entered in the *Direction 1* panel.

14. Check the **Thin Feature** option box in the *PropertyManager*.

15. Enter **15 mm** in the *Thickness* option window on the *Thin Feature* panel.

16. Click the **Reverse Direction** button on the *Thin Feature* panel.

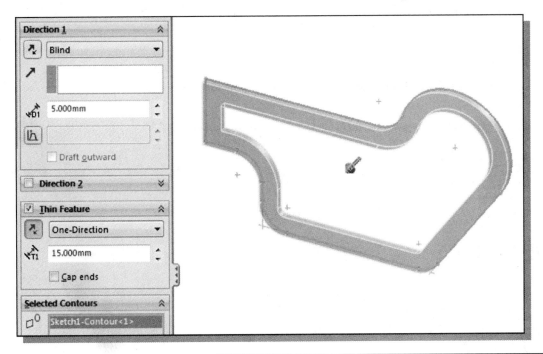

17. Click **OK** in the *PropertyManager* to accept the settings and create the *Extrude-Thin* feature.

➢ Notice the part created is identical to the part we created in the previous section.

18. Save the **Gasket2** part file.

➢ We now have two part files. The first was created by creating two sketches, one offset from the other by 15 mm, and two features, a *Boss Extrude* and a *Cut Extrude*. The second was created using one sketch and one *Boss Extrude* using the Thin Feature option with a thickness of 15 mm. The final parts are identical.

## Questions:

1.  Can we create a profile with extra 2D geometry entities?

2.  How do we access the *SolidWorks* **Edit Sketch** option?

3.  How do we create a *profile* in *SolidWorks*?

4.  Can we build a profile that consists of self-intersecting curves?

5.  Describe the procedure to create an offset copy of a sketched 2D geometry.

6.  Describe the **Selected Contours** option in *SolidWorks*.

7.  Identify and briefly describe the following commands:

    (a)

    (b)

    (c)

    (d)

## Exercises:

1. Dimensions are in inches. Plate Thickness: 0.25

2. Dimensions are in inches.  Plate thickness:  .25

3. Dimensions are in millimeters.

4. Dimensions are in inches.

## Chapter 7
# Parent/Child Relationships and the BORN Technique

## Learning Objectives

- ♦ **Understand the Concept and Usage of the BORN Technique**
- ♦ **Understand the Importance of Parent/Child Relations in Features**
- ♦ **Use the *Suppress Feature* Option**
- ♦ **Resolve Undesired Feature Interactions**

## Certified SolidWorks Associate Exam Objectives Coverage

### Sketch Entities – Lines, Rectangles, Circles, Arcs, Ellipses, Centerlines

Objectives:  Creating Sketch Entities.

### Sketch Tools – Offset, Convert, Trim

Objectives:  Using Sketch Tools.

### Boss and Cut Features – Extrudes, Revolves, Sweeps, Lofts

Objectives:  Creating Basic Swept Features.

## Introduction

The parent/child relationship is one of the most powerful aspects of *parametric modeling*. In *SolidWorks*, each time a new modeling event is created previously defined features can be used to define information such as size, location, and orientation. The referenced features become **PARENT** features to the new feature, and the new feature is called the **CHILD** feature. The parent/child relationships determine how a model reacts when other features in the model change, thus capturing design intent. It is crucial to keep track of these parent/child relations. Any modification to a parent feature can change one or more of its children.

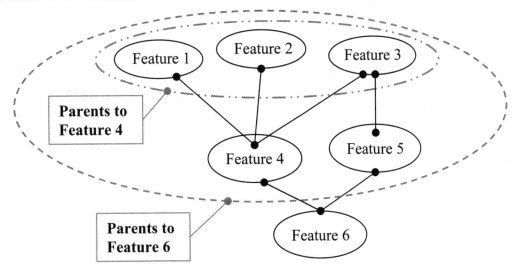

Parent/child relationships can be created *implicitly* or *explicitly*; implicit relationships are implied by the feature creation method and explicit relationships are entered manually by the user. In the previous chapters, we first select a sketching plane before creating a 2D profile. The selected surface becomes a parent of the new feature. If the sketching plane is moved, the child feature will move with it. As one might expect, parent/child relationships can become quite complicated when the features begin to accumulate. It is therefore important to think about modeling strategy before we start to create anything. The main consideration is to try to plan ahead for possible design changes that might occur which would be affected by the existing parent/child relationships. Parametric modeling software, such as SolidWorks, also allows us to adjust feature properties so that any feature conflicts can be quickly resolved.

## The BORN Technique

In the previous chapters, we have used a technique of creating solid models known as the **"Base Orphan Reference Node"** (**BORN**) technique. The basic concept of the BORN technique is to use a *Cartesian coordinate system* as the first feature prior to creating any solid features. With the *Cartesian coordinate system* established, we then have three mutually perpendicular datum planes (namely the *XY or 'front'*, *YZ or 'right'*, and *ZX or 'top' planes*) available to use as sketching planes. The three datum planes can also be used as references for dimensions and geometric constructions. Using this technique, the first node in the design tree is called an "orphan," meaning that it has no history to be replayed. The technique of creating the reference geometry in this "base node" is therefore called the "Base Orphan Reference Node" (BORN) technique.

*SolidWorks* automatically establishes a set of reference geometry when we start a new part, namely a *Cartesian coordinate system* with three work planes, three work axes, and an origin. All subsequent solid features can then use the coordinate system and/or reference geometry as sketching planes. This approach is also very useful in creating assembly models, which will be illustrated in *Chapter 12*.

## The *U-Bracket* Design

> Based on your knowledge of *SolidWorks* so far, how many features would you use to create the model? Which feature would you choose as the **base feature**? What is your choice for arranging the order of the features? Would you organize the features differently if the rectangular cut at the center is changed to a circular shape (Radius: 80mm)?

## Starting SolidWorks

1. Select the **SolidWorks** option on the *Start* menu or select the **SolidWorks** icon on the desktop to start *SolidWorks*. The *SolidWorks* main window will appear on the screen.

2. Select the **New** icon with a single click of the left-mouse-button on the *Menu Bar*. The *New SolidWorks Document* dialog box should appear in Advanced mode. If it appears in Novice mode, click once with the left-mouse-button on the **Advanced** icon.

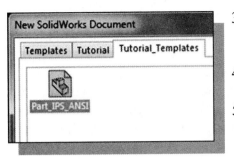

3. Select the **Tutorial_Templates** tab. (**NOTE:** You added this tab in Chapter 4.)

4. Select the **Part_IPS_ANSI** template as shown.

5. Click on the **OK** button to open a new document using the Part_IPS_ANSI template. The *Dimensioning Standard* will automatically be ANSI and the units will be set to inch, pound, second (IPS) as defined in the template.

## Applying the BORN Technique

❖ In the *FeatureManager Design Tree* panel, notice a new part name (Part1) appears with four work features established. The four work features include three *workplanes*, and the *origin*. By default, the three workplanes are aligned to the **world coordinate system** and the origin is aligned to the *origin* of the **world coordinate system**.

1. Inside the *FeatureManager Design Tree* panel, move the cursor on top of the first work plane, the **Front (XY) Plane**. Notice a rectangle, representing the workplane, appears in the graphics window.

2. Inside the *FeatureManager Design Tree* panel, click once with the right-mouse-button on Front (XY) Plane to display the option menu. Click on the **Show** icon to toggle *ON* the display of the plane.

3. On your own, repeat the above steps and toggle *ON* the display of all of the *workplanes* on the screen.

4. On your own, use the *Viewing* options (Rotate, Zoom and Pan) to view the planes.

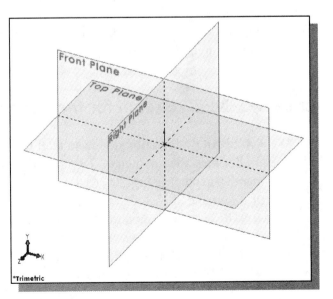

❖ By default, the basic set of planes is aligned to the world coordinate system; the workplanes are the first features of the part. We can now proceed to create solid features referencing the three mutually perpendicular datum planes. We will sketch the first feature, the base feature, in the top (XZ) plane. We will sketch the second feature in the front (XY) plane. Due to the symmetry in the shape of the part, we will use the right (YZ) plane and the front (XY) planes as planes of symmetry for the part. Thus before starting, we have decided on the orientation and the location of the part in relation to the basic workplanes.

5.  Move the cursor inside the graphics area, but away from the planes, and click once with the **left-mouse-button** to make sure no plane is selected.

6.  Select the **Sketch** button on the *Sketch* toolbar to create a new sketch.

7.  In the *Edit Sketch Property-Manager*, the message *"Select a plane on which to create a sketch for the entity"* is displayed. Move the cursor over the edge of the Top Plane in the graphics area. When the Top Plane is highlighted, click once with the **left-mouse-button** to select the **Top (XZ) Plane** as the sketch plane for the new sketch.

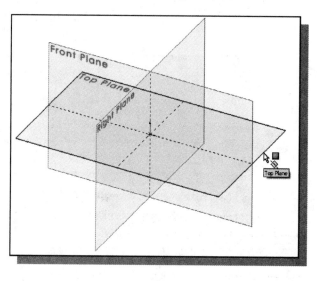

8.  On your own, turn *OFF* the visibility of the three planes. (**HINT:** Right-click on each plane in the *FeatureManager Design Tree* and select Hide.)

## Creating the 2D Sketch for the Base Feature

❖ We will begin by sketching the base feature. The symmetry of the feature will be used in defining the geometry. Two methods, one using the Dynamic Mirror command, the other using the Mirror command, will be demonstrated. The Dynamic Mirror command allows sketch objects to be automatically mirrored as they are drawn. The Mirror command is used to mirror existing objects.

1.  **Left-click** on the arrow next to the **Line** button on the *Sketch* toolbar to reveal additional commands.

2. Select the **Centerline** command from the pop-up menu.

3. Move the cursor to a point directly above the *origin*. The Vertical relation will be automatically highlighted as shown. Click once with **the left-mouse-button** to select the first endpoint of the centerline.

4. Move the cursor to a point directly below the *origin*. The Vertical relation will be highlighted as shown. Click once with the **left-mouse-button** to select the second endpoint of the centerline.

5. Inside the graphics window, right-mouse-click to bring up the option menu.

6. In the option menu, select **Select** to end the Centerline command.

❖ The **Mirror** and **Dynamic Mirror** commands can be used to generate sketch objects with symmetry about a centerline.

7. Select the **Tools** pull-down menu, then click on **Sketch Tools**. A complete list of sketch tools will appear. (Some of these also appear in the *Sketch* toolbar.)

8. Select **Dynamic Mirror** as shown.

9. The message *"Please select a sketch line or linear edge to mirror about"* appears in the *Mirror PropertyManager*. Move the cursor over the centerline in the graphics area and click once with the **left-mouse-button** to select it as the line to mirror about.

➤ Notice the *hash marks* which appear on the centerline to indicate that the Dynamic Mirror command is active.

10. Click on the **Line** icon in the *Sketch* toolbar.

11. Move the cursor to a point on the centerline, above the *origin*. The Coincident relation will be highlighted as shown. Click once with the **left-mouse-button** to select the first endpoint of the line.

12. Move the cursor to a point to the right, activating the Horizontal relation, as shown. Click once with the **left-mouse-button** to select the second endpoint of the line.

13. Inside the graphics window, right-mouse-click to bring up the option menu. In the option menu, select **Select** to end the Line command.

➤ Notice the mirror image of the line appears to the left of the centerline.

14. On your own, repeat these steps to create a similar horizontal line below the origin. Be sure that the Horizontal and Vertical relations are active for the second endpoint as shown in the image to the right.

15. **Left-click** on the arrow next to the **Arc** button on the *Sketch* toolbar to reveal additional commands.

16. Select the **Tangent Arc** command from the pop-up menu.

17. Select the right endpoint of the top horizontal line, as shown below.

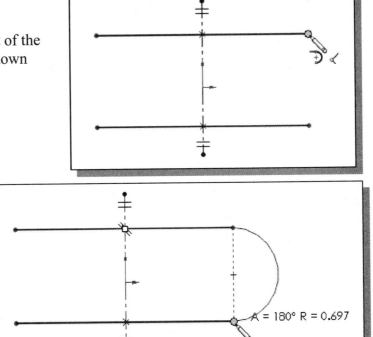

18. Select the right endpoint of the bottom horizontal line, as shown below.

19. Inside the graphics window, right-mouse-click to bring up the option menu. In the option menu, select **Select** to end the Tangent Arc command.

❖ *SolidWorks* offers the option to *autotransition* from the Line to the Tangent Arc command (and vice versa) without selecting the Arc command. We will redraw the second line and the arc to demonstrate this utility.

20. Click once with the left mouse button on the **Undo** command on the *Menu Bar* to reverse the last action – the creation of the arc.

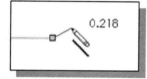

21. Click a second time on the **Undo** command to reverse the creation of the line.

❖ Notice that the Dynamic Mirror tool has been disabled by the Undo command.

22. On your own, **turn *ON*** the Dynamic Mirror tool. (**HINT:** Perform steps 7 - 9.)

23. Execute the **Line** command and select a point on the centerline to restart the second horizontal line. Be sure that the Horizontal and Vertical relations are active for the endpoint as shown in the image to the right, then click once to select the endpoint.

24. Move the cursor away from the endpoint of the horizontal line. **Do not click.** Notice the preview shows another line.

25. Move the cursor back to the endpoint. **Do not click.**

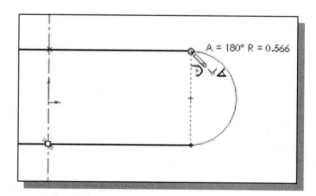

26. Move the cursor away again. Notice the preview now shows a tangent arc.

27. Select the right endpoint of the top horizontal line to end the arc.

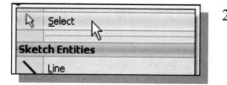

28. Inside the graphics window, right-mouse-click to bring up the option menu. In the option menu, select **Select** to end the Line/Tangent Arc command.

29. On your own, **turn *OFF*** the Dynamic Mirror command. (**HINT:** Perform steps 7 and 8.)

❖ We will now constrain the center of the arc to be on a horizontal line with the origin.

30. **Left-click** on the arrow next to the **Display/Delete Relations** button on the *Sketch* toolbar to reveal additional sketch relation commands.

31. Select the **Add Relation** command from the pop-up menu. Notice the *Add Relations PropertyManager* appears.

32. Pick the **centerpoint** of the tangent arc to the right side by left-mouse-clicking once on the geometry.

33. Pick the **origin**.

34. Click once with the left-mouse-button on the **Horizonal** icon in the *Add Relations PropertyManager* as shown. This activates the **Horizontal** relation.

35. Click the **OK** icon in the *PropertyManager*, or hit the [**Esc**] key once, to end the Add Relations command.

36. On your own, draw the circle as shown. Make sure the centerpoint for the circle is selected at the center of the tangent arc.

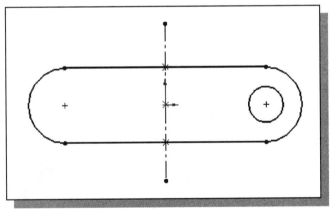

37. Press the [**Esc**] key to ensure no sketch features are selected.

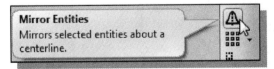

38. Select the **Mirror Entities** command on the *Sketch* toolbar.

(**NOTE:** The Mirror command could alternately be executed by selecting it with the *Sketch Tools* option on the *Tools* pull-down menu.)

39. In the *Options* panel of the *Mirror PropertyManager*, the *Entities to mirror:* text box is highlighted. Move the cursor over the **new circle** in the graphics area and click once with the **left-mouse-button** to select it as the object to mirror.

40. Move the cursor into the *Mirror about:* text box in the *Mirror PropertyManager* and click once with the **left-mouse-button**.

41. Move the cursor over the **centerline** in the graphics area and click once with the **left-mouse-button** to select it as the object to mirror about.

42. Select **OK** in the *Mirror PropertyManager*.

❖ We have now completed the rough sketch, and applied the appropriate geometric relations. Remember the concept is 'shape before size'.

43. On your own, apply the *Smart Dimensions* as shown below. Notice the sketch is now **Fully Defined**.

44. Select the **Sketch** icon on the *Sketch* toolbar to exit the **Sketch** option.

## Creating the First Extrude Feature

1. On your own, use the **Boss Extrude** command to create a base with a height of **0.5** inches.

2. On your own, turn the visibility of the three major planes back *ON*. (**HINT:** Right-click on each plane in the *FeatureManager Design Tree* and select **Show**.)

➤ Notice the orientation of the base in relation to the major workplanes of the world coordinate system.

## The Implied Parent/Child Relationships

• The *FeatureManager Design Tree* display includes the **Front**, **Top**, and **Right Planes**, the **Origin** (default work features) and the base feature (**Extrude1** shown in the figure) we just created. The parent/child relationships were established implicitly when we created the base feature: (1) Top (*XZ*) *workplane* was selected as the sketch plane; (2) **Origin** was used as the reference point to align the 2D sketch of the base feature.

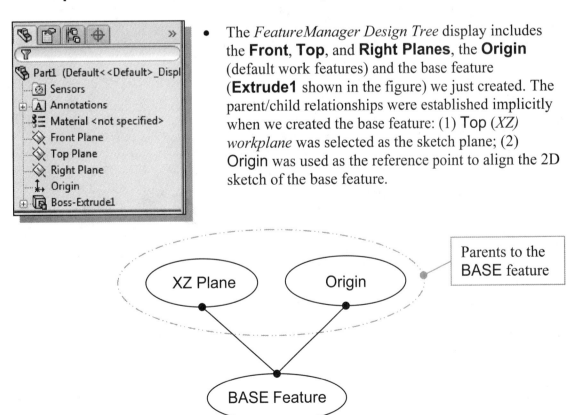

## Creating the Second Solid Feature

- For the next solid feature, we will create the top section of the design. Note that the center of the base feature is aligned to the **Origin** of the default work features. This was done intentionally so that additional solid features can be created referencing the default work features. For the second solid feature, the Front *(XY) workplane* will be used as the sketch plane.

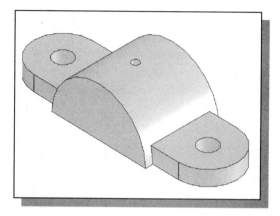

1. Move the cursor inside the graphics area, but away from the planes and click once with the **left-mouse-button** to make sure no plane is selected.

2. In the *Sketch* toolbar select the **Sketch** command by left-clicking once on the icon.

3. In the *Edit Sketch PropertyManager*, the message *"Select a plane on which to create a sketch for the entity"* is displayed. Move the cursor over the edge of the Front Plane in the graphics area. When the Front Plane is highlighted, click once with the **left-mouse-button** to select the **Front (XY) Plane** as the sketch plane for the new sketch.

4. Change the display to wireframe by clicking once with the **left-mouse-button** on the **Wireframe** icon on the *Display Style* pull-down menu on the *Heads-up View* toolbar.

5. **Left-click** on the arrow next to the **Arc** button on the *Sketch* toolbar to reveal additional commands.

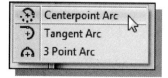

6. Select the **Centerpoint Arc** command from the pop-up menu.

7. Pick the **Origin** as the center location of the new arc.

8. On your own, create a semi-circle of arbitrary size, with both endpoints aligned to the X-axis, as shown below.

 9. Move the cursor on top of the **Smart Dimension** icon. Left-click once on the icon to activate the Smart Dimension command.

10. On your own, create and adjust the radius dimension of the arc to **1.75**.

 11. Select the **Line** command in the *Sketch* toolbar.

12. Create a line connecting the two endpoints of the arc as shown in the figure below.

13. On your own, add a **Coincident** relation between the origin and the horizontal line. The sketch should now be Fully Defined.

14. On your own, turn *OFF* the visibility of the workplanes.

 15. Select the **Sketch** icon on the *Sketch* toolbar to exit the Sketch option.

16. On your own, change the display style back to '*Shaded with edges*'.

17. Make sure the sketch – Sketch2 – is selected in the *FeatureManager Design Tree*.

18. In the *Features* toolbar, select the **Extruded Boss/Base** command by clicking once with the left-mouse-button on the icon. The *Extrude PropertyManager* is displayed in the left panel.

19. In the *Extrude PropertyManager* panel, click the drop down arrow to reveal the options for the *End Condition* (the default end condition is Blind) and select **Mid Plane** as shown.

20. In the *Extrude PropertyManager* panel, enter **2.5** as the extrusion distance. Notice that the sketch region is automatically selected as the extrusion profile.

21. Make sure the **Merge result** box is checked.

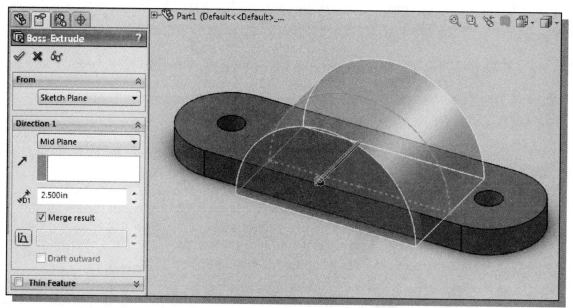

22. Click on the **OK** button to proceed with the **Extrude** operation.

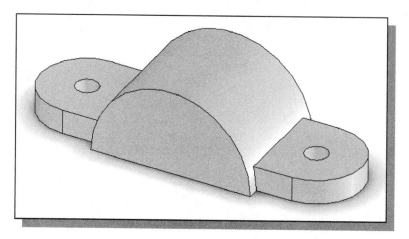

# Creating the First Extruded Cut Feature

- A rectangular cut will be created as the next solid feature.

1. In the *Sketch* toolbar select the **Sketch** command by left-clicking once on the icon.

2. In the *Edit Sketch PropertyManager*, the message "*Select a plane on which to create a sketch for the entity*" is displayed. Pick the front vertical face of the solid model shown.

3. We will use the origin as an endpoint for one of the dimensions. Make sure the **View Origins** option is toggled *ON* using the *Hide/Show Items* pull-down menu on the *Heads-up View* toolbar.

4. On your own, create a rectangle and apply the dimensions as shown. (**HINT:** To apply the horizontal dimension from the midpoint of the lower edge, select the **origin** of the world coordinate system as an endpoint. *Solidworks* will automatically project the origin onto the workplane.)

5. On your own, exit the sketch and use the **Extruded Cut** command with the **Through All** end condition option to create a cutout that cuts through the entire 3D solid model as shown.

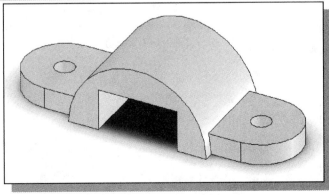

## Creating the Second Extruded Cut Feature

1. In the *Sketch* toolbar select the **Sketch** command by left-clicking once on the icon.

2. In the *Edit Sketch PropertyManager*, the message "*Select a plane on which to create a sketch for the entity*" is displayed. Select the horizontal face of the last cut feature as the *sketching plane*.

3. Left-click on the **View Orientation** icon on the *Heads-up View* toolbar to reveal the *View Orientation* pull-down menu. Select the **Normal To** command.

❖ The Normal To command can be used to switch to a 2D view of a selected surface. Since the surface defining the current sketch plane was pre-selected, this surface is automatically used for the 2D view.

4. Select the **Circle** command by clicking once with the left-mouse-button on the icon in the *Sketch* toolbar.

5. Pick the projected origin to align the center of the new circle.

6. Create a circle of arbitrary size.

7. On your own, add the size dimension of the circle and set the dimension to **0.25**.

8. Select the **Sketch** icon on the *Sketch* toolbar to exit the **Sketch** option.

9. Make sure the sketch – Sketch4 – is selected in the *FeatureManager Design Tree*.

 10. In the *Features* toolbar, select the **Extruded Cut** command by clicking once with the left-mouse-button on the icon.

11. In the *Cut-Extrude PropertyManager* panel, click the arrow to reveal the pull-down options for the *end condition* (the default end condition is Blind) and select **Through All**.

12. Click the **OK** button (green check mark) in the *Cut-Extrude PropertyManager* panel.

13. On your own, change the view orientation to Isometric.

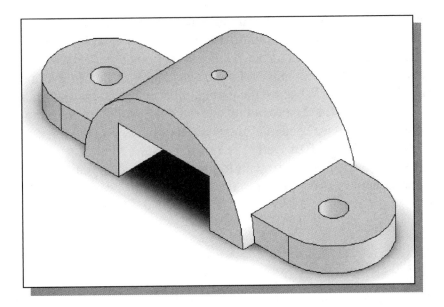

## Examining the Parent/Child Relationships

1.  On your own, rename the feature names to: **Base**, **Main_Body**, **Rect_Cut** and **Center_Drill** as shown in the figure.

❖  The *FeatureManager Design Tree* window now contains several items, including the major planes, the **Origin** (default work features) and four solid features. All of the parent/child relationships were established implicitly as we created the solid features. As more features are created, it becomes much more difficult to make a sketch showing all the parent/child relationships involved in the model. On the other hand, it is not really necessary to have a detailed picture showing all the relationships among the features. In using a feature-based modeler, the main emphasis is to consider the interactions that exist between the **immediate features**. Treat each feature as a unit by itself, and be clear on the parent/child relationships for each feature. Thinking in terms of *features* is what distinguishes *feature-based modeling* and the previous generation solid modeling techniques. Let us take a look at the last feature we created, the **Center_Drill** feature. What are the parent/child relationships associated with this feature? (1) Since this is the last feature we created, it is not a parent feature to any other features. (2) Since we used one of the surfaces of the rectangular cutout as the sketching plane, the **Rect_Cut** feature is a parent feature to the **Center_Drill** feature. (3) We also used the projected Origin as a reference point to align the center; therefore, the **Origin** is also a parent to the **Center_Drill** feature.

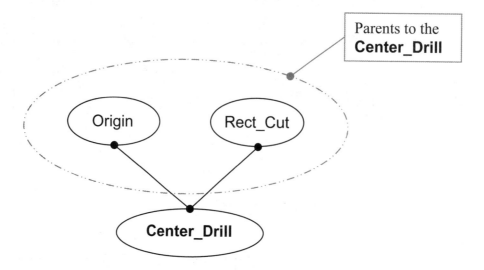

## Modify a Parent Dimension

❖ Any changes to the parent features will affect the child feature. For example, if we modify the height of the **Rect_Cut** feature from 1.0 to 0.75, the depth of the child feature (**Center_Drill** feature) will be affected.

1. In the *FeatureManager Design Tree* window, move the cursor on top of **Annotations** and click once with the **right-mouse-button** to bring up the option menu.

2. In the option menu, select **Show Feature Dimensions**.

3. Select the height dimension (1.0) by double-clicking on the dimension.

4. Enter **0.75** as the new height dimension as shown.

5. Select **OK** in the *Modify* window.

6. Click on the **Rebuild** button in the *Menu Bar* to proceed with updating the solid model.

➢ Note that the position of the **Center_Drill** feature is also adjusted as the placement plane is lowered. The drill-hole still goes through the main body of the *U-Bracket* design. The parent/child relationship assures the intent of the design is maintained.

7. On your own, adjust the height of the **Rect_Cut** feature back to **1.0 inch** before proceeding to the next section.

8. Repeat steps 1 and 2 to turn off the **Show Feature Dimensions** option.

## A Design Change

➢ Engineering designs usually go through many revisions and changes. For example, a design change may call for a circular cutout instead of the current rectangular cutout feature in our model. *SolidWorks* provides an assortment of tools to handle design changes quickly and effectively. In the following sections, we will demonstrate some of the more advanced tools available in *SolidWorks*, which allow us to perform the modification of changing the rectangular cutout (2.0 × 1.0 inch) to a circular cutout (radius: 1.25 inch).

❖ Based on your knowledge of *SolidWorks* so far, how would you accomplish this modification? What other approaches can you think of that are also feasible? Of the approaches you came up with, which one is the easiest to do and which is the most flexible? If this design change were anticipated right at the beginning of the design process, what would be your choice in arranging the order of the features? You are encouraged to perform the modifications prior to following through the rest of the tutorial.

## Feature Suppression

❖ With *SolidWorks*, we can take several different approaches to accomplish this modification. We could (1) create a new model, or (2) change the shape of the existing cut feature, or (3) perform **feature suppression** on the rectangular cut feature and add a circular cut feature. The third approach offers the most flexibility and requires the least amount of editing to the existing geometry. **Feature suppression** is a method that enables us to disable a feature while retaining the complete feature information; the feature can be reactivated at any time. Prior to adding the new cut feature, we will first suppress the rectangular cut feature.

1.  Move the cursor inside the *FeatureManager Design Tree* window. Click once with the **right-mouse-button** on top of **Rect_Cut** to bring up the option menu.

2.  Pick **Suppress** in the pop-up menu.

❖ We have literally *gone back in time*. The Rect_Cut and Center_Drill features have disappeared in the graphics area and both are shaded grey (meaning they are suppressed) in the *FeatureManager Design Tree*. The child feature cannot exist without its parent(s), and any modification to the parent (Rect_Cut) influences the child (Center_Drill).

3.  Move the cursor inside the *FeatureManager Design Tree* window. Click once with the **right-mouse-button** on top of **Center_Drill** to bring up the option menu.

4.  Pick **Unsuppress** in the pop-up menu.

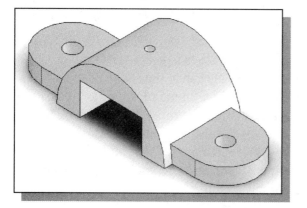

> In the display area and the *Model Tree* window, both the **Rect_Cut** feature and the **Center_Drill** feature are re-activated. The child feature cannot exist without its parent(s); the parent (Rect_Cut) must be activated to enable the child (Center_Drill).

## A Different Approach to the CENTER_DRILL Feature

❖ The main advantage of using the BORN technique is to provide greater flexibility for part modifications and design changes. In this case, the Center_Drill feature can be placed on the Top (XZ) Workplane and therefore not be linked to the Rect_Cut feature. Again, we can take several different approaches to accomplish this modification. We could (1) delete the Center_Drill feature and the corresponding sketch, create a new sketch on the Top (XZ) Workplane, and recreate the Center_Drill feature, or (2) redefine the sketch plane for the existing sketch associated with the Center_Drill feature. We will perform the second option.

1. Move the cursor inside the *FeatureManager Design Tree* window. Click once with the **left-mouse-button** on the tree to reveal the Sketch defining the Center_Drill feature as shown.

2. Move the cursor inside the *FeatureManager Design Tree* window. Click once with the **right-mouse-button** on top of **Sketch4** to bring up the option menu.

3. Pick **Edit Sketch Plane** in the pop-up menu. This will allow us to redefine the workplane for Sketch4.

❖ The *Sketch Plane PropertyManager* appears, with the *Sketch Plane/Face* text box highlighted. The original sketch plane for Sketch4 (Face<1>) appears in the field.

4.  Notice the Part1 icon of the design tree now appears at the upper left corner of the graphics area. **Left-click** on the box next to the Part1 icon to reveal the design tree as shown.

5.  Move the cursor over the **Top Plane** icon. When the Top Plane is highlighted, click once with the **left-mouse-button** to select the Top (XZ) Plane as the sketch plane for Sketch4.

6.  Top Plane now appears in the *Sketch Plane/Face* field of the *Sketch Plane PropertyManager*. Click once with the **left-mouse-button** on the **OK** icon to accept the new definition of the sketch plane.

## Suppress the Rect_Cut Feature

❖  Now the **Center_Drill** feature is no longer a child of the **Rect_Cut** feature, any change to the **Rect_Cut** feature does not affect the **Center_Drill** feature.

1.  Move the cursor inside the *Model Tree* window. Click once with the right-mouse-button on top of **Rect_Cut** to bring up the option menu.

2.  Pick **Suppress** in the pop-up menu.

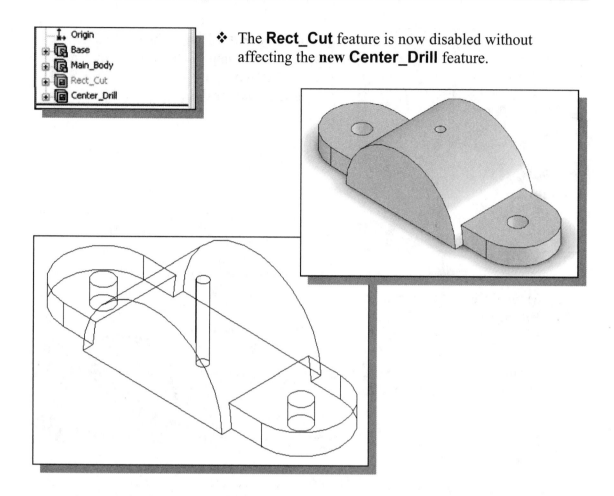

❖ The **Rect_Cut** feature is now disabled without affecting the **new Center_Drill** feature.

## Creating a Circular Extruded Cut Feature

1. Left-click once in the graphics area, away from the model, to ensure no features are selected.

2. In the *Sketch* toolbar select the **Sketch** command by left-clicking once on the icon.

3. In the *Edit Sketch PropertyManager*, the message *"Select a plane on which to create a sketch for the entity"* is displayed. **Left-click** on the FeatureManager Design Tree tab to reveal the design tree as shown.

4.  Move the cursor over the edge of the **Front Plane** icon in the *FeatureManager Design Tree*. When the Front Plane is highlighted, click once with the **left-mouse-button** to select the Front (XY) Plane as the sketch plane for the new sketch.

5.  Select the **Circle** command by clicking once with the left-mouse-button on the icon in the *Sketch* toolbar.

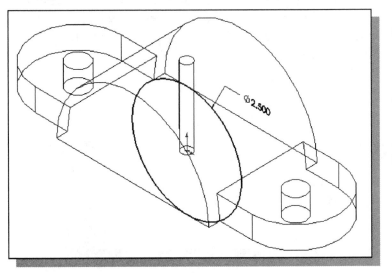

6.  Pick the **Origin** to align the center of the new circle.

7.  Create a circle of arbitrary size.

8.  On your own, create the size dimension of the circle and set the dimension to **2.5**, as shown in the figure.

9.  On your own, complete the cut feature using the **Extruded Cut** command. Use the **Mid Plane** *end condition* option and **2.5** in. (or greater) for the *depth.*

10. Rename the feature **Circular_Cut**.

❖ Note that the parents of the Circular_Cut feature are the Front (XY) Plane and the Origin.

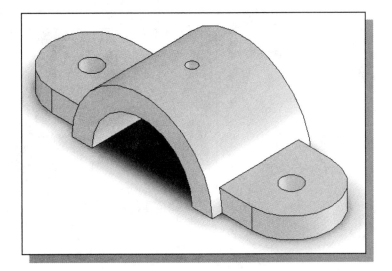

## A Flexible Design Approach

In a typical design process, the initial design will undergo many analyses, testing, reviews and revisions. *SolidWorks* allows the users to quickly make changes and explore different options of the initial design throughout the design process.

The model we constructed in this chapter contains two distinct design options. The *feature-based parametric modeling* approach enables us to quickly explore design alternatives and we can include different design ideas into the same model. With parametric modeling, designers can concentrate on improving the design and the design process to be much more quickly and effortlessly. The key to successfully using parametric modeling as a design tool lies in understanding and properly controlling the interactions of features, especially the parent/child relations.

## Save Part File

1.  Select **Save as** in the *File* pull-down menu as shown.

2.  Enter **U-Bracket** for the *File name*.

3.  Enter **2-1/2" U-Bracket** for the *Description* as shown.

4.  Click **Save**.

## Questions:

1.  Why is it important to consider the parent/child relationships in between features?

2.  Describe the procedure to **Suppress** a feature.

3.  What is the basic concept of the BORN technique?

4.  What happens to a feature when it is suppressed?

5.  How do you identify a suppressed feature in a model?

6.  What is the main advantage of using the BORN technique?

7.  Create sketches showing the steps you plan to use to create the models shown on the next page:

**Exercises:** (Dimensions are in inches)

1.

2.

3.

# Chapter 8
# Part Drawings and Associative Functionality

## Learning Objectives

- ◆ **Create Drawing Layouts from Solid Models**
- ◆ **Understand Associative Functionality**
- ◆ **Using the default Sheet Formats**
- ◆ **Arrange and Manage 2D Views in Drawing Mode**
- ◆ **Display and Hide Feature Dimensions**
- ◆ **Create Reference Dimensions**
- ◆ **Understand *Edit Sheet* and *Edit Sheet Format* Modes**
- ◆ **Use Property Links**

## Certified SolidWorks Associate Exam Objectives Coverage

# Drawings from Parts and Associative Functionality

With the software/hardware improvements in solid modeling, the importance of two-dimensional drawings is decreasing. Drafting is considered one of the downstream applications of using solid models. In many production facilities, solid models are used to generate machine tool paths for *computer numerical control* (CNC) machines. Solid models are also used in *rapid prototyping* to create 3D physical models out of plastic resins, powdered metal, etc. Ideally, the solid model database should be used directly to generate the final product. However, the majority of applications in most production facilities still require the use of two-dimensional drawings. Using the solid model as the starting point for a design, solid modeling tools can easily create all the necessary two-dimensional views. In this sense, solid modeling tools are making the process of creating two-dimensional drawings more efficient and effective.

*SolidWorks* provides associative functionality in the different *SolidWorks* modes. This functionality allows us to change the design at any level, and the system reflects it at all levels automatically. For example, a solid model can be modified in the *Part Modeling* mode and the system automatically reflects that change in the *Drawing* mode. And we can also modify a feature dimension in the *Drawing* mode, and the system automatically updates the solid model in all modes.

In this lesson, the general procedure of creating multi-view drawings is illustrated. The *U_Bracket* design from last chapter is used to demonstrate the associative functionality between the model and drawing views.

## Starting SolidWorks

1.  Select the **SolidWorks** option on the *Start* menu or select the **SolidWorks** icon on the desktop to start *SolidWorks*. The *SolidWorks* main window will appear on the screen.

2.  Select the **Open** icon on the *Menu Bar* with a single click of the left-mouse-button.

3.  In the *Open* window, select the **U-Bracket.SLDPRT** file. Use the *browser* to locate the file if it is not displayed in the *File name* list box.

4.  Click on the **Open** button in the *Startup* dialog box to accept the selected settings.

## Drawing Mode

➢ *SolidWorks* allows us to generate 2D engineering drawings from solid models so that we can plot the drawings to any exact scale on paper. An engineering drawing is a tool that can be used to communicate engineering ideas/designs to manufacturing, purchasing, service, and other departments. Until now we have been working in **Model** mode to create our design in ***full size***. We can arrange our design on a two-dimensional sheet of paper so that the plotted hardcopy is exactly what we want. This two-dimensional sheet of paper is saved in a ***drawing*** file in *SolidWorks*. We can place borders and title blocks, objects that are less critical to our design, in the *drawing*. In general, each company uses a set of standards for drawing content, based on the type of product and also on established internal processes. The appearance of an engineering drawing varies depending on when, where, and for what purpose it is produced. However, the general procedure for creating an engineering drawing from a solid model is fairly well defined. In *SolidWorks*, creation of 2D engineering drawings from solid models consists of four basic steps: drawing sheet formatting, creating/positioning views, annotations, and printing/plotting.

1. Click on the arrow next to the **New** icon on the *Menu Bar* and select **Make Drawing from Part/Assembly** in the pull-down menu.

➢ We must now select a drawing template. A drawing template is the foundation for drawing information in *SolidWorks*. The template contains specifications including sheet size and orientation, and the *SolidWorks* sheet format. The sheet format includes borders, title blocks, bill of materials table format, etc. The user can select from the *SolidWorks* 'Standard' drawing template, the *SolidWorks* 'Tutorial' drawing template, user-defined custom templates, or use no template. We will use the SolidWorks 'Tutorial' drawing template.

2. In the *New SolidWorks Document* window, select the **Tutorial** tab.

3. Select the **draw** template file icon.

4. Select **OK** to open a drawing using the *draw* template.

5.  If the *Sheet Format/Size* window appears, select any size and click **OK**.  (We will reset the paper size and formatting in subsequent steps.)

➢  Note that a new graphics window appears on the screen. We can switch between the solid model and the drawing by clicking the corresponding file from the *Window* pull-down menu.

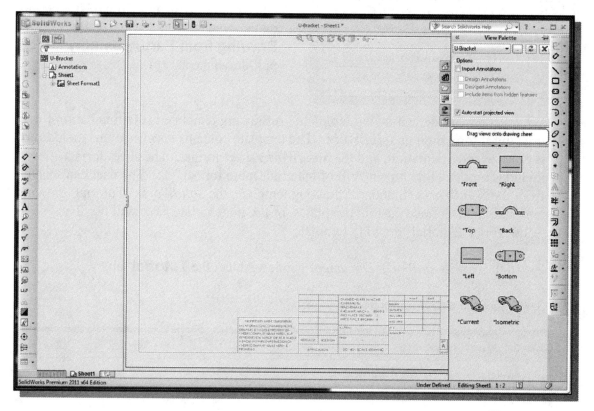

➢  The **View Palette** appears in the task pane.  This can be used to insert drawing views. We will first set the document properties and sheet properties for the drawing.

➢  In the graphics window, *SolidWorks* displays a default drawing sheet that includes a title block.   The title block also indicates the paper size being used.

➢  In the *FeatureManager Design Tree* area, the **Drawing** icon is displayed at the top, which indicates that we have switched to *Drawing* mode. The default filename is the filename of the solid part file from which we created the drawing – U-Bracket. *Sheet1* is the current drawing sheet that is displayed in the graphics window.

## Setting Document Properties

➤ The document properties, such as dimensioning standard, units, text fonts, etc., must be set for the new drawing file. If a set of document properties will be used regularly, a new drawing file template can be saved which contains these settings.

1. Select the **Options** icon from the *Menu Bar* to open the options dialog box.

2. Under the **System Options** tab, select **Display Style** as shown.

3. Under '*Display style for new views*', select **Hidden lines visible**. This will be the default display style for orthographic views (e.g., front view) added to the drawing.

4. Select the **Document Properties** tab.

5. Select **ANSI** in the drop-down selection window under the *Dimensioning standard* panel as shown.

6. Click **Units** as shown below.

7. Select **IPS (inch, pound, second)** under the *Unit system* options.

8. Select **.12** in the *Decimals* spin boxes for the *Length* and *Dual Dimension Length* units as shown to define the degree of accuracy with which the units will be displayed to 2 decimal places.

9. Click **OK** in the options dialog box to accept the selected settings.

## Setting Sheet Properties using the Pre-Defined Sheet Formats

➤ Another set of properties are set for each sheet in the drawing file. These settings include sheet size, sheet orientation, scale, and projection type.

**Sheet (Sheet1)**
- Edit Sheet Format
- Lock Sheet Focus
- Add Sheet...
- Copy
- Delete
- Properties...

1. Move the cursor onto the graphics area and click once with the **right-mouse-button** to open the pop-up menu.

2. Select **Properties** from the pop-up menu as shown to edit the properties for Sheet1.

**Sheet Properties**

Name: Sheet1

3. Scale 2:1

4. Third angle

Scale: 2 : 1

Type of projection
- First angle
- ● Third angle    Next datum    A

Sheet Format/Size
- ● Standard sheet size
  - ☐ Only show standard format

5. C (ANSI) Landscape

A (ANSI) Landscape
A (ANSI) Portrait
B (ANSI) Landscape
C (ANSI) Landscape
D (ANSI) Landscape
E (ANSI) Landscape
A0 (ANSI) Landscape

c - landscape.slddrt    Browse...

☑ Display sheet format

Preview

Width: 22.00in    Height: 17.00in

- ○ Custom sheet size
  - Width: ____    Height: ____

Use custom property values from model shown
Default ▼    OK    Cancel

3. In the *Sheet Properties* window, set the scale to **2:1** as shown.

4. Set the *Type of projection* to **Third angle**.

5. Set the *Standard sheet size* to **C (ANSI) Landscape**.

6. Click **OK** in the *Sheet Properties* window to accept the selected settings.

➤ We are now ready to add drawing views. We will do this using commands on the *Drawing* toolbar. By default, the *Drawing* toolbar is displayed vertically at the left of the *SolidWorks* window when a drawing document is open.

## Open the Drawing Toolbar

❖ If the *Drawing* toolbar is not displayed, move the cursor over the *Menu Bar* and click once with the **right-mouse-button**. Select the *Drawing* toolbar from the list of toolbars.

Display States
Drawing
Explode Sketch

## Creating Three Standard Views

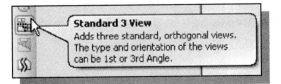

1. Select the **Standard 3 View** button on the *Drawing* toolbar.

➤ The *Standard 3 View PropertyManager* appears. In the *Open documents* field of the *Part/Assembly to Insert* option window, the **U-Bracket** part file appears and is highlighted. The *U-Bracket* model is the only model opened. By default, all of the 2D drawings will be generated from this model file.

2. Left-click on the **OK** icon to accept the *U-Bracket* part file as the document used to create the three views. The three standard views for the *U-Bracket* appear on the active sheet.

➤ The three new views now appear in the *FeatureManager Design Tree*. Notice the icon for Drawing View9. This icon indicates Drawing View9 is a base view. The icons for Drawing View10 and Drawing View11 indicate that these views are projected from the base view.

## Repositioning Views

1. Move the cursor on top of the front view and watch for the **four-arrow Move symbol** as the cursor is near the border indicating the view can be dragged to a new location as shown in the figure.

2. Press and hold down the left-mouse-button and reposition the view to a new location.

3. On your own, reposition the views we have created so far. Note that the top view can be repositioned only in the vertical direction. The top view remains aligned to the base view, the front view. Similarly, the right side view can be repositioned only in the horizontal direction.

## Adding a New Sheet

1. Move the cursor into the graphics area and click once with the **right-mouse-button** to reveal the pop-up menu.

2. Select **Add Sheet** from the pop-up menu as shown.

> The new sheet appears in the graphics area as the active sheet.

3. Move the cursor onto the graphics area and click once with the **right-mouse-button** to open the pop-up menu.

4. Select **Properties** from the pop-up menu as shown to edit the properties for Sheet2.

5. In the *Sheet Properties* window, set the scale to **1:1** as shown.

6. Set the *Type of projection* to **Third angle**.

7. Set the *Standard sheet size* to **B-Landscape**.

8. Click **OK** in the *Sheet Properties* window to accept the selected settings.

> The active sheet can be changed by left-clicking on the sheet tabs at the bottom of the graphics area.

## Adding a Base View

❖ In *SolidWorks Drawing* mode, the first drawing view we create is called a **base view**. A *base view* is the primary view in the drawing; other views can be derived from this view. When creating a *base view*, *SolidWorks* allows us to specify the view to be shown. By default, *SolidWorks* will treat the *world XY plane* as the front view of the solid model. Note that there can be more than one *base view* in a drawing.

1.  Make sure **Sheet2** is the active drawing sheet.

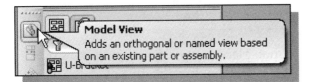

2.  Click on the **Model View** icon on the *Drawing* toolbar.

3.  The *Model View PropertyManager* appears with the **U-Bracket** part file selected as the part from which to create the base view. Click the **Next** arrow as shown to proceed with defining the base view.

4.  In the *Model View PropertyManager*, select **Single View** for the *Number of Views* and the **Front View** for the *Orientation*, as shown.

5.  Scroll down in the *PropertyManager* to the *Display Style* panel. Notice the default display style is *Hidden Lines Visible*. This was defined in the *Document Settings*.

6.  Under the *Scale* option, select **Use custom scale**.

7.  Select **1:1** from the pull-down window, as shown.

8. Move the cursor inside the graphics area and left-click to place the *base* view near the lower left corner of the drawing sheet as shown below.

9. Upon placement of the base view, *SolidWorks* automatically enters the **Projected View** command. Move the cursor above the base view and select a location to position the projected top view of the model.

10. Click **OK** in the *PropertyManager* to exit the Projected View command.

❖ In *SolidWorks Drawing* mode, **projected views** can be created with a first-angle or third-angle projection, depending on the drafting standard used for the drawing. We must have a base view before a projected view can be created. Projected views can be orthographic projections or isometric projections. Orthographic projections are aligned to the base view and inherit the base view's scale and display settings.

➢ **NOTE:** In your drawing, the inserted views may include *center marks*, *centerlines*, and/or *dimensions*. If so, these were added with the **auto-insert** option. To access these options, click **Options** (*Standard* toolbar), select the **Document Properties** tab, and then select **Detailing**. This lesson was done with only the **Center marks-holes-part** auto-insert option selected. Other center marks, centerlines, and dimensions will be added individually.

➢ Notice the hidden lines are visible. The dash lengths and spaces can be adjusted in the document properties.

11. Select the **Options** icon from the *Menu Bar* to open the options window.

12. Select the **Document Properties** tab.

13. Select **Line Style**.

14. Select the **Dashed** line style.

15. Adjust the *Line length and spacing values* to, for example, **A,0.75,-0.25**. (This will scale the dash length by 0.75 and the space by 0.25.)

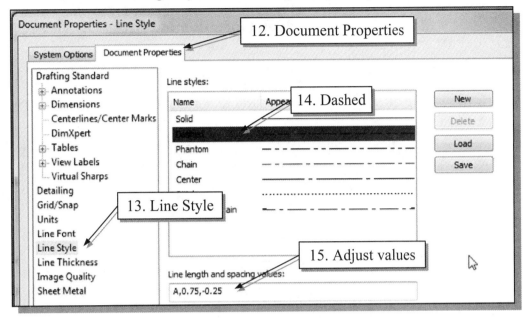

16. Left-click on the **OK** button to accept the settings.

17. Press the **[F]** key to fit the drawing to the graphics viewing area.

## Adding an Isometric View using the View Palette

❖ We will add an isometric view. The isometric view could be added as a *Projected View* based on the existing *Front View*. We will add the isometric view as a second base view. It can be added using the **Model View** command as was used for the *Front View*. An alternate method to add a base view is to use the **View Palette**. We will use this option.

1. Click on the **View Palette** icon to the right of the graphics area.

2. The *View Palette* appears in the task pane. Select the **U-Bracket** part at the top of the View Palette.

3. Views can be dragged from the *View Palette* onto the drawing sheet to create a base drawing view. Click on the **Isometric** view in the *View Palette* as shown. Hold the **left-mouse-button** down and **drag** the view to the upper right corner of the sheet to position the isometric view. SolidWorks places the view on the sheet and opens the *Drawing View PropertyManager*.

➤ In general, hidden lines are not used in isometric views.

4. In the *Drawing View PropertyManager*, select the **Hidden Lines Removed** option for the *Display Style*.

5. Left-click on the **OK** icon in the *Drawing View PropertyManager* to accept the view.

## Adjusting the View Scale

❖ *SolidWorks* allows us to easily adjust the drawing view settings. Simply selecting a drawing view will open the corresponding *PropertyManager*.

1. Move the cursor on top of the isometric view and watch for the box around the entire view indicating the view is selectable as shown in the figure. **Left-mouse-click** once to bring up the *PropertyManager*.

2. Under the *Scale* options in the *Drawing View PropertyManager*, select **Use custom scale**.

3. Select **User Defined** from the pull-down options (scroll to the top of the list), as shown.

4. Enter **3:4** as the user defined scale.

5. Left-click on the **OK** icon in the *Drawing View PropertyManager* to accept the new settings.

6. If necessary, reposition the views to appear as shown below.

## Displaying Feature Dimensions

- By default, feature dimensions are not displayed in 2D views in *SolidWorks*. The dimensions used to create the part can be imported into the drawing using the **Model Items** command. We can also add dimensions to the drawing manually using the **Smart Dimension** command. The **Model Items** command appears on the *Annotation* toolbar.

1. By default the *Annotation* toolbar appears at the left of the *SolidWorks* window (below or next to the *Drawing* toolbar). If it is not displayed, right-click on the *Menu Bar* and select the **Annotation** icon to display the *Annotation* toolbar.

2.  Left-mouse-click on the **Model Items** icon on the *Annotation* toolbar. This command allows us to import dimensions from the referenced model into selected drawing views.

3.  In the *Source/ Destination* options panel of the *Model Items PropertyManager*, select the **Entire model** option from the *Import from* pull-down menu and check **Import items into all views** as shown.

4.  Under the *Dimensions* options panel, select the **Marked for drawing** icon and check **Eliminate duplicates** as shown.

5.  Click the **OK** icon in the *Model Items PropertyManager*. Notice dimensions are automatically placed on the front and top drawing views.

## Repositioning, Appearance, and Hiding of Feature Dimensions

1.  Move the cursor on top of the width dimension text **5.00** and watch for when the dimension text becomes highlighted as shown in the figure, indicating the dimension is selectable.

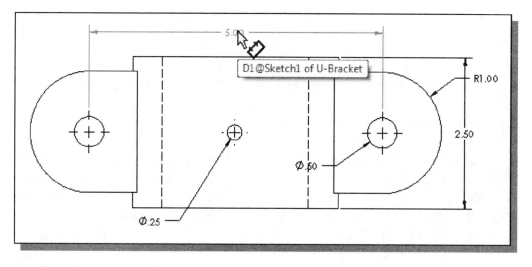

2.  Reposition the dimension by using the left-mouse-button to drag the dimension text to a new location. (**NOTE:** *SolidWorks* may execute snaps to align the text automatically. To negate these, hold down the **[Alt]** key while dragging the text and it will move freely.)

3. Move the cursor on top of the diameter dimension **0.50** and click once with the left-mouse-button to select the dimension.

4. Left-click on the arrow at the end of the leader line and drag to lengthen the bent leader line as shown.

❖ The default bent leader length can be adjusted to improve the appearance of the current view. This is done using the **Document Settings**. There are many document settings, including dimension settings, line style, etc., which can be adjusted to achieve the desired drawing display.

5. On your own, change the **Bent leader length** to **0.2 in**. (Select the **Options** icon from the *Menu Bar* to open the *Options* window. Select the **Document Properties** tab. Select **Dimensions**. In the **Leader length:** field, enter **0.2 in**. Click **OK**.)

6. Move the cursor on top of the diameter dimension **0.50** and click once with the left-mouse-button to select the dimension.

7. Select the **Leaders** tab in the *Dimension PropertyManager*.

8. Select the **Smart** display button.

    8. Smart

9. Check the **Use document bend length** box.

10. Click **OK** in the *PropertyManager*.

➢ Notice the bent leader length (that we lengthened in step 4) now reverts to the length we set in the *Document Settings*.

11. On your own, reposition the dimensions displayed in the *top* view as shown.

➢ Any feature dimensions can be removed from the display just as they are displayed.

   12. Move the cursor on top of the vertical **2.50** dimension and **right-mouse-click** once to bring up the option menu.

| Dimension (D1@Main_Body@U-Bracket-1...) |
| --- |
| Hide |
| Display Options |

13. Select **Hide** from the pop-up option menu.

## Adding Additional Dimensions – Reference Dimensions

• Besides displaying the **feature dimensions**, dimensions used to create the features, we can also add additional **reference dimensions** in the drawing. *Feature dimensions are used to control the geometry, whereas *reference dimensions* are controlled by the existing geometry. In the drawing layout, therefore, we can **add** or **delete** *reference dimensions* but we can only **hide** the *feature dimensions*. One should try to use as many *feature dimensions* as possible and add *reference dimensions* only if necessary. It is also more effective to use *feature dimensions* in the drawing layout since they are created when the model was built. Note that additional *Drawing* mode entities, such as lines and arcs, can be added to drawing views. Before *Drawing* mode entities can be used in a reference dimension, they must be associated to a *drawing view*.

1. Left-mouse-click on the **Smart Dimension** icon on the *Annotation* toolbar.

2. Select the *top edge* in the top view.

3. Select the *bottom edge* in the top view.

4. Move the cursor to the left of the top view and **left-click** to position the dimension as shown.

5. Click **OK** in the *Dimension PropertyManager* to create the reference dimension without parentheses.

6. On your own, add the **2.50** horizontal dimension and arrange the display of the top view to look like the figure below.

7. In the front view, left click on the **R1.75** dimension to select the radius dimension.

8. In the *Dimension PropertyManager*, select the **Leaders** tab.

9. In the *Witness/Leader Display* panel, select the **Inside** option as shown.

10. On your own, select the Ø**2.50** dimension and select the **Smart** display option.

11. On your own, adjust the front view dimension display to appear as in the figure below. (**NOTE:** The 0.50 vertical feature dimension was replaced with a reference dimension to allow the visible gap between the object lines and the extension lines.)

## Tangent Edge Display

❖ Another important setting for drawing views is the way tangent edges – where a curved surface meets tangent to a flat surface – are represented. In the figure above, the tangent edges (the vertical lines coincident with the centerlines of the two hidden holes) are visible.

1. Press the [**Esc**] key to ensure no objects are selected.

2. Move the cursor over the *front view* in the graphics area and **right-click** to open the pop-up option menu.

3. Select **Tangent Edge**, then **Tangent Edges Removed** from the pop-up menu, as shown.

4. Click **OK** in the *Property-Manager* or press the [**Esc**] key to accept the setting.

❖ Notice the tangent edges are no longer visible.

5. On your own, remove the tangent edges from the isometric view.

## Adding Center Marks, Center Lines, and Sketch Objects

  1. Click on the **Center Mark** button in the *Annotation* toolbar.

2. Click on the larger arc in the front view to add the center mark.

3. A preview of the center mark appears in the graphics area and the *Center Mark PropertyManager* is opened.

❖ The default center mark included extended lines in all four directions. Since the feature is semicircular, we will turn *OFF* the default extended lines and sketch them where desired.

4. In the *Display Attributes* panel of the *Center Mark PropertyManager*, **uncheck** the **Use document defaults** box, and **uncheck** the **Extended lines** box.

5. Left-Click **OK** in the *PropertyManager* to accept the settings and end the **Center Mark** command.

6. If the *Sketch* toolbar is not displayed, move the cursor over the *Menu Bar* (or any open toolbar) and click once with the **right-mouse-button**. Notice a pop-up menu appears containing a list of toolbars.

7. Select the *Sketch* toolbar. Notice the *Sketch* toolbar opens. By default it appears at the right edge of the *SolidWorks* window.

8. Left-click on the **Line** button on the *Sketch* toolbar.

9. Move the cursor over the center mark, then move the cursor above the center to engage the **Vertical** relation. Click once with the **left-mouse-button** to locate the first point for the line.

10. Move the cursor vertically to locate the endpoint for the line. Click once with the **left-mouse-button** to locate the endpoint.

11. Click once with the **right-mouse-button** to open the pop-up menu.

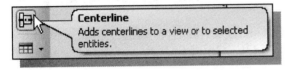

12. Left-click on the **Select** option on the pop-up menu to end the **Line** command.

13. On your own, sketch the two horizontal lines as shown in the figure below.

14. Click on the **Centerline** button in the *Annotation* toolbar. (**NOTE:** This is different from the Centerline command on the *Sketch* toolbar.)

15. Inside the graphics window, click on the two hidden edges of the **Hole** on the left as shown in the figure.

16. On your own, repeat the above step and create another centerline on the right side of the front view as shown below.

17. Left-click the **OK** icon in the *Centerline PropertyManager* or press the **[Esc]** key to end the Centerline command.

18. On your own, adjust your settings and endpoint locations until the top view appears as in the figure below. Add the three center marks if they were not added automatically. Drag the endpoint of the *Extended Lines* to desired locations. For the central hole, **uncheck** the Use document defaults option, **check** the Extended lines option, and **check** the Centerline font option in the *PropertyManager*.

19. Click on the **Save** icon in the *Menu Bar* as shown.

20. Note the message "*The following models referenced ...*" appears in the *Save Modified Documents* window and the drawing (U-Bracket.SLDDRW) and part (U-Bracket.SLDPRT) files are selected.  Select the **Save All** option.

**Save Modified Documents**

The following models referenced in this document have been modified. They will be saved when the document is saved.

| | Filename | Read-only | In Use By |
|---|---|---|---|
| ☑ 🔲 | U-Bracket.SLDDRW | | |
| ☑ 🧊 | U-Bracket.SLDPRT | | |

20.  Save All

☐ Don't ask me again when saving      [ Save All ]   [ Cancel ]   [ Help ]

21. Save the drawing with the filename **U-Bracket**.

| File name: | U-Bracket |
| --- | --- |
| Save as type: | Drawing (*.drw;*.slddrw) |
| Description: | Add a description |

☐ Save as copy        References...        Display States (linked) ▾

▲ Hide Folders                                    Save        Cancel

## Edit Sheet vs. Edit Sheet Format

❖ There are two modes in a *SolidWorks* drawing: *Edit Sheet* and *Edit Sheet Format*. To this point we have been operating in the *Edit Sheet* mode. The *Edit Sheet* mode is used to make detail drawings, including adding and modifying views, adding and modifying dimensions, and adding and modifying drawing notes. *The Edit Sheet Format* mode is used to add and edit title blocks, borders, and standard text that appear in every drawing. The correct mode must be selected in order to execute the corresponding commands.

1. Move the cursor into the graphics area and **right-click** to open the pop-up option menu.

2. Select **Edit Sheet Format** from the pop-up option menu to change to *Edit Sheet Format* mode.

❖ Notice the title block is highlighted.

Sheet (Sheet2)
  Edit Sheet Format
  Lock Sheet Focus
  Add Sheet...
  Copy
  Delete
  Properties...
  Relations/Snaps Options...

## Completing the Drawing Sheet

1. On your own, use the **Zoom** and **Pan** commands to adjust the display as shown, this is so that we can complete the title block.

❖ There are many notes added as entries in the default title block. Some are simple **Text** notes; some include **Property Links** to automatically display document properties. In the following steps, we will learn to (1) edit existing notes, (2) insert new notes, (3) control **Property Links**. We will first edit a simple text note.

2. Zoom in on the tolerance specification box. This note contains only simple text entries. **Double-click** with the **left-mouse-button** on the text to enter the text editor.

3. Highlight the FRACTIOANAL ± line as shown by clicking and dragging with the left-mouse-button.

4. Press the **[Delete]** key twice to delete the line.

5. Move the cursor to a location to the right of the MACH ± text, and click once with the **left-mouse-button** to select a location to enter text.

6. Enter **0.1**.

7. In the *Text Format* panel of the *Note PropertyManager*, select the **Add Symbol** icon.

8. In the *Symbols* pop-up window, select **Degree** and click **OK** to insert a degree symbol.

9. On your own, continue editing the text in the tolerance box until it appears as shown.

DIMENSIONS ARE IN INCHES
TOLERANCES:
ANGULAR: MACH ± 0.1°
TWO PLACE DECIMAL    ± 0.01
THREE PLACE DECIMAL  ± 0.003

10. Select the **OK** icon in the *Note PropertyManager* or press the **[Esc]** key to accept the change to the note.

11. We will not insert a new note. Left-mouse-click on the **Note** icon on the *Annotation* toolbar.

12. Select the **No Leader** option in the *Leader* panel of the *Note Property Manager*.

13. Move the cursor into the MATERIAL box and click once with the **left-mouse-button** to select the location for the new note.

14. Enter the text **1060 ALLOY**.

15. **Highlight** the text **1060 ALLOY**.

16. Change the font size to **6** in the *Formatting* window as shown and press the **[Enter]** key to reset the font size.

17. Select the **OK** icon in the *Note PropertyManager* or press the **[Esc]** key to accept the note.

18. Click and drag on the new note to locate it as shown. (**NOTE:** *SolidWorks* may execute snaps to align the text automatically. To negate these, hold down the **[Alt]** key while dragging the text and it will move freely.)

## Property Links

*SolidWorks* allows notes to be linked to properties for automatic display. In *SolidWorks*, these properties are classified as system-defined **System Properties** and user-defined **Custom Properties**. Each system or custom property has a property name. There are system and custom properties associated with each *SolidWorks* **Part**, **Assembly**, or **Drawing** file. Each **Property Link** contains (1) the definition of the source and (2) the property name. The source can be (1) the current document, (2) a model specified in a sheet, (3) a model in a specified drawing view, or (4) a component to which the annotation is attached. Several linked properties are automatically included in the default *SolidWorks* sheet formats.

1.  Move the cursor over the note in the center of the DWG. NO. box, as shown. A letter **A** appears indicating a note. A pop-up dialog box appears which reads *$PRP: "SW-File Name"*. This is the definition of a **Property Link**. The prefix *$PRP:* defines the source as the current document. The Property Name is *SW-File Name*. This is an example of a **System Property**. Based on this Property Link, the filename – **U-Bracket** – of the current file is displayed.

2.  We will change the file name. Select **Save as** from the *Menu Bar* pull-down menu.

3.  Enter **MET 3001** for the *File name*.

4.  Enter **U-Bracket Detail** for the *Description*.

5.  Click **Save**.

  6.  If the text in the DWG. NO. box does not change, select the **Rebuild** icon on the *Menu Bar*.

7. Notice the new file name is now displayed in the DWG. NO. box. Click once with the left-mouse-button on the **MET 3001** note to open the *Note PropertyManager*.

8. Click the **Font** button in the *Text Format* panel of the *Note PropertyManager*.

9. In the *Choose Font* pop-up window, select **Points** under the *Height* option.

10. Select **16** as the font size.

11. Click **OK** in the *Choose Font* pop-up window.

12. Press the **[Esc]** key to accept the change and unselect the note.

13. Move the cursor over the center of the box above the Title: box. A letter **A** appears indicating a note. A pop-up dialog box appears identifying a Property Link which reads **$PRP: "CompanyName"**. The prefix **$PRP:** defines the source as the current document. The Property Name is **CompanyName**. This is an example of a **Custom Property**. The note is currently blank because the *CompanyName Custom Property* has not been defined.

Print Preview...
Print...

Pack and Go...
Send To...

Properties...

1 MET 3001.SLDDRW

14. Select **Properties** from the *File* pull-down menu on the *Menu Bar*.

15. In the *Summary Information* window select the **Custom** tab. Notice the *Custom Property* **Description** appears in the table. We defined this property when we saved the drawing file.

16. Move the cursor over the cell below the cell containing **Description** and click once with the **left-mouse-button**. An arrow button will appear at the right end of the cell.

17. Left-click once on the drop down **arrow** button to reveal the pull-down selection options for *Property Name*.

18. Select **CompanyName** from the menu. (NOTE: If the pull-down selection options do not appear, type **CompanyName** in the cell.)

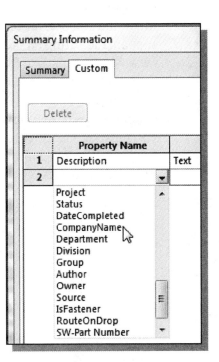

19. Enter the **company name** to appear in the title block in the **Value / Text Expression** cell as shown.

|   | Property Name | Type | | Value / Text Expression | Evaluated Value |
|---|---------------|------|---|------------------------|-----------------|
| 1 | Description | Text | ▼ | U-Bracket Detail | U-Bracket Detail |
| 2 | CompanyName | Text | ▼ | University of New Orleans | |

20. Click **OK** to accept the user-defined property.

University of New Orleans

TITLE:

21. Notice the entry now automatically appears in the title block. On your own, adjust the font size to fit in the box (see steps 6-10 above).

22. Move the cursor over the box next to **Drawn** as shown. A note containing a link to the *Custom Property* **DrawnBy** is contained in this box.

|  | NAME | DATE |  |
|--|------|------|--|
| DRAWN |  |  |  |
| CHECKED |  | A | TIT |
| ENG APPR. | $PRP:"DrawnBy" |  |  |

23. On your own, go to the *File Properties* window and enter your name or initials as the entry for the **DrawnBy** *Custom Property*.

24. On your own, determine the *Property Link* in the **Drawn Date** box. Enter the date for the *Custom Property*.

| | NAME | DATE |
|---|---|---|
| DRAWN | A. Smith | 01/08/11 |
| CHECKED | | |

25. Move the cursor over the **Title** (it should read **2-1/2″ U-Bracket**). A letter **A** appears indicating a note. A pop-up dialog box appears identifying a *Property Link* which reads **$PRPSHEET: "Description"**. The prefix **$PRPSHEET:** defines the source as the model (part file) appearing in the sheet. The *Property Name* is **Description**. This is a **Custom Property**. We defined this description when we saved the **U-Bracket** part file. If 2-1/2″ U-Bracket does not appear, you must define the description. Go to the part file (select **U-Bracket.SLDPRT** from the *Window* pull-down menu). Follow the same procedure as we did in the drawing file to change the **Description** property. Then return to the drawing window.

26. On your own investigate the rest of the title block to determine where other *Property Links* appear.

| | | | UNLESS OTHERWISE SPECIFIED: | | NAME | DATE | University of New Orleans | |
|---|---|---|---|---|---|---|---|---|
| | | | DIMENSIONS ARE IN INCHES TOLERANCES: ANGULAR: MACH ± 0.1° TWO PLACE DECIMAL ± 0.01 THREE PLACE DECIMAL ± 0.003 | DRAWN | A. Smith | 01/08/11 | | |
| | | | | CHECKED | | | TITLE: | |
| | | | | ENG APPR. | | | | |
| | | | | MFG APPR. | | | 2-1/2″ U-Bracket | A |
| | | | INTERPRET GEOMETRIC TOLERANCING PER: | Q.A. | | | | |
| | | | | COMMENTS: | | | | |
| | | | MATERIAL    1060 ALLOY | | | | SIZE | DWG. NO.    REV |
| NEXT ASSY | USED ON | | FINISH | | | | B | MET 3001 |
| APPLICATION | | | DO NOT SCALE DRAWING | | | | SCALE: 1:1  WEIGHT: | SHEET 2 OF 2 |
| 4 | | 3 | | | 2 | | | 1 |

27. Press the **[F]** key to scale the view to fit the graphics area.

28. Move the cursor into the graphics area and **right-click** to open the pop-up option menu.

**Sheet (Sheet Format2)**
> Define Title Block
> Edit Sheet
> Add Sheet...

29. Select **Edit Sheet** from the pop-up option menu to change to *Edit Sheet* mode.

## Associative Functionality – Modifying Feature Dimensions

- *SolidWorks' associative functionality* allows us to change the design at any level, and the system reflects the changes at all levels automatically.

1. Select the **U-Bracket** part window from the *Window* pull-down menu to switch to *Part Modeling* mode.

2. In the *FeatureManager Design Tree*, **right-click** on **Annotations** to open the option menu.

3. Select **Show Feature Dimensions** in the popup option menu.

4. Double-click on the diameter dimensions (**0. 50**) of the hole on the base feature as shown in figure. (Change the display to *Wireframe* mode if necessary.)

5. In the *Edit Dimension* dialog box, enter **0.625** as the new diameter dimension.

6. Click on the **OK** button to accept the new setting.

7. Select the **Rebuild** icon on the *Menu Bar*. Notice both holes are increased to 0.625 due to the Mirror relation.

8. Select the **MET 3001- Sheet2** drawing window from the *Window* pull-down menu to switch to *Drawing* mode.

9. If the *SolidWorks 2011* pop-up window appears, select **Yes** to update the drawing file to include the changes made to the model.

> Notice the change made to the model – the changed hole diameter – is reflected in the drawing.

10. Inside the graphics window, left-click on the **0.63** dimension in the *top* view to bring up the *Dimension PropertyManager*.

11. In the *Tolerance/Precision* panel of the *Dimension PropertyManager*, set the **Unit Precision** option to **3 digits after the decimal point** as shown.

12. Click **OK** in the *PropertyManager* to accept the new setting. Notice the accurate dimension of **.625** is now displayed.

13. Inside the graphics window, **double-click** with the **left-mouse-button** on the **R 1.75** dimension in the *front* view to bring up the *Modify* pop-up option window.

14. Change the dimension to **1.625**.

15. Click on the **check mark** button in the *Modify* window to accept the setting.

16. In the *Dimension PropertyManager*, set the **Unit Precision** option to **3 digits after the decimal point**.

17. Click **OK** in the *PropertyManager* to accept the new setting.

> Notice the views become shaded with cross-hatching. This is an indication by *SolidWorks* that changes have been made and a rebuild is needed to update the drawing and model.

18. Select the **Rebuild** icon on the *Menu Bar*.

❖ Note the geometry of the cut feature is updated in all views automatically.

❖ On your own, switch to the *Part Modeling* mode and confirm the design is updated as well.

## Saving the Drawing File

1. Go to *Drawing* mode with **MET 3001.SLDDRW** as the active document.

2. Select the **Save** icon on the *Menu Bar*. This command will save the **MET 3001.SLDDRW** file. This file includes the document properties, the sheet format, and the drawing views.

3. In the *Save Modified Documents* window, select **Save All**.

4. If the *Confirm drawing view update* window appears, select **Yes**.

## Saving a Drawing Template

❖ In *SolidWorks*, each new drawing is created from a template. During the installation of *SolidWorks*, a default drafting standard was selected which sets the default template used to create drawings. We can use this template or another predefined template, modify one of the predefined templates, or create our own templates to enforce drafting standards and other conventions. Any drawing file can be used as a template; a drawing file becomes a template when it is saved as a template (*.drwdot) file. Once the template is saved, we can create a new drawing file using the new template.

❖ We will create a custom *SolidWorks* drawing template file with the document properties (e.g., ANSI dimension standard, English units, etc.) and sheet format (size B paper size, etc.) we have created. The template can include the layout of the drawing views, but we will want to choose different views in future drawings. We will therefore delete the views. **NOTE:** Do not save MET 3001.SLDDRW after these changes.

1. We will want only the sheet format in *Sheet2* in the template. Move the cursor over **Sheet1** in the *FeatureManager Design Tree* and click once with the **right-mouse-button**.

2. Select **Delete** from the pop-up option menu.

3. Select **Yes** in the *Confirm Delete* window.

4. On your own, delete the three drawing views (the front view, top view, and isometric view). **Right-click** on the view in the graphics area or the corresponding icon in the *FeatureManager Design Tree*; then select **Delete** from the pop-up option menu; then select **Yes** in the *Confirm Delete* window.

5. Select the **Document Properties** tab.

6. Click **Units** as shown.

7. Verify that **IPS (inch, pound, second)** is selected under the *Unit system* options.

8. Verify that **.12** is selected in the *Decimals* spin boxes.

9. Click **Dimensions** as shown.

10. Verify that **.12** is selected in the *Primary precision* spin box.

11. Click **Detailing** as shown below.

12. **Uncheck** all of the *Auto insert on view creation* options at the right of the window as shown.

13. Click **OK** in the options dialog box to accept the selected settings

14. Select **Save as** from the *File* pull-down menu as shown. (**NOTE:** Use the *File* pull-down menu instead of the *Menu Bar* to ensure you do not accidentally click **Save**. This would write over the MET 3001.SLDDRW file.)

15. Click in the *Save as type:* entry box and select **Drawing Template** from the pull-down options.

| File name: | MET 3001 |
|---|---|
| Save as type: | Drawing (*.drw;*.slddrw) |
| Description: | Drawing (*.drw;*.slddrw) |
| | Detached Drawing (*.slddrw) |
| | Drawing Templates (*.drwdot) |
| | Dxf (*.dxf) |

16. The folder selection will automatically change to the default **Templates** folder. Use the browser to change the folder selection to the **Tutorial Templates** folder you created in Chapter 4.

17. Enter **ANSI-B-Inch** for the *File name*.

18. Enter **ANSI B Inch** for the *Description*.

19. Select **Save**.

20. If the *SolidWorks 2009* pop-up window appears, click **OK**.

❖ Exit *SolidWorks*. This drawing template will now be available for use to create future drawings.

## Questions:

1. What does *SolidWork*'s *associative functionality* allow us to do?

2. How do we move a view on the *Drawing Sheet*?

3. How do we display feature/model dimensions in the *Drawing* mode?

4. What is the difference between a *feature dimension* and a *reference dimension*?

5. How do we reposition dimensions?

6. What is a *base view*?

7. Identify and describe the following commands:

   (a)

   (b)

   (c)

   (d)

**Exercises:** (Create the solid models and the associated 2D drawings.)

1.   Dimensions are in inches.

2.   Dimensions are in inches.

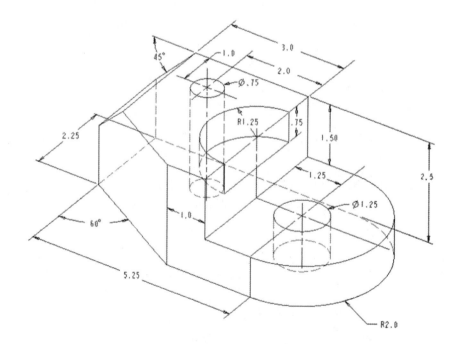

3. Dimensions are in inches.

4. Dimensions are in inches.

**NOTES:**

# Chapter 9
# Reference Geometry and Auxiliary Views

## Learning Objectives

- ♦ **Understand the Concepts and the Use of Reference Geometry**
- ♦ **Use the Different Options to Create Reference Geometry**
- ♦ **Create Auxiliary Views in 2D Drawing Mode**
- ♦ **Create and Adjust Centerlines**
- ♦ **Create Shaded Images in the 2D Drawing mode**

## Certified SolidWorks Associate Exam Objectives Coverage

### Sketch Relations
Objectives: Using Geometric Relations.

### Reference Geometry – Planes, Axis, Mate References
Objectives:  Creating Reference Planes, Axes, and Mate References.

### Drawing Sheets and Views
Objectives: Creating and Setting Properties for Drawing Sheets; Inserting and Editing Standard Views.

## Reference Geometry

*Feature-based parametric modeling* is a cumulative process. The relationships that we define between features determine how a feature reacts when other features are changed. Because of this interaction, certain features must, by necessity, precede others. A new feature can use previously defined features to define information such as size, shape, location and orientation. *SolidWorks* provides several tools to automate this process. *Reference geometry* can be thought of as user-definable datum, which are updated with the part geometry. We can create planes, axes, points, or local coordinate systems that do not already exist. Reference geometry can also be used to align features or to orient parts in an assembly. In this chapter, the use of the **Offset** option and the **Angled** option to create new reference planes, surfaces that do not already exist, are illustrated. By creating parametric reference geometry, the established feature interactions in the CAD database assure the capturing of the design intent. The default planes, which are aligned to the origin of the coordinate system, can be used to assist the construction of the more complex geometric features.

## Auxiliary Views in 2D Drawings

An important rule concerning multiview drawings is to draw enough views to accurately describe the design. This usually requires two or three of the regular views, such as a front view, a top view and/or a side view. However, many designs have features located on inclined surfaces that are not parallel to the regular planes of projection. To truly describe the feature, the true shape of the feature must be shown using an **auxiliary view**. An *auxiliary view* has a line of sight that is perpendicular to the inclined surface, as viewed looking directly at the inclined surface. An *auxiliary view* is a supplementary view that can be constructed from any of the regular views. Using the solid model as the starting point for a design, auxiliary views can be easily created in 2D drawings. In this chapter, the general procedure of creating auxiliary views in 2D drawings from solid models is illustrated.

## The *Rod-Guide* Design

❖ Based on your knowledge of *SolidWorks* so far, how would you create this design? What are the more difficult features involved in the design? Take a few minutes to consider a modeling strategy and do preliminary planning by sketching on a piece of paper. You are also encouraged to create the design on your own prior to following through the tutorial.

## Modeling Strategy

## Starting SolidWorks

1. Select the **SolidWorks** option on the *Start* menu or select the **SolidWorks** icon on the desktop. The *SolidWorks* main window will appear on the screen.

2. Select the **New** icon with a single click of the left-mouse-button on the *Menu Bar*. The *New SolidWorks Document* dialog box should appear in Advanced mode. If it appears in Novice mode, click once with the left-mouse-button on the **Advanced** icon.

3. Select the **Tutorial_Templates** tab. (**NOTE:** You added this tab in Chapter 4.)

4. Select the **Part_IPS_ANSI** template as shown.

5. Click on the **OK** button to open a new document using the Part_IPS_ANSI template.

## Applying the BORN Technique

1. Select the **Hide/Show Items** icon on the *Heads-up View* toolbar to reveal the pull-down menu. In the pull-down menu, toggle on the **View Planes** and **View Origins** buttons.

2. In the *FeatureManager Design Tree* window, select the **Front, Top, and Right Planes** by holding down the [**Shift**] key and clicking with the left-mouse-button.

3. Click on any of the planes to display the option menu. Click on **Show** to toggle *ON* the display of the planes.

4. On your own, toggle *ON* the display of the **Origin**.

5. On your own, use the viewing options (Rotate, Zoom and Pan) to view the work features established.

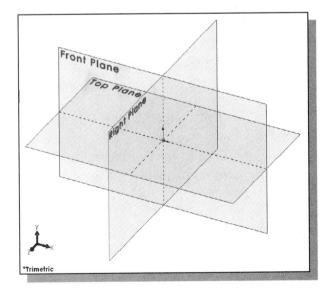

6.  Move the cursor into the graphics area, away from the planes, and click once with the **left-mouse-button** to ensure no planes are selected.

7.  Select the **Sketch** button on the *Sketch* toolbar to create a new sketch.

8.  In the *Edit Sketch Property-Manager*, the message "*Select a plane on which to create a sketch for the entity*" is displayed. Move the cursor over the edge of the **Top Plane** in the graphics area. When the Top Plane is highlighted, click once with the **left-mouse-button** to select the Top (XZ) Plane as the sketch plane for the new sketch.

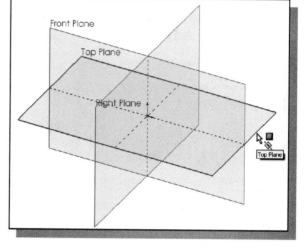

9.  On your own, **hide** the three planes.

## Creating the Base Feature

1.  Select the **Rectangle** command by clicking once with the left-mouse-button on the icon in the *Sketch* toolbar.

2.  Create a rectangle of arbitrary size with the origin inside the rectangle as shown.

3.  Click on the **Sketch Fillet** icon in the *Sketch* toolbar.

4.  Enter **0.25 in** for the fillet radius in the *Fillet Parameters* panel of the *Sketch Fillet Property-Manager*.

| Fillet Parameters | ⋀ |
|---|---|
| ⟋   0.250in | ▲ ▼ |
| ☑ Keep constrained corners | |
| ☐ Dimension each fillet | |

5.  Create four rounded corners as shown.  Each fillet can be created by moving the cursor into the graphics area and (1) clicking on the corner, or (2) clicking on the two lines forming the corner.

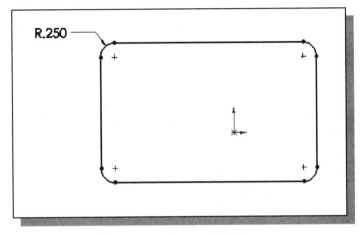

6.  Select **OK** in the *PropertyManager* or press the **[Esc]** key to exit the Sketch Fillet command.

7.  On your own, create four circles of the same diameter and with the centers aligned to the centers of arcs.  (**NOTE:** Use the *Link Value* option for the diameter dimensions – see page 5-24.) Also create and modify the six dimensions as shown in the figure below.  Note that these dimensions fix the center of the base at the origin.  (**NOTE:**  If you cannot select the origin, make sure the visibility is toggled *ON* in the *FeatureManager Design Tree*.)

8.  Select the **Sketch** icon on the *Sketch* toolbar to exit the Sketch option.

9.  Make sure the sketch – Sketch1 – is selected.

10. In the *Features* toolbar, select the **Extruded Boss/Base** command by clicking once with the left-mouse-button on the icon.

11. Create a **Blind** extrusion with a distance of **0.75** in.

12. Click **OK** in the *Extrude PropertyManager* to accept the settings and create the extrusion.

## Creating an Angled Reference Plane

 1. In the *Display Style* pull-down menu on the *Heads-up View* toolbar, select the **Wireframe** option to set the display mode to *Wireframe*.

❖ *SolidWorks* allows the creation of a plane through an edge, axis, or sketch line at an angle to a face or plane, using the **At Angle** option of the **Plane** command. Using the **At Angle** option requires selection of an existing edge, axis, or sketch line and an existing face or plane. We will create a reference axis along the Y-direction, and create a plane that can be visualized by rotating the Front Plane about the reference (Y) axis.

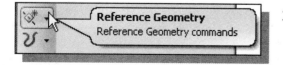 2. In the *Features* toolbar, select the **Reference Geometry** command by left-clicking the icon.

3.　In the pull-down option menu of the Reference Geometry command, select the **Axis** option.

4.　In the *Selections* panel of the *Axis PropertyManager*, select the **Two Planes** option. (We will define the Y-axis as the intersection of the Front and Right Planes.)

5.　Select the **Front Plane** and **Right Plane** in the *Design Tree* appearing in the graphics area.

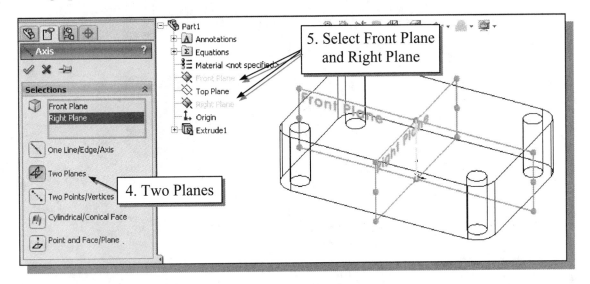

5. Select Front Plane and Right Plane

4. Two Planes

6.　Click **OK** in the *PropertyManager* to create the new reference axis.

7.　Press the **[Esc]** key to make sure no objects are selected.

➢　Notice the reference axis, named **Axis1**, has been created. It is aligned with the Y-axis and passes through the center of the base feature.

8.　Select the **Reference Geometry** command from the *Features* toolbar, and select the **Plane** option from the pull-down menu.

➢　Notice the message "*Select references and constraints*" appears and the *First Reference* window is highlighted.

9.  In the *Design Tree* appearing in the graphics area, select **Axis1** (the reference axis created above) as the *First Reference* and **Front Plane** as the *Second Reference*.

10. In the *Second Reference* panel of the *Plane PropertyManager*, select the **At Angle** option button.

11. Enter **30 deg** as the angle in the *PropertyManager*.

12. Check the **Flip** box.

13. Check that the preview of the reference plane appears as shown above.

14. Click **OK** in the *PropertyManager* to create the new reference plane.

❖ Note that the *angle* is measured relative to the selected reference plane, the Front (XY) Plane.

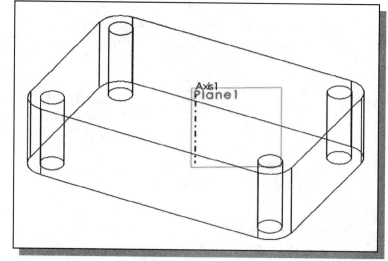

## Creating a 2D Sketch on the Reference Plane

1. Press the [Esc] key twice to ensure no objects are selected.

2. In the *Sketch* toolbar, select the **Sketch** command by left-clicking once on the icon.

3. Select the angled reference plane **Plane1** as the sketch plane.

## Using the Convert Entities Option

❖ Projected geometry is another type of *reference geometry*. The Convert Entities tool can be used to project entities from previously defined sketches or features onto the sketch plane. The position of the projected geometry is fixed to the feature from which it was projected. We can use the Convert Entities tool to project geometry from a sketch or feature onto the active sketch plane.

Typical uses of the Convert Entities command include:
- Project a silhouette of a 3D feature onto the sketch plane for use in a 2D profile.
- Project a sketch from a feature onto the sketch plane so that the projected sketch can be used to constrain a new sketch.

1. Move the cursor over the top rear edge of the base feature. When the edge is highlighted, click once with the **left-mouse-button** to select the edge.

2. In the *Sketch* toolbar, select the **Convert Entities** command by left-clicking the icon.

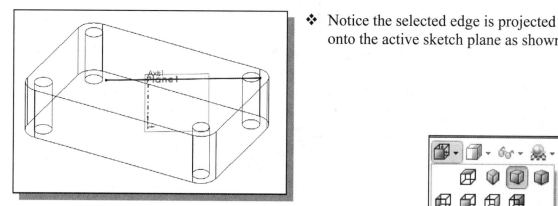

❖ Notice the selected edge is projected onto the active sketch plane as shown.

3.  Left-click on the **View Orientation** icon on the *Heads-up View* toolbar to reveal the *View Orientation* pull-down menu.  Select the **Normal To** command.

4.  **Left-click** on the arrow next to the **Line** button on the *Sketch* toolbar to reveal additional commands.

5.  Select the **Centerline** command from the pop-up menu.

6.  Draw a vertical centerline with one end coincident with the origin and the other end above the top of the base as shown.

7.  Press the **[Esc]** key twice to exit the Centerline command and unselect the centerline you created.

❖ The **Dynamic Mirror** command will be used to generate sketch objects with symmetry about a centerline.

8.  Select the **Tools** pull-down menu, then click on **Sketch Tools**.  A complete list of sketch tools will appear. (Some of these also appear in the *Sketch* toolbar.)

9.  Select **Dynamic Mirror** as shown.

10. The message *"Please select a sketch line or linear edge to mirror about"* appears in the *Mirror PropertyManager*. Move the cursor over the **centerline** in the graphics area and click once with the **left-mouse-button** to select it as the line to mirror about.

➢ Notice the hash marks which appear on the centerline to indicate that the Dynamic Mirror command is active.

 11. Click on the **Line** icon in the *Sketch* toolbar.

12. On your own, create a rough sketch using the projected edge as the bottom line as shown in the figure. (Note that all edges are either horizontal or vertical.)

13. Press the **[Esc]** key to exit the Line command.

14. On your own, **turn OFF** the Dynamic Mirror command. (**HINT:** Perform steps 9 and 10.)

15. Press the **[Esc]** key twice to ensure no entities are selected.

16. Select the **Add Relation** command from the *Display/Delete Relations* pop-up menu on the *Sketch* toolbar.

17. Select the lower and upper vertical lines in the sketch as shown.

Select

Select

18. Select the **Collinear** option in the *Add Relations* panel of the *Add Relations PropertyManager*.

19. Press the **[Esc]** key to exit the Add Relations command.

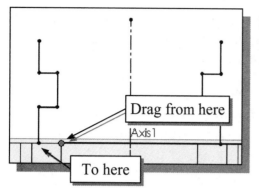

20. Move the cursor over the left endpoint of the projected edge. Press and drag the **left-mouse-button** to move the endpoint until it is coincident with the lower endpoint of the left vertical line as shown.

21. On your own, drag the right endpoint of the projected edge to be coincident with the lower endpoint of the right vertical line.

22. **Left-click** on the arrow next to the **Arc** button on the *Sketch* toolbar and select the **Centerpoint Arc** command from the pop-up menu.

23. On your own, create the arc with the centerpoint coincident with the centerline and aligned with the top endpoints of the vertical lines as shown.

24. Use the **Add Relation** command to create a **Tangent** relation between the arc and the upper right vertical line.

25. On your own, create the Smart Dimensions as shown.

26. On your own, add a **0.75** inch circle concentric with the arc and complete the sketch as shown in the figure.

❖ The *Status Bar* should now read *Fully Defined*, because the geometric and dimensional constraints fully define the sketch.

## Completing the Solid Feature

1. Select the **Sketch** icon on the *Sketch* toolbar to exit the Sketch option.

2. In the *Features* toolbar, select the **Extruded Boss/Base** command by clicking once with the left-mouse-button on the icon. The *Extrude PropertyManager* is displayed in the left panel.

3. Select the **Midplane** option.

4. Enter **1 inch** for the extrusion distance.

5. Check the **Merge result** option.

6. Click **OK** in the *PropertyManager* to accept the settings and create the extrusion.

7. Using the *Heads-up View* toolbar, set the display style to **Shaded with edges**.

## Creating an Offset Reference Plane

1. Select the **Reference Geometry** command from the *Features* toolbar, and select the **Plane** option from the pull-down menu.

❖ In the *Status Bar* area, the message: "*Select valid entities to define a plane (plane, face, edge, line, or point*" is displayed. *SolidWorks* expects us to select any existing geometry, which will be used as a reference to create the new work plane.

2. Move the cursor over the top face of the base feature. Notice the top face of the base feature is highlighted. Click once with the **left-mouse-button** to select the face.

3. Notice the top face, called **Face<1>**, appears in the *First Reference* panel of the *Plane PropertyManager*, and the **Offset Distance** option is automatically selected.

4. Enter **0.75 in** as the offset distance.

5. Click **OK** in the *ProperyManager* to accept the settings and create the new reference plane.

6. Press the **[Esc]** key to unselect the new plane.

## Creating another Extruded Cut Feature using the Reference Plane

 1. In the *Sketch* toolbar, select the **Sketch** command by left-clicking once on the icon.

2. Select the offset reference plane **Plane2** as the sketch plane.

3. In the *Display Style* pull-down menu on the *Heads-up View* toolbar, select the **Wireframe** option to set the display mode to *Wireframe*.

4. In the *View Orientation* pull-down menu on the *Heads-up View* toolbar, select the **Normal To** command.

5. On your own, create a **Ø 0.25** inch circle aligned to the origin as shown in the figure.

6. Select the **Sketch** icon on the *Sketch* toolbar to exit the sketch.

7. On your own, create the **Extruded Cut** feature. Use the **Through All** option and click the Reverse Direction button if necessary.

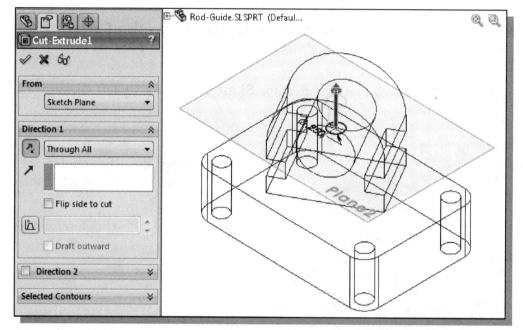

8. Click **OK** in the *PropertyManager* to create the extruded cut feature.

9. On your own, hide all planes, hide Axis1, and set the display to **Shaded With Edges**.

10. Press the **[F]** key to fit the view to the graphics area.

11. Select the **Save As** option from the *File* pull-down menu.

12. In the *Save As* pop-up window, enter **Rod-Guide** for the *File name*.

13. Enter **3/4″ Rod Guide** for the *Description*.

14. Click **Save** to save the file.

| File name: | Rod-Guide |
|---|---|
| Save as type: | Part (*.prt;*.sldprt) |

Description: 3/4″ Rod Guide

## Starting a New 2D Drawing and Adding a Base View

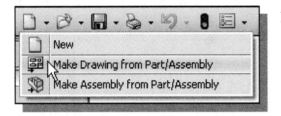

1. Click on the arrow next to the **New** icon on the *Menu Bar* and select **Make Drawing from Part/Assembly** in the pull-down menu.

2. In the *New SolidWorks Document* window, select the **Tutorial_Templates** tab.

3. Select the **ANSI-B-Inch** template file icon. This is the custom drawing template you created in Chapter 8.

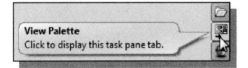

4. Select **OK** in the *New SolidWorks Document* window to open the new drawing file.

➢ The new drawing file opens using the **ANSI-B-Inch.SLDDOT** template. The B-size drawing sheet appears. The *View Palette* appears in the *task pane*.

❖ In *SolidWorks*, the first drawing view we create is called a **base view**. A *base view* is the primary view in the drawing; other views can be derived from this view. In *SolidWorks*, a base view can be added using the **Model View** command on the *Drawing* toolbar, or using the **View Palette**. By default, *SolidWorks* will treat the *world XY plane* as the front view of the solid model. Note that there can be more than one *base view* in a drawing.

5. If the *View Pallette* is collapsed, select the **View Pallette** tab at the right of the graphics area.

6. Select the **Top** view in the *View Palette* by clicking on the icon with the **left-mouse-button** as shown.

7. Hold down the **left-mouse-button** and **drag** the top view from the *View Palette* into the graphics window and place the **base view** near the upper left corner of the graphics window as shown below.

➤ When the base view is placed, *SolidWorks* automatically executes the **Projected View** command and the *Projected View PropertyManager* appears.

8. Press the **[Esc]** key to exit the Projected View command.

## Creating an Auxiliary View

❖ In *SolidWorks Drawing* mode, the **Projected View** command is used to create standard views such as the *top* view, *front* view or *isometric* view. For non-standard views, the **Auxiliary View** command is used. *Auxiliary views* are created using orthographic projections. Orthographic projections are aligned to the base view and inherit the base view's scale and display settings.

1. If the *Drawing* toolbar is not open, open it. (Move the cursor over the *Menu Bar* and click once with the **right-mouse-button** to access the menu of toolbars.)

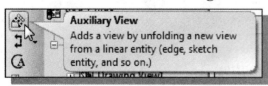

**Auxiliary View**
Adds a view by unfolding a new view from a linear entity (edge, sketch entity, and so on.)

2. Click on the **Auxiliary View** button in the *Drawing* toolbar.

3. The message "*Please select a Reference Edge to continue*" appears in the *Auxiliary View Property-Manager*. Pick the front edge of the upper section of the model as shown.

❖ The orthographic projection direction will be perpendicular to the selected edge.

4. Move the cursor below the base view and select a location to position the auxiliary view of the model as shown. Click once with the left-mouse-button to place the view.

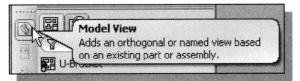

5. In the *Auxiliary View PropertyManager* **uncheck** the box next to the **Arrow** option. This will turn *OFF* the display of the direction arrow.

6. Press the **[Esc]** key to accept the settings and exit the Auxiliary View command.

7. Click on the **Model View** icon *Drawing* toolbar.

8. The *Model View PropertyManager* appears with the *Rod-Guide* part file selected as the part from which to create the base view. Click the **Next** arrow as shown to proceed with defining the base view.

9. In the *Model View PropertyManager*, select the **Isometric** view for the *Orientation*, as shown.

➢ In general, hidden lines are not used in isometric views.

10. In the *Model View PropertyManager*, select the **Hidden Lines Removed** option for the *Display Style*.

11. Move the cursor toward the upper right corner of the sheet and select a location to position the isometric view of the model as shown below.

12. Left-click on the **OK** icon in the *Drawing View PropertyManager* to accept the view.

## Displaying Feature Dimensions

➢ In your drawing, the inserted views may include *center marks*, *centerlines*, and/or *dimensions*. If so, these were added with the **auto-insert** option. To access these options, click **Options** (*Standard* toolbar), select the **Document Properties** tab, and then select **Detailing**. This lesson was done with no auto-insert options selected. The center marks, centerlines, and dimensions will be added individually. The dimensions used to create the part can be imported into the drawing using the **Model Items** command. We can also add dimensions to the drawing manually using the **Smart Dimension** command.

➢ Before we apply dimensions using the Model Items command we will adjust the size/position of the *Reference Plane 1*. The Model Items command will use the mid-line of the plane to locate the angle dimension.

1. Select the **Rod-Guide.SLDPRT** part window from the *Window* pull-down menu to switch to *Part Modeling* mode.

2. In the *View Orientation* pull-down menu on the *Heads-up View* toolbar, select the **Top View** command.

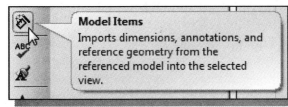

3. On your own, toggle *ON* the visibility of **Plane1**.

4. Using the left-mouse-button, **click and drag** the end of **Plane1** and position it such that the mid-point of the plane coincides with the center of the hole. This point will be used as the reference point for applying the angle dimension when the Model Items command is executed.

5. On your own, switch back to *Drawing* mode.

6. Press the **[Esc]** key to make sure no items are selected.

7. If the *Annotation* toolbar is not open, open it. (Move the cursor over the *Menu Bar* and click once with the **right-mouse-button** to access the menu of toolbars.)

**Model Items**

Imports dimensions, annotations, and reference geometry from the referenced model into the selected view.

8. Left-mouse-click on the **Model Items** icon on the *Annotation* toolbar.

**Source/Destination**

Source:

Entire model

☑ Import items into all views

9. In the *Source/ Destination* options panel of the *Model Items PropertyManager*, select the **Entire model** option from the *Import from* pull-down menu and check **Import items into all views** as shown.

**Dimensions**

☑ Eliminate duplicates

10. Under the *Dimensions* options panel, select the **Marked for drawing** icon. (**NOTE:** This option may be selected by default.) Check **Eliminate duplicates** as shown.

11. Click the **OK** icon in the *Model Items PropertyManager*. Notice dimensions are automatically placed on the top and auxiliary drawing views.

## Adjusting the View Scale

1.  Move the cursor over the top view and click once with the **left-mouse-button**. The *Drawing View1 PropertyManager* appears.

2.  Under the *Scale* options in the *Drawing View PropertyManager*, select **Use custom scale**.

3.  Select **User Defined** from the pull-down options, as shown.

4.  Enter **3:2** as the user defined scale.

5.  Left-click on the **OK** icon in the *Drawing View PropertyManager* to accept the new settings. Notice the auxiliary view is automatically scaled.

6.  If necessary, reposition the views so they do not overlap.

## Repositioning, Appearance, and Hiding of Feature Dimensions

1.  Zoom in on the top view.

2.  **Right-click** on the **R.25** *radius* dimension of the round, and select **Hide** from the pop-up option menu.

3. On your own, hide the diameter dimensions of 3 of the 4 corner holes, leaving the dimension on the upper left hole.

4. On your own, reposition the dimensions to appear as shown in the figure.

5. **Pan** to the auxiliary view. On your own, hide and reposition dimensions as shown in the figure.

❖ The appearance of dimensions can be adjusted independently.

6. Move the cursor over the **0.25** dimension shown in the figure and click once with the **left-mouse-button** to select the dimension. The *Dimension PropertyManager* will appear.

7. In the *Dimension PropertyManager*, select the **Leaders** tab.

8. In the *Witness/Leader Display* panel, select the **Outside** option as shown. This will result in the arrows being located inside the extension lines.

9.  Reposition the dimension as shown.

10. Press the **[Esc]** key to exit the Dimension command and unselect the dimension.

 11. Left-mouse-click on the **Smart Dimension** icon on the *Annotation* toolbar.

12. Select the *curved top edge* in the auxiliary view.

13. Move the cursor to and **left-click** to position the dimension as shown.

❖ By default, reference dimensions are displayed in parentheses. However, we are using the dimension as an alternate placement for the hidden feature dimension. We will not use the parentheses.

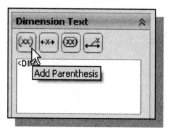

14. If parentheses appear by default with the reference dimension, go to the *Dimension PropertyManager*, scroll down to the *Dimension Text* panel and **unselect** the **Add Parenthesis** option as shown.

15. Click **OK** in the *Dimension PropertyManager* to create the reference dimension without parentheses.

16. Adjust the dimensions to appear as shown in the figure. Also notice the note which was automatically added containing the custom scale for the auxiliary view.

## Tangent Edge Display

1. Move the cursor over the auxiliary view and click once with the **right-mouse-button**.

2. In the pop-up option menu, select **Tangent Edge**, then **Tangent Edges Removed**.

## Adding Center Marks and Center Lines

> In your drawing, the inserted views may include *center marks*. If so, these were added with the **auto-insert** option. This lesson was done with no auto-insert options selected. The center marks will be added individually. If your drawing already has the center marks, you can delete them and proceed with the lesson, or select them and adjust the *Display Attributes* in the Center *Mark PropertyManager* as described below.

1. Click on the **Center Mark** button in the *Annotation* toolbar.

2. In the *Display Attributes* panel of the *Center Mark PropertyManager*, **uncheck** the **Use document defaults** box, enter **0.075** for the Mark size, and **check** the Extended lines box.

3. Click on the five circles in the top view to add the center marks as shown.

4. Click **OK** in the *PropertyManager* to exit the **Center Mark** command.

5. Notice the extension lines for some of the dimensions interfere with the center mark for the central hole. Select the **1.50** dimension as shown.

6. Move the endpoint of the extension line by **clicking and dragging** to reveal the center mark.

7. On your own, repeat this for the other extension lines to reveal the center mark as shown in the figure.

**Centerline**
Adds centerlines to a view or to selected entities.

8. Click on the **Centerline** button in the *Annotation* toolbar.

9. Inside the graphics window, click on the two hidden edges of one of the **Drill** features and create a center line in the auxiliary view as shown in the figure.

10. On your own, repeat the above step and create additional centerlines as shown.

11. Click **OK** in the *PropertyManager* to exit the Centerline command.

    12. Click on the **Center Mark** button in the *Annotation* toolbar.

13. In the *Display Attributes* panel of the *Center Mark PropertyManager*, **uncheck** the Use document defaults box, enter **0.075** for the Mark size, and **check** the Extended lines box.

14. Click on the circle in the auxiliary view. Notice the orientation of the center mark.

15. If the center mark is not aligned with the auxiliary view base as shown, go to the *Angle* panel of the *Center Mark PropertyManager*, enter **0.0** as the angle.

16. Click **OK** in the *PropertyManager* to exit the Center Mark command.

17. On your own, adjust line endpoints to appear approximately as shown in the figure.

## Controlling the View and Sheet Scales

➢ The scale for the Sheet is set at 1:1. This setting automatically appears in the title block due to the Property Link described as *$PRP:"SW-Sheet Scale"*. The prefix *$PRP:* defines the source as the current document. The Property Name is *SW-Sheet Scale*. This is a **System Property**. Each view can be set to use the default sheet scale or to use a custom scale defined for the view. When we created the top and auxiliary views, a custom scale of 3:2 was created. For the isometric view the default sheet scale of 1:1 was used. We will change the sheet scale to 3:2.

1. Move the cursor over **Sheet2** in the *FeatureManager Design Tree* and **right-click** to open the option menu.

2. Select **Properties**.

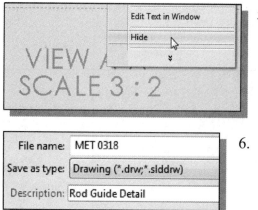

3. Enter **3:2** as the Scale in the *Sheet Properties* window.

4. Click **OK** in the *Sheet Properties* window.

➢ Notice the scale note in the title block now reads **3:2**. Also notice the scale of the isometric view has changed due to the **Use sheet scale** option.

5. Since the sheet scale is labeled as **3:2** in the title block, the view scale note is not necessary. Right click on the note and select **Hide** from the pop-up option menu.

6. On your own, save the drawing file with **MET 0318** as the *File name* and **Rod Guide Detail** as the *Description*.

7. If the *SolidWorks* pop-up window appears, click **Save All**.

## Completing the Drawing Sheet

1. Move the cursor into the graphics area and **right-click** to open the pop-up option menu.

2. Select **Edit Sheet Format** from the pop-up option menu to change to *Edit Sheet Format* mode.

❖ Notice the title block is highlighted.

3. On your own, use the **Zoom** and **Pan** commands to adjust the display to work on the title block area. Most of the information is accurate due to Property Links.

4. The date probably is inaccurate. Select **Properties** from the *File* pull-down menu on the *Menu Bar*.

5. In the *Summary Information* window select the **Custom** tab. Notice the *Custom Properties* appearing in the list. We defined these properties and saved them in the template file.

Summary Information

| Summary | Custom |
|---------|--------|

BOM quantity:

| | Property Name | Type | Value / Text Expression | Evaluated Value |
|---|---------------|------|-------------------------|-----------------|
| 1 | Description | Text | Rod Guide Detail | Rod Guide Detail |
| 2 | CompanyName | Text | University of New Orleans | University of New Orlean |
| 3 | DrawnBy | Text | A. Smith | A. Smith |
| 4 | DrawnDate | Text | 01/08/10 | 01/08/10 |
| 5 | | | | |

6. Change the DrawnDate Value / Text Expression to the current date.

7. Click **OK** in the *Summary Information* window to accept the change.

8.  On your own, correct any other entries to the title block if necessary.

| UNLESS OTHERWISE SPECIFIED: | | NAME | DATE | University of New Orleans | | |
|---|---|---|---|---|---|---|
| DIMENSIONS ARE IN INCHES | DRAWN | A. Smith | 01/08/11 | | | |
| TOLERANCES: ANGULAR: MACH± 0.1° TWO PLACE DECIMAL ± 0.01 THREE PLACE DECIMAL ± 0.003 | CHECKED | | | TITLE: | | |
| | ENG APPR. | | | 3/4" Rod Guide | | |
| | MFG APPR. | | | | | |
| INTERPRET GEOMETRIC TOLERANCING PER: | Q.A. | | | | | |
| | COMMENTS: | | | SIZE | DWG. NO. | REV |
| MATERIAL        1060 ALLOY | | | | B | MET 0318 | |
| FINISH | | | | | | |
| DO NOT SCALE DRAWING | | | | SCALE: 3:2 | WEIGHT: | SHEET 1 OF 1 |

9.  Left-mouse-click on the **Note** icon on the *Annotations CommandManager*.

10. On your own, also create a general note at the lower left corner of the border as shown.

## Editing the Isometric view

1.  Press the [**F**] key to scale the view to fit the graphics area.

2.  Move the cursor into the graphics area and **right-click** to open the pop-up option menu.

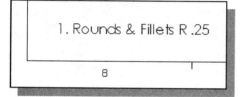

3.  Select **Edit Sheet** from the pop-up option menu to change to *Edit Sheet* mode.

4.  Left-mouse-click inside the *isometric* view to bring up the *Drawing View PropertyManager*.

5.  In the *Display Style* panel of the *Drawing View PropertyManager*, select **Shaded with Edges**.

6.  Click **OK** in the *PropertyManager* to accept the setting.

7.  On your own, save the final version of the drawing file.

## Questions:

1. What are the different types of reference geometry features available in *SolidWorks*?

2. Why are reference geometry features important in parametric modeling?

3. Describe the purpose of auxiliary views in 2D drawings?

4. What are the required elements in order to generate an auxiliary view?

5. Describe the method used to create centerlines in the chapter.

6. Can we change the View Scale of existing views? How?

7. Identify and describe the following commands:

(a)

(b)

(c)

(d)

**Exercises:**  (Create the Solid models and the associated 2D drawings.)

1.   Dimensions are in inches.

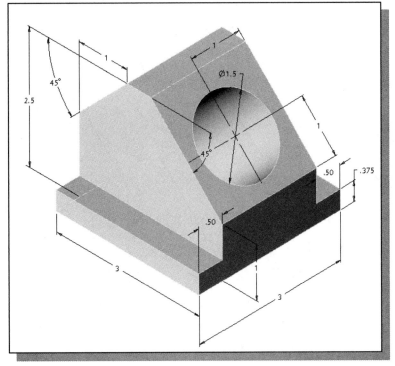

2.   Dimensions are in millimeters.

3.　Dimensions are in inches.

4.　Dimensions are in inches.

## Chapter 10
# Symmetrical Features in Designs

## Learning Objectives

- ◆ **Create Revolved Features**
- ◆ **Use the Mirror Feature Command**
- ◆ **Create New Borders and Title Blocks**
- ◆ **Create Circular Patterns**
- ◆ **Create and Modify Linear Dimensions**
- ◆ **Use SolidWorks' Associative Functionality**
- ◆ **Identify Symmetrical Features in Designs**
- ◆ **Create a Section View in a Drawing**

## Certified SolidWorks Associate Exam Objectives Coverage

## Introduction

In parametric modeling, it is important to identify and determine the features that exist in the design. *Feature-based parametric modeling* enables us to build complex designs by working on smaller and simpler units. This approach simplifies the modeling process and allows us to concentrate on the characteristics of the design. Symmetry is an important characteristic that is often seen in designs. Symmetrical features can be easily accomplished by the assortments of tools that are available in feature-based modeling systems, such as *SolidWorks*.

The modeling technique of extruding two-dimensional sketches along a straight line to form three-dimensional features, as illustrated in the previous chapters, is an effective way to construct solid models. For designs that involve cylindrical shapes, shapes that are symmetrical about an axis, revolving two-dimensional sketches about an axis can form the needed three-dimensional features. In solid modeling, this type of feature is called a *revolved feature*.

In *SolidWorks*, besides using the **Revolved Boss/Base** command to create revolved features, several options are also available to handle symmetrical features. For example, we can create multiple identical copies of symmetrical features with the **Circular Pattern** command, or create mirror images of models using the **Mirror** command. We can also use *construction geometry* to assist the construction of more complex features. In this lesson, the construction and modeling techniques of these more advanced options are illustrated.

## A Revolved Design: *PULLEY*

❖ Based on your knowledge of *SolidWorks*, how many features would you use to create the design? Which feature would you choose as the **base feature** of the model? Identify the symmetrical features in the design and consider other possibilities in creating the design. You are encouraged to create the model on your own prior to following through the tutorial.

# Modeling Strategy – A Revolved Design

## Starting SolidWorks

1. Select the **SolidWorks** option on the *Start* menu or select the **SolidWorks** icon on the desktop to start *SolidWorks*. The *SolidWorks* main window will appear on the screen.

2. Select the **New** icon with a single click of the left-mouse-button on the *Menu Bar*. The *New SolidWorks Document* dialog box should appear in Advanced mode. If it appears in Novice mode, click once with the left-mouse-button on the **Advanced** icon.

3. Select the **Tutorial_Templates** tab. (**NOTE:** You added this tab in Chapter 4.)

4. Select the **Part_IPS_ANSI** template as shown.

5. Click on the **OK** button to open a new document using the Part_IPS_ANSI template.

## Creating the 2D Sketch for the Base Feature

1. Select the **Sketch** button on the *Sketch* toolbar to create a new sketch.

2. In the *Edit Sketch Property-Manager*, the message "*Select a plane on which to create a sketch for the entity*" is displayed. Move the cursor over the edge of the Front Plane in the graphics area. When the Front Plane is highlighted, click once with the **left-mouse-button** to select the Front (XY) Plane as the sketch plane for the new sketch.

3. Click on the **Line** icon in the *Sketch* toolbar.

4. Create a closed-region sketch as shown below. (Note that the *Pulley* design is symmetrical about a horizontal axis as well as a vertical axis, which allows us to simplify the 2D sketch as shown below.)

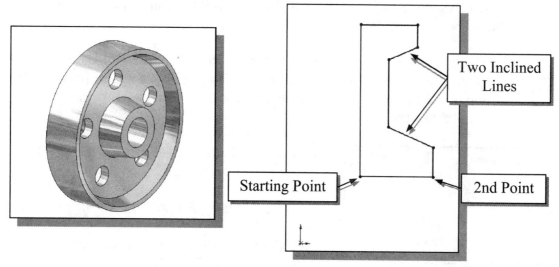

Two Inclined Lines

Starting Point

2nd Point

5. We want the left vertical edge to be aligned with the Y-axis. Select the **Add Relation** command from the *Display/Delete Relations* pop-up menu on the *Sketch* toolbar.

Display/Delete Relations
Add Relation
Fully Define Sketch

6. On your own, select the **left vertical edge** and the **origin** and add a **Coincident** relation.

➢ The X-axis is an axis of symmetry. It will serve as the rotation axis for the revolve feature, and we will use it to apply dimensions. A centerline will be created along the X-axis for these purposes.

Line
Centerline

7. Select the **Centerline** command from the *Line* pop-up menu on the *Sketch* toolbar.

8. Left-click on the origin as the first endpoint of the centerline.

9. Move the cursor to the right and left-click to create a horizontal centerline along the X-axis.

10. Press the [**Esc**] key to exit the Centerline command.

11. Select the **Smart Dimension** command in the *Sketch* toolbar.

12. Pick the **centerline** as the first entity to dimension as shown in the figure below.

13. Select the **bottom horizontal line** as the second object to dimension.

14. Locate the dimension **below the centerline**. This will automatically create a diameter dimension bisected by the centerline.

13. Select the bottom horizontal edge

12. Select the centerline

14. Locate dimension below centerline

15. In the *Modify* pop-up window enter **.75** for the dimension.

16. Select **OK** in the *Modify* pop-up window.

- **To create a dimension that will account for the symmetrical nature of the design: pick the centerline (axis of symmetry), pick the entity, and then place the dimension on the side of the centerline opposite the entity.**

17. Pick the **centerline** as the first entity to dimension as shown in the figure below.

18. Select the **corner point** as the second object to dimension as shown in the figure below.

19. Locate the dimension **below the centerline**. This will automatically create a diameter dimension bisected by the centerline.

18. Select this corner

17. Select the centerline

19. Locate dimension below centerline

20. In the *Modify* pop-up window enter **1.25** for the dimension.

21. Select **OK** in the *Modify* pop-up window.

22. On your own, create and adjust the vertical size/location dimensions as shown.

23. Select the **Sketch** icon on the *Sketch* toolbar to exit the Sketch option.

24. Select the **View Orientation** button on the *Heads-up View* toolbar by clicking once with the left-mouse-button.

25. Select the **Isometric** icon in the *View Orientation* pull-down menu.

## Creating the Revolved Feature

1.  Make sure the sketch – Sketch1 – is selected in the *FeatureManager Design Tree*.

2.  In the *Features* toolbar, left-click on the **arrow** next to the **Extruded Boss/Base** icon and select the **Revolved Boss/Base** command from pop-up menu.

3.  The *Revolve PropertyManager* appears. In the *Revolve Parameters* panel; the centerline is automatically selected as the revolve axis. The default revolution is **360°**. Click the **OK** icon to accept these parameters and create the revolved feature.

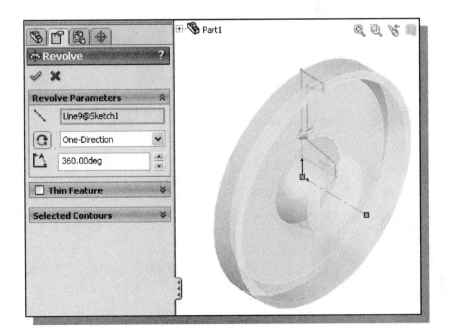

## Mirroring Features

- In *SolidWorks*, features can be mirrored to create and maintain complex symmetrical features. We can mirror a feature about a work plane or a specified surface. We can create a mirrored feature while maintaining the original parametric definitions, which can be quite useful in creating symmetrical features. For example, we can create one quadrant of a feature, then mirror it twice to create a solid with four identical quadrants.

1. In the *Features* toolbar, left-click on the **arrow** next to the **Linear Pattern** icon and select the **Mirror** command from pop-up menu.

2. In the *Mirror PropertyManager* appears. The *Mirror Face/Plane* panel is highlighted and the message "*Select a plane or planar face about which to mirror ...*" appears in the *Status Bar* area. Press the right arrow button [→] several times to rotate the model so that we are viewing the back surface as shown.

3. Select the surface as shown in the figure as the planar surface about which to mirror. The selection appears in the *Mirror Face/Plane* panel.

4. The ***Features to Mirror*** panel in the *PropertyManager* should contain **Revolve1** as the feature to mirror because this was pre-selected when we entered the Mirror command. If it does not, select the Revolve1 feature as the feature to mirror.

5. Click **OK** in the *PropertyManager* to accept the settings and create the mirrored feature.

6. On your own, return to an isometric view.

> Now is a good time to save the model. It is a good habit to save your model periodically, just in case something might go wrong while you are working on it. You should also save the model after you have completed any major constructions.

7. On your own, save the *.sldprt* file, entering **Pulley** for the filename and **4″ Pulley** for the Description.

## Creating an Extruded Cut Feature using Construction Geometry

- In *SolidWorks*, we can also use **construction geometry** to help define, constrain, and dimension the required geometry. **Construction geometry** can be lines, arcs, and circles that are used to line up or define other geometry, but are not themselves used as the shape geometry of the model. When profiling the rough sketch, *SolidWorks* will separate the construction geometry from the other entities and treat them as construction entities. Construction geometry can be dimensioned and constrained just like any other profile geometry. When the profile is turned into a 3D feature, the construction geometry remains in the sketch definition but does not show in the 3D model. Using construction geometry in profiles may mean fewer constraints and dimensions are needed to control the size and shape of geometric sketches. In *SolidWorks*, any sketch entity can be converted to construction geometry. Points and centerlines are always construction entities. We will illustrate the use of the construction geometry to create a cut feature.

- The *Pulley* design requires the placement of five identical holes on the base solid. Instead of creating the five holes one at a time, we can simplify the creation of these holes by using the **Circular Pattern** command, which allows us to create duplicate features. Prior to using the Circular Pattern command, we will first create a *pattern leader*, which is a regular extruded feature.

1. Press the [**Esc**] key to ensure that no objects are selected.

  2.  In the *Sketch* toolbar select the **Sketch** command by left-clicking once on the icon.

3. Use the *Design Tree* in the graphics area to select the **Right** (YZ) **Plane** as shown.

4.  Select the **View Orientation** button on the *Heads-up View* toolbar and select the **Normal to** option. The view will change to be normal to the sketch plane.

5.  Select the **Circle** command by clicking once with the left-mouse-button on the icon in the *Sketch* toolbar.

6.  Create a circle of arbitrary size as shown.

7.  Select the **Line** command in the *Sketch* toolbar.

8.  Create 2 *lines* by left-clicking on (1) the center of the circle we just created, (2) the *origin*, and (3) a point to the right of the origin creating a horizontal line, as shown below.

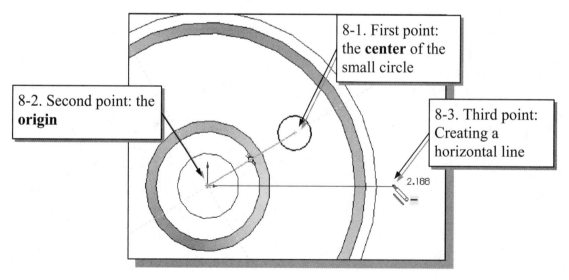

8-1. First point: the **center** of the small circle

8-2. Second point: the **origin**

8-3. Third point: Creating a horizontal line

2.188

9.  Press the [**Esc**] key to exit the Line command.

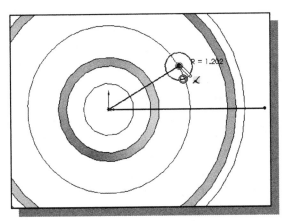

10. Select the **Circle** command on the *Sketch* toolbar.

11. Place the center at the ***origin***.

12. Pick the center of the small circle to set the size of the circle as shown.

13. Press the **[Esc]** key to exit the *Circle* command.

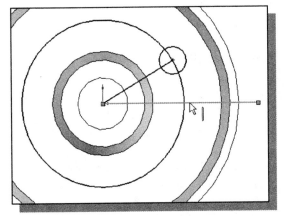

14. In the graphics area, left-click on the ***horizontal line*** to select it.

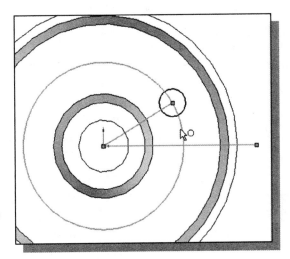

15. Press and hold down the **[Ctrl]** key and left-click on the **angled line** and **the last circle** drawn. The two lines and the circle are all highlighted. All three appear as selected entities (*Arc2, Line1, Line2*) in the *Properties PropertyManager*.

16. **Check** the box next to the **For construction** option in the options panel of the *Properties PropertyManager*.

17. Click **OK** in the *PropertyManager* to accept the setting. Notice the entities have been converted to construction geometry and appear with the same line style as centerlines.

18. Select the **Smart Dimension** command in the *Sketch* toolbar.

19. Pick the horizontal construction line as the first entity to dimension.

20. Select the angled construction line as the second entity to dimension.

21. Place the dimension text to the right of the model as shown.

22. Enter **30 deg** for the angle dimension.

23. Click **OK** in the *Modify* window.

➢ Note that the location of the small circle is adjusted as the location of the construction line is adjusted by the *angle dimension* we created.

24. On your own, create the two diameter dimensions, **.5** and **2.5**, as shown below.

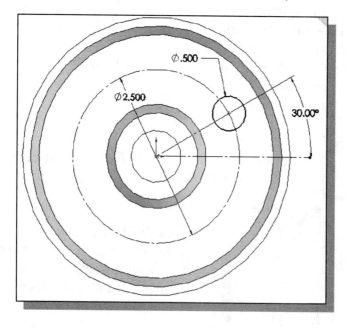

25. Select the **Sketch** icon on the *Sketch* toolbar to exit the **Sketch** option.

26. On your own, create the **Extruded Cut** feature.  Use the **Mid Plane** option and enter **0.25** for the distance.

27. Click **OK** in the *PropertyManager* to create the extruded cut feature.

28. On your own, adjust the angle dimension applied to the construction line of the cut feature to **90** and observe the effect of the adjustment. (**HINT:** Access the **Show Feature Dimensions** option by right-clicking on *Annotations* in the *FeatureManager Design Tree*.  Don't forget to use the **Rebuild** command.)

29. Reset the angle dimension to **30** degrees before continuing to the next section.

## Circular Pattern

> ➤ In *SolidWorks*, existing features can be easily duplicated. The **Linear Pattern** and **Circular Pattern** commands allow us to create rectangular and polar arrays of features. The patterned features are parametrically linked to the original feature; any modifications to the original feature are also reflected in the arrayed features.

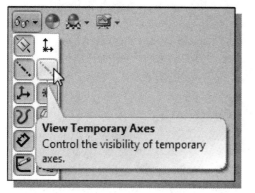

1. Select the **View Temporary Axes** option from the *Hide/Show* pull-down menu on the *Heads-up View* toolbar. Temporary axes are those created implicitly by cones and cylinders in the model. We will use the central axis for our circular pattern.

> ➤ Alternately, the visibility can be toggled *ON* by selecting **Temporary Axes** on the *View* pull-down menu.

2. Press the **[Esc]** key to ensure no feature is selected.

3. In the *Features* toolbar, left-click on the **arrow** next to the **Linear Pattern** icon and select the **Circular Pattern** command from pop-up menu.

4. The message "*Select edge or axis for direction reference...*" is displayed in the *Status Bar* area. *SolidWorks* expects us to select an axis to pattern about. Select the **axis** at the center of the *Pulley* as shown. Notice the axis (**Axis<1>**) appears in the *Pattern Axis* box in the *Parameters* panel of the *Circular Pattern PropertyManager*.

5. In the *Parameters* panel, check the **Equal Spacing** box, enter **5** in the *Number of Instances* box, and enter **360** in the *Angle* box as shown.

6. **Left-click** in the *Features to Pattern* text box as shown to begin selection of features to pattern.

7. Select the **circular cut feature** when it is highlighted as shown.

8. Select **OK** in the *Circular Pattern PropertyManager* to accepts the settings and create the circular pattern.

9. On your own, turn *OFF* the visibility of the Temporary Axes and the Origins. (See Step 1 above.)

10. Select **Save** in the *Menu Bar*; we can also use the "**Ctrl-S**" combination (press down the [Ctrl] key and hit the [S] key once) to save the part as ***Pulley***.

## Drawing Mode – Defining a New Border and Title Block

1. Click on the arrow next to the **New** icon on the *Menu Bar* and select **Make Drawing from Part/Assembly** in the pull-down menu.

2. In the *New SolidWorks Document* window, select the **Tutorial_Templates** tab.

3. Select the **ANSI-B-Inch** template file icon. This is the custom drawing template you created in Chapter 8.

4. Select **OK** in the *New SolidWorks Document* window to open the new drawing file.

➢ We will use the *Document Properties* in this template, but will create a new *Sheet Format*.

5. Right-click on the **Sheet** icon in the *FeatureManager Design Tree* to reveal the pop-up option menu.

6. Select **Properties** from the menu.

**Sheet Properties**

| Name: | Sheet2 | |
| Scale: | 1 | : | 1 |

Sheet Format/Size
◉ Standard sheet size
☐ Only show standard format

A (ANSI) Landscape
A (ANSI) Portrait
B (ANSI) Landscape

7. Set the scale to **1:1** and select **A (ANSI) Landscape** for the *Sheet Format/Size* in the *Sheet Properties* window.

8. Select **OK** in the *Sheet Properties* window.

**Sheet (Sheet2)**
Edit Sheet Format
Lock Sheet Focus
Add Sheet...
Copy
Delete
Properties...

Relations/Snaps Options...

9. Move the cursor into the graphics area and **right-click** to open the pop-up option menu.

10. Select **Edit Sheet Format** from the pop-up option menu to change to *Edit Sheet Format* mode. (Notice this method could also be used to access the *Sheet Properties*.)

11. Inside the graphics area, click and drag to create a window selecting all the entities in the title block, leaving only the border.

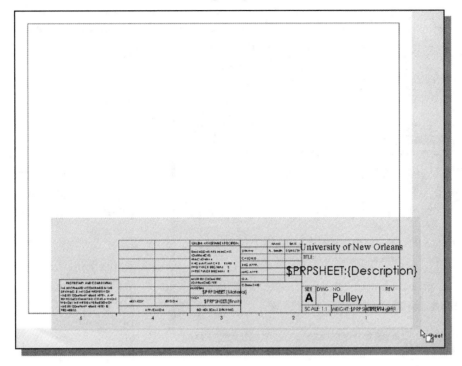

12. Press the **[Delete]** key to delete these entities.

13. On your own, create a title block using the **Line** and **Smart Dimension** commands in the *Sketch* toolbar and the **Note** command in the *Annotation* toolbar.  (If these toolbars are not open, open them by right-clicking on any open toolbar and selecting them.)

| UNIVERSITY OF NEW ORLEANS | | AP. BY: | | DATE: | ID CODE: |
|---|---|---|---|---|---|
| DR. BY: | CK. BY: | | SCALE: | SHEET: | DWG. No. |

.25

.50

2.00 — 2.00 — 1.92 — 1.10 — 1.60 — 1.68

➢ We will now add a Note with a Property Link.

14. Left-mouse-click on the **Note** icon on the *Annotation* toolbar.

15. Select a location inside the central empty box in the new title block as shown.

.25

.50

| | | | DAT |
|---|---|---|---|
| AP. BY: | | SCALE: | SHEE |

1.92 — 1.10

16. In the *Text Format* panel of the *Note PropertyManager*, select the **Link to Property** icon as shown.

➢ We will link to the **Description** entered as a user-defined property for the model part file *Pulley.SLDPRT*.

17. In the *Link to Property* window, select **Model in view specified in sheet properties**, as shown.

18. In the *Link to Property* window, select **Description** from the pull-down menu as shown.

19. Left-click **OK** in the *Link to Property* window to accept the selection.

20. Left-click **OK** in the *Note PropertyManager* to create the note.

➢ Notice the Property Link appears in the title block as **$PRPSHEET:{Description}**. The prefix **$PRPSHEET:** defines the source as the model (part file) appearing in the sheet. The Property Name is **Description**. This is a *Custom Property*.

```
|     | $PRPSHEET:{Description}  |
| AP. BY: |          | SCALE: |
```

21. On your own, delete the dimensions you created to set up the title block.

22. Move the cursor into the graphics area and **right-click** to open the pop-up option menu.

| Sheet (Sheet Format2) |
| Define Title Block |
| Edit Sheet |
| Add Sheet... |

23. Select **Edit Sheet** from the pop-up option menu to change to *Edit Sheet* mode.

24. Press the **[F]** key to fit the view to the graphics area.

## Creating a New Drawing Template

1. Select **Save as** from the *File* pull-down menu.

2. Click in the *Save as type:* entry box and select **Drawing Template** from the pull-down options.

3. The folder selection will automatically change to the default Templates folder. Use the browser to change the folder selection to the **Tutorial Templates** folder you created in Chapter 4.

4. Enter **A-Custom** for the *File name*.

5. Enter **ANSI A Inch Custom** for the *Description*.

6. Select **Save**.

7. If the *SolidWorks 2011* pop-up window appears, click **OK**.

8. Select the **Rebuild** icon on the *Menu Bar*.

## Creating Views

1. Click on the **Model View** icon in the *Drawing* toolbar.

2. The *Model View PropertyManager* appears with the *Pulley* part file selected as the part from which to create the base view. Click the **Next** arrow as shown to proceed with defining the base view.

3. In the *Model View PropertyManager*, select **Single View** for the *Number of Views* and the **Left View** for the *Orientation*, as shown.

4. Under the *Scale* options in the *Drawing View PropertyManager*, select **Use custom scale**.

5. Select **User Defined** from the pull-down options, as shown.

6. Enter **3:4** as the user defined scale.

7. Move the cursor inside the graphics area and place the **base view** toward the left side of the border as shown.

➢ When the base view is placed, *SolidWorks* automatically executes the **Projected View** command and the *Projected View PropertyManager* appears.

8. Press the **[Esc]** key to exit the Projected View command.

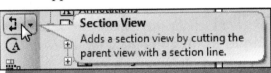 9. Select the **Rebuild** icon on the *Menu Bar*.

➢ Notice the Description we entered for the *Pulley* model part file – **4″ Pulley** – appears in the title block due to the Property Link.

**Section View**
Adds a section view by cutting the parent view with a section line.

10. Select the **Section View** icon in the *Drawing* toolbar.

11. Inside the graphics window, align the cursor to the center of the base view and create the vertical cutting plane line as shown.

5.93, 90°

**Display Style**
☐ Use parent style
Hidden Lines Removed
**Scale**

12. In the *Section View PropertyManager*, select the **Hidden Lines Removed** option for the *Display Style*.

13. Next, *SolidWorks* expects us to place the projected section. Select a location that is toward the right side of the base view as shown in the figure.

14. Select **OK** in the *PropertyManaager* to create the *Section View*.

> We will add an isometric view using the **Projected View** command.

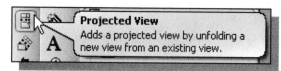

15. Select the **Projected View** icon from the *Drawing* toolbar.

16. **Left-click** to select the base view for the projection as shown.

17. In the *Projected View PropertyManager*, select the **Hidden Lines Removed** option for the *Display Style*.

18. Place the projected isometric view by moving the cursor to the left and above the base view as shown and clicking once with the **left-mouse-button**. (**NOTE:** When it is created, the projected isometric view is automatically aligned along a line at a 45° angle from the base view. We can relocate the isometric view after it is created.)

19. Press the **[Esc]** key to exit the Projected View command.

SECTION A-A
SCALE 3 : 4

| UNIVERSITY OF NEW ORLEANS | | | 4" Pulley | | DATE: | ID CODE: |
| DR. BY: | CK. BY: | AP. BY: | | SCALE: | SHEET: | DWG. No. |

➤ On your own, reposition the views so that they appear as shown.

## Retrieve Dimensions – Model Items Command

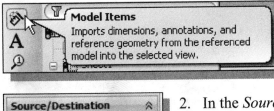

1. Left-mouse-click on the **Model Items** icon on the *Annotation* toolbar.

2. In the *Source/ Destination* options panel of the *Model Items PropertyManager*, select the **Entire model** option from the *Import from* pull-down menu and check **Import items into all views** as shown.

3. Under the *Dimensions* options panel, select the **Marked for drawing** icon and check **Eliminate duplicates** as shown.

4. Click the **OK** icon in the *Model Items PropertyManager*. Notice dimensions are automatically placed on the side and section drawing views.

5. On your own, adjust the drawing to appear as shown below. You will have to reposition some dimensions, hide some dimensions, and add some reference dimensions. You may also have to reposition the views.

## Save the Drawing File

1. Select **Save as** from the *File* pull-down menu.

2. Select **Drawing** (*.slddrw) as the file type.

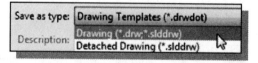

3. Use the browser to select the directory. Save the drawing file in the same directory as the part file.

4. Enter **Pulley** for the *File name* and **Pulley Detail** for the *Description*.

| File name: | Pulley |
| Save as type: | Drawing (*.drw;*.slddrw) |
| Description: | Pulley Detail |

5. Click **Save**.

6. If the *SolidWorks* window appears enter **Save All**.

## Associative Functionality – A Design Change

❖ *Solidworks' associative functionality* allows us to change the design at any level, and the system reflects the changes at all levels automatically. We will illustrate the associative functionality by changing the circular pattern from five holes to six holes.

1. Inside the *FeatureManager Design Tree* window, right-click on the **Drawing View** icon to bring up the option menu.

2. Select **Open pulley.sldprt** in the popup menu to switch to the associated solid model.

3. Inside the *FeatureManager Design Tree* window, right-click on the **CircularPattern1** feature to bring up the option menu.

4. Select **Edit Feature** in the popup menu to bring up the associated feature option.

5. In the *Circular Pattern PropertyManager*, change the number to **6** as shown.

6. Click on the **OK** button to accept the setting.

❖ The solid model is updated showing the 6 equally spaced holes as shown.

7. Switch back to the *Pulley* drawing by selecting it in the *Window* pull-down menu. (**NOTE:** The **\*** appearing next to the filename indicates that this file has been modified but not saved. When you save the file, this **\*** will no longer appear and notice the drawing is also updated.)

❖ Notice the drawing views are shaded, indicating that they have not been updated to include the changes to the model.

8. Select the **Rebuild** icon on the *Menu Bar*.

❖ Notice, in the *Pulley* drawing, the circular pattern is also updated automatically in all views.

## Adding Centerlines to the Pattern Feature

In your drawing, the inserted views may include *center marks*. If so, these were added with the **auto-insert** option. This lesson was done with no auto-insert options selected. If your drawing already has the center marks, you can delete them and proceed with Step 1, or select them and proceed to Step 6.

1. Click on the **Center Mark** button in the *Annotation* toolbar.

2. In the *Options* panel of the *Center Mark PropertyManager*, select the **Circular Center Mark** option, and **check** the **Circular lines**, **Radial lines**, and **Base center mark** option boxes.

➤ The **Centered Pattern** option allows us to add centerlines to a patterned feature.

3. Inside the graphics area, select the four circular edges of the base feature as shown.

4. Select **OK** in the *Center Mark PropertyManager* to create the center marks.

5. Notice the base circle center mark interferes with the cutting plane line. **Select** any of the newly created center marks or the associated centerlines to reopen the *PropertyManager*.

6. In the *Options* panel of the *Center Mark PropertyManager*, **uncheck** the **Base center mark** option box.

7. Select **OK** in the *PropertyManager* to accept the new setting.

8. On your own, extend the segments of the centerlines so that they appear as shown.

## Completing the Drawing

1. Right-click on the **30°** angular dimension and select **Hide** from the pop-up option menu.

2. Use the **Smart Dimension** command to create the 60° dimension as shown.

3. Select the **Ø2.50** dimension to open the *PropertyManager*.

4. Select the **Inside** option for the arrow placement under the **Leaders** tab in the *PropertyManager* as shown below.

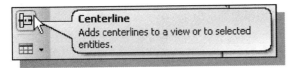

5. Click on the **Centerline** button in the *Annotation* toolbar.

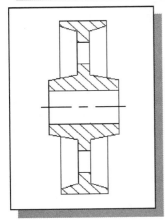

6. Inside the graphics window, click on the two edges of the *Section View* to create a centerline through the view as shown in the figure.

7. Repeat the above step and create the centerlines through the other two holes.

8. On your own, complete the title block and complete the drawing to appear as shown on the next page. Remember to switch to *Edit Sheet Format* mode to modify the title block.

9. Be sure to switch back to *Edit Sheet* mode.

10. Select the **Save** icon on the *Menu Bar*. This command will save the Pulley.SLDDRW file. This file includes the document properties, the sheet format, and the drawing views.

➢ Because the Pulley.SLDPRT model part file was not saved after the design change, the *Save Modified Documents* window will appear.

Save Modified Documents

The following models referenced in this document have been modified. They will be saved when the document is saved.

| | Filename | Read-only | In Use By |
|---|---|---|---|
| ☑ | Pulley.SLDDRW | | |
| | ☑ Pulley.SLDPRT | | |

☐ Don't ask me again when saving    Save All    Cancel    Help

11. Select **Save All** to save the Pulley.SLDDRW drawing file and the Pulley.SLDPRT model part file.

SECTION A-A
SCALE 3 : 4

Ø4.00
Ø3.75
Ø3.50
Ø1.50
Ø1.25
1.00
.25
Ø.75
Ø2.50
Ø.50
60.00°

| UNIVERSITY OF NEW ORLEANS | | DATE: 01/08/11 | ID CODE: ENME |
|---|---|---|---|
| DR.BY: Your Name | CK.BY: A. SMITH | | |
| | | 4" Pulley | |
| | AP.BY: B. JONES | SCALE: 3:4 | SHEET: 1 of 1 | DWG. No.EN2101 |

## Questions:

1. List the different symmetrical features created in the *Pulley* design.

2. What are the advantages of using a *drawing template*?

3. Describe the steps required in using the Mirror command.

4. Why is it important to identify symmetrical features in designs?

5. When and why should we use the Circular Pattern command?

6. What are the required elements in order to generate a sectional view?

7. How do we create a linear *diameter dimension* for a revolved feature?

8. What is the difference of *construction geometry* and *normal geometry*?

9. Identify and describe the following commands:

   (a)

   (b)

   (c)

   (d)

## Exercises: (All dimensions are in inches.)

1.

2.

4.

5.

**NOTES:**

# Chapter 11
# Advanced 3D Construction Tools

## Learning Objectives

- ♦ **Understand the Concepts Behind the Different 3D Construction Tools**
- ♦ **Setup Multiple Reference Planes**
- ♦ **Create Swept Features**
- ♦ **Create Lofted Features**
- ♦ **Use the Shell Command**
- ♦ **Create 3D Rounds & Fillets**

## Certified SolidWorks Associate Exam Objectives Coverage

## Introduction

*SolidWorks* provides an assortment of three-dimensional construction tools to make the creation of solid models easier and more efficient. As demonstrated in the previous lessons, creating **extruded** features and **revolved** features are the two most common methods used to create 3D models. In this next example, we will examine the procedures for using the **Sweep** commands, the **Loft** commands, and the **Shell** command, and also for creating **3D rounds** and **fillets** along the edges of a solid model. These types of features are common characteristics of molded parts.

The **Sweep** options (*Swept Boss/Base* and *Cut Sweep*) are defined as moving a cross-section through a path in space to form a three-dimensional object. To define a sweep in *SolidWorks*, we define two sections: the trajectory and the cross-section.

The **Loft** commands (*Lofted Boss/Base* and *Cut Loft*) allow us to blend multiple profiles with varying shapes on separate planes to create complex shapes. Profiles are usually on parallel planes, but non-perpendicular planes can also be used. We can use as many profiles as we wish but, to avoid twisting the loft shape, we should map points on each profile that align along a straight vector.

The **Shell** option is defined as hollowing out the inside of a solid, leaving a shell of specified wall thickness.

## A Thin-Walled Design: *Dryer Housing*

## Modeling Strategy

## Starting SolidWorks

1.  Select the **SolidWorks** option on the *Start* menu or select the **SolidWorks** icon on the desktop to start *SolidWorks*. The *SolidWorks* main window will appear on the screen.

2.  Select the **New** icon with a single click of the left-mouse-button on the *Menu Bar*. The *New SolidWorks Document* dialog box should appear in Advanced mode. If it appears in Novice mode, click once with the left-mouse-button on the **Advanced** icon.

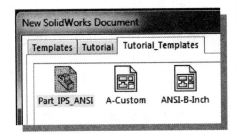

3.  Select the **Tutorial_Templates** tab. (**NOTE:** You added this tab in Chapter 4.)

4.  Select the **Part_IPS_ANSI** template as shown.

5.  Click on the **OK** button to open a new document using the Part_IPS_ANSI template.

## Creating the 2D Sketch for the Base feature

1.  Select the **Sketch** button on the *Sketch* toolbar to create a new sketch.

2.  In the *Edit Sketch PropertyManager*, the message *"Select a plane on which to create a sketch for the entity"* is displayed. Move the cursor over the edge of the Front Plane in the graphics area. When the Front Plane is highlighted, click once with the **left-mouse-button** to select the Front (XY) Plane as the sketch plane for the new sketch.

3.  Select the **Circle** command by clicking once with the left-mouse-button on the icon in the *Sketch* toolbar.

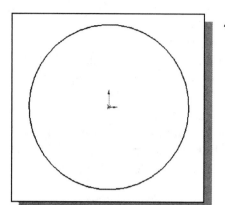

4. Create a **circle** of arbitrary size, with its center aligned to the *Origin* as shown.

5. Click on the **Line** icon in the *Sketch* toolbar.

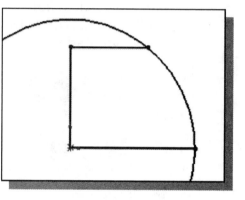

6. Create the three line segments as shown. The lines are either horizontal or vertical with the **lower left corner** aligned to the **projected *Origin***.

7. Select the **Trim** icon in the *Sketch* toolbar.

8. Select the **Power Trim** option in the *Trim PropertyManager*.

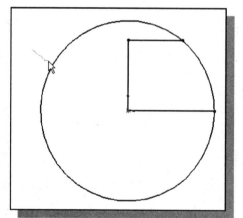

➢ To trim entities, with the **Power Trim** option, hold down and drag the cursor across the entity.

9. Left-click in the graphics area outside the portion of the circle to be trimmed.

10. Hold down and drag the mouse across the circle to execute the power trim.

11. Click **OK** in the *PropertyManager* to exit the **Trim** command.

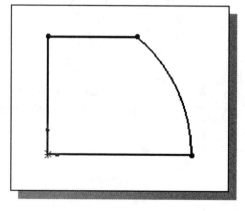

12. On your own, use the **Smart Dimension** command to create the dimensions as shown in the figure below. (**HINT:** Modify the radius dimension first.)

 13. Click on the **Sketch Fillet** icon in the *Sketch* toolbar.

14. In the *Fillet Parameters* panel of the *Sketch Fillet PropertyManager,* set the ***radius*** to **0.25**.

15. Select the top horizontal line and the arc to create a rounded corner as shown.

16. Select **OK** in the *PropertyManager* to exit the **Sketch Fillet** command.

 17. Select the **Sketch** icon on the *Sketch* toolbar to exit the **Sketch** option.

## Create a Revolved Boss Feature

1. Make sure the sketch – Sketch1 – is selected in the *FeatureManager Design Tree.*

2. In the *Features* toolbar, left-click on the **arrow** next to the **Extruded Boss/Base** icon and select the **Revolved Boss/Base** command from pop-up menu.

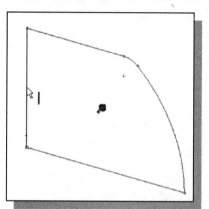

3. The *Revolve PropertyManager* appears. In the *Revolve Parameters* panel, the *Axis of Revolution* box is highlighted. *Solidworks* expects us to select the revolution axis for the revolved feature. Select the **vertical edge** of the sketch as the axis of rotation as shown.

4. The default revolution is **360°**. Click the **OK** icon in the *PropertyManager* to accept these parameters and create the revolved feature.

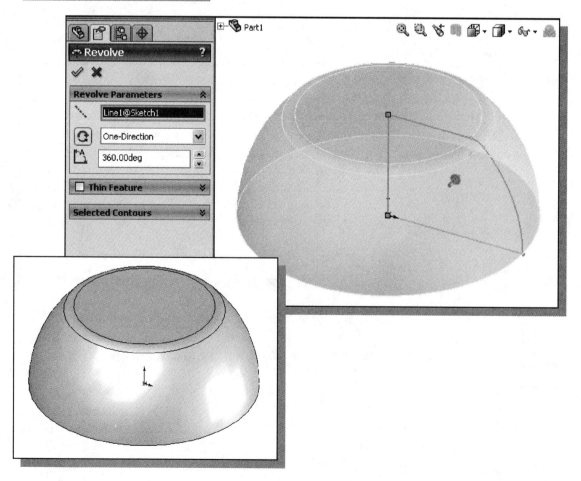

## Creating Offset Reference Planes

1. In the *Display Style* pull-down menu on the *Heads-up View* toolbar, select the **Wireframe** option to set the display mode to *Wireframe*.

2. In the *FeatureManager Design Tree*, click on the **Front Plane** icon to reveal the pop-up option menu.

3. Select **Show** from the pop-up option menu to turn *ON* the visibility of the Front Plane.

4. Press the **[Esc]** key to ensure that no objects are selected.

5. Select the **Reference Geometry** command from the *Features* toolbar, and select the **Plane** option from the pull-down menu.

6. Select the Front Plane as the *Reference Entity* by clicking on the **Front Plane** in the graphics area.

➢ Notice the **Front Plane** appears in the *First Reference* panel of the *Plane PropertyManager*, and the **Offset Distance** option is automatically selected.

7. Enter **2.5 in** as the offset distance.

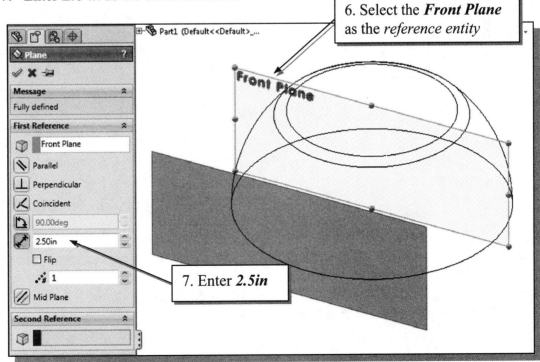

6. Select the *Front Plane* as the *reference entity*

7. Enter *2.5in*

8.  Select **OK** in the *PropertyManager* to accept the settings and create the new reference plane.

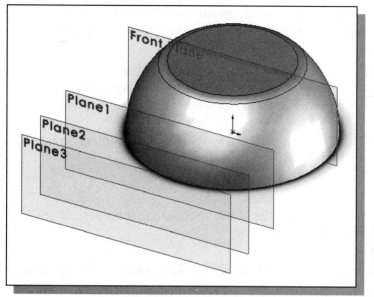

9.  On your own, repeat steps 4 - 8 and create two additional work planes that are **3.5** inches and **4.25** inches away from the Front (XY) Plane.

➢ **NOTE:** Remember to press [**Esc**] (Step 4) to unselect the previous plane before executing the Reference Geometry command, or it will be used as the *First Reference*.

## Creating 2D Sketches on the Reference Planes

1.  Click in the graphics area, away from the model to ensure no planes are selected.

2.  In the *Sketch* toolbar select the **Sketch** command by left-clicking once on the icon.

3.  Select the **Front Plane** as the sketch plane.

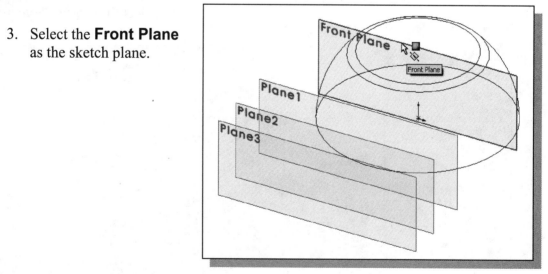

4.  Select the **Rectangle** command by clicking once with the left-mouse-button on the icon in the *Sketch* toolbar.

5. Click on the projected *Origin* to align the first corner of the rectangle. (**NOTE:** If the origin is not visible, use the *Hide/Show* menu on the *Heads-up View* toolbar to turn the visibility *ON*.)

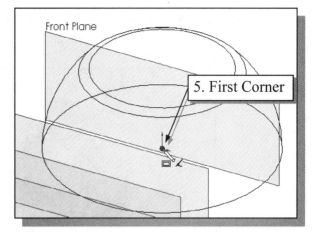

6. Create a rectangle of arbitrary size by selecting a location that is toward the right side of the graphics window as shown.

7. On your own, create and modify the two dimensions as shown in the figure.

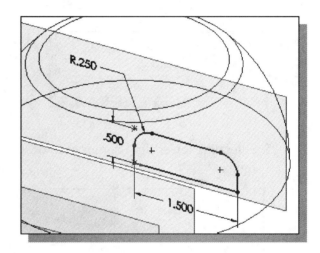

8. On your own, use the **Sketch Fillet** command to create two rounded corners (**radius 0.25**) as shown.

9. Select the **Sketch** icon on the *Sketch* toolbar to exit the Sketch option.

10. Click in the graphics area, away from the model to ensure no planes are selected.

11. In the *Menu Bar* select the **Sketch** command by left-clicking once on the icon.

12. Select **Plane1**, by left-clicking once on any edge of the first offset work plane in the graphics window as shown.

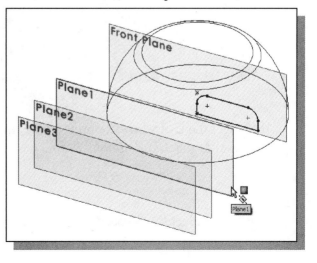

13. On your own, use the **Rectangle**, **Smart Dimension**, and **Sketch Fillet** commands to create the sketch as shown.  Do **not** align the sketch to the origin.

14. We will now align the lower right corners of the two sketches.  Select the **Add Relation** command from the *Display/ Delete Relations* pop-up menu on the *Sketch* toolbar.

15. Select the lower right corner each of the sketches we just created, as shown in the figure.

16. Select the **Coincident** option in the *Add Relations* panel of the *Add Relations PropertyManager*.

17. Select the **Sketch** icon on the *Sketch* toolbar to exit the Sketch option.

18. On your own, repeat the above steps and create two additional sketches on **Plane2** and **Plane3** as shown in the figure below. Align the **lower right corners** of the four sketches in the Z-direction through the use of coincident relations. (**NOTE:** Remember to ensure the previous plane is not selected prior to beginning a new sketch.)

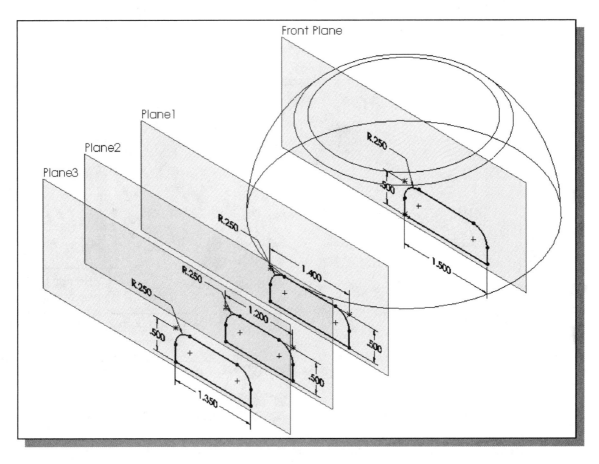

## Creating a Lofted Feature

➢ The **Loft** option allows us to blend multiple profiles with varying shapes on separate planes to create complex shapes. Profiles are usually on parallel planes, but any non-perpendicular planes can also be used. We can use as many profiles as we wish, but to avoid twisting the loft shape, we should map points on each profile that align along a straight vector.

1. Click in the graphics area, away from the model to ensure no planes are selected.

2. In the *Features* toolbar, left-click on the **arrow** next to the **Extruded Boss/Base** icon and select the **Lofted Boss/Base** command from pop-up menu. The *Loft PropertyManager* is displayed in the left panel.

3.  In the *Loft PropertyManager*, the **Profiles** option is activated. *SolidWorks* expects us to select a number of existing profiles, which will be used to create the lofted feature.

4.  Pick the four sketched sections, in the order that they were created, by clicking on the lower right corners of the sketches. Three arrows are displayed showing the blending direction of the sketches. Note that, to avoid twisting the loft shape, we are mapping the same corner points on the sketches to align along a straight vector.

5.  Click on the **OK** button to accept the settings and create the lofted feature.

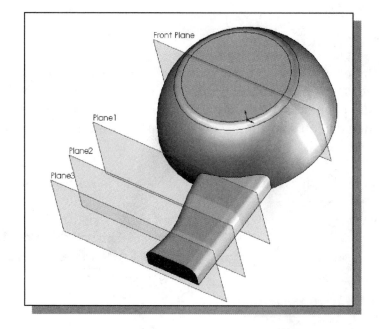

## Creating an Extruded Boss Feature

1. In the *FeatureManager Design Tree*, click on the **Right Plane** icon to reveal the pop-up option menu.

2. Select **Show** from the pop-up option menu to turn *ON* the visibility of the Right Plane.

3. Click in the graphics area, away from the model to ensure no planes are selected.

4. In the *Sketch* toolbar select the **Sketch** command by left-clicking once on the icon.

5. Select the **Right (YZ) Plane** as the sketch plane.

6. Click on the **Line** icon in the *Sketch* toolbar.

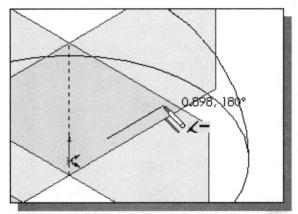

7. Create a line along the horizontal axis as shown.

8. Select the **Centerpoint Arc** command in the *Sketch* toolbar as shown.

9. On your own create an arc aligned to the **mid-point** and **endpoints** of the previously created line as shown in the figure.

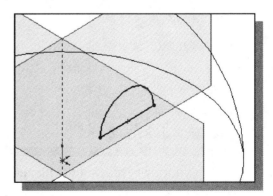

10. On your own, create and modify the dimensions as shown in the figure. The radius of the arc is **0.75 in** and the distance from the origin to the midpoint of the line is **1.125 in**.

11. Select the **Sketch** icon on the *Sketch* toolbar to exit the Sketch option.

## Completing the Extruded Boss Feature

1. In the *Features* toolbar, select the **Extruded Boss/Base** command.

2. In the *Extrude PropertyManager* window, enter **5.5** as the extrusion distance.

3. In the *Extrude* dialog box, click the **Reverse Direction** button to set the extrusion direction as shown, confirm the **Merge Result** option box is checked, and then click on the **OK** button to accept the settings to create the feature.

4. On your own, hide all the planes and change the display style to **Shaded with Edges**.

## Creating 3D Rounds and Fillets

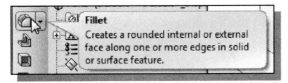

**Fillet**
Creates a rounded internal or external face along one or more edges in solid or surface feature.

1. In the *Features* toolbar, select the **Fillet** command by left-clicking once on the icon.

2. In the *Fillet PropertyManager*, set the ***Radius*** option to a radius of **0.15 in** as shown below.

3. Click on the **three edges** as shown.

4. Click on the **OK** button to accept the settings and create the 3D rounds and fillets.

## Creating a Shell Feature

• The **Shell** command can be used to hollow out the inside of a solid, leaving a shell of specified wall thickness.

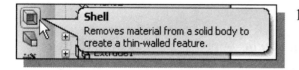

1.  In the *Features* toolbar, select the **Shell** command by left-clicking once on the icon.

2.  On your own, use the **arrow** keys display the back faces of the model as shown below. (Use the **arrow** keys to rotate the view vertically or horizontally. Hold down [Alt] key and use the **left-right arrow** keys to rotate clockwise or counterclockwise.)

3.  In the *Shell PropertyManager*, set the *Thickness* to **0.125 in**, select the **two faces** as shown, and click on the **OK** button to accept the settings and create the shell feature.

Pick these two surfaces

## Creating a Rectangular Extruded Cut Feature

- The *Dryer Housing* design requires the placement of identical holes on the top face of the solid. Instead of creating the holes one at a time, we can simplify the creation of these holes by using the **Linear Pattern** command to create duplicate features. Prior to using the Linear Pattern command, we will first create a *pattern leader*, which is a regular cut feature.

1. In the *View Orientation* pull-down menu on the *Heads-up View* toolbar, select the **Isometric** option.

2. In the *Sketch* toolbar select the **Sketch** command by left-clicking once on the icon.

3. Pick the top face of the base feature as shown.

4. In the *View Orientation* pull-down menu on the *Heads-up View* toolbar, select the **Normal To** option.

5.  On your own, create the **Rectangle** and add **Smart Dimensions** as shown in the figure below.

6.  Select the **Sketch** icon on the *Sketch* toolbar to exit the Sketch option.

7.  In the *View Orientation* pull-down menu on the *Heads-up View* toolbar, select the **Isometric** option.

8.  In the *Features* toolbar, select the **Extruded Cut** command by clicking once with the left-mouse-button on the icon.

9.  Create a Blind cut extrusion with a distance of **0.13 in**.

10. Select **OK** in the *PropertyManager* to create the extruded cut.

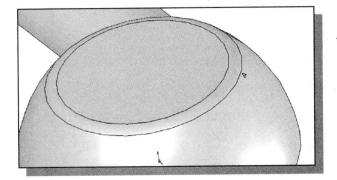

♦ Note that the pattern leader creates a fairly small cut on the solid model.

## Creating a Linear Pattern

In *SolidWorks*, existing features can be easily duplicated. The **Linear Pattern** command allows us to create rectangular arrays of features. The patterned features are parametrically linked to the original feature; any modifications to the original feature are also reflected on the arrayed features. An edge or an axis can be selected to define a pattern direction. We will create a reference axis and create a rectangular pattern using an edge to define one direction and the reference axis to define the other.

1. Select the **Reference Geometry** command from the *Features* toolbar, and select the **Axis** option from the pull-down menu..

2. In the *Selections* panel of the *Axis PropertyManager*, select the **Two Planes** option. (We will define the Z-axis as the intersection of the Top and Right Planes.)

3. Select the **Top Plane** and **Right Plane** in the *Design Tree* appearing in the graphics area.

4. Click **OK** in the *PropertyManager* to create the new reference axis.

5. Click in the graphics area, away from the model to ensure no axes are selected.

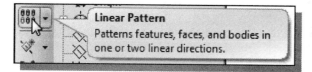

6. In the *Features* toolbar, select the **Linear Pattern** command by left-clicking once on the icon.

7. In the *Linear Pattern PropertyManager*, notice the *Pattern Direction* box in the *Direction 1* panel is activated. Click on an **edge** along the swept feature as shown in the figure.

➤ Notice **Edge<1>** appears in the *Pattern Direction* box.

8. In the *Direction 1* panel of the *PropertyManager*, click the **Reverse Direction** button (if necessary) to align the direction as shown in the figure.

9. In the *Direction 1* panel enter **0.6 in** for the *Spacing* and **5** for the *Number of Instances*.

10. In the *Linear Pattern PropertyManager*, notice the *Pattern Direction* box in the *Direction 2* panel is now activated. Select the **reference axis** we just created by expanding the *design tree* in the graphics area and clicking on the **Axis1** icon.

➢ Notice **Axis1** appears in the *Pattern Direction* box.

11. Check that the direction is aligned as shown in the figure below.  **If necessary**, click the **Reverse Direction** button in the *Direction 2* panel of the *PropertyManager* to align the direction.

12. In the *Direction 2* panel enter **0.25 in** for the *Spacing* and **10** for the *Number of Instances*.

13. In the *Linear Pattern PropertyManager*, notice the *Features to Pattern* box is now activated.  Select **Cut-Extrude1**, the cut feature created in the last section, in the *Design Tree* appearing in the graphics area.

➢ Notice **Cut-Extrude1** appears in the *Features to Pattern* panel in the *Linear Pattern PropertyManager*.

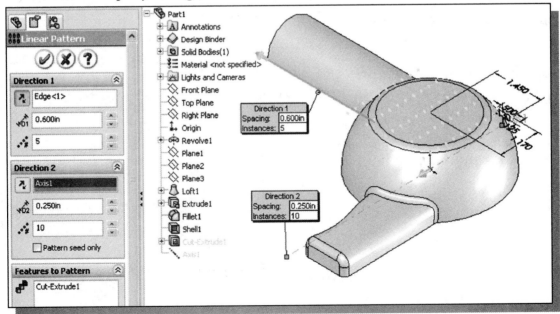

14. Click on the **OK** button to accept the settings and create the *linear pattern*.

# Creating a Swept Feature

❖ The **Sweep** operation is defined as moving a planar section through a planar (2D) or 3D path in space to form a three-dimensional solid object. The path can be an open curve or a closed loop, but must be on an intersecting plane with the profile. The **Extrusion** operation, which we have used in the previous lessons, is a specific type of sweep. The **Extrusion** operation is also known as a *linear sweep* operation, in which the sweep control path is always a line perpendicular to the two-dimensional section. Linear sweeps of unchanging shape result in what are generally called *prismatic solids* which means solids with a constant cross-section from end to end. In *SolidWorks*, we create a *swept feature* by defining a 2D sketch of a cross section and a planar path. To create the path, we can use a sketch, existing model edges, or curves. The sketched profile is then swept along the planar path. The **Sweep** operation is used for objects that have uniform shapes along a trajectory. We will define a **Cut Sweep** feature using existing model edges to define the path.

## Define the Sweep Section

1. In the *Menu Bar* select the **Sketch** command by left-clicking once on the icon.

2. Select the small circular surface of the model as shown.

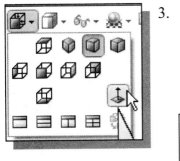

3. In the *View Orientation* pull-down menu on the *Heads-up View* toolbar, select the **Normal to** option

4. On your own, create the **Rectangle** and add **Smart Dimensions** as shown in the figure below.

5. On your own, use the **Add Relation** command to add a **Midpoint** relation between the bottom edge of the rectangle and the corner of the half-cylinder, as shown below.

❖ **NOTE:** The sketched profile to be swept has been located in a manner to overlap the edge which will be selected for the sweep path. In theory this is not necessary. However, since our sweep path includes small radius curves (the fillets), rounding of calculated values sometimes leads to a thin shell being left on the curves of the swept path. Our sketch will cut a 0.0625 x 0.125 inch rectangular extrusion along the path. The 0.0625 inch overlap will ensure no shell is left.

6. The sketch should be Fully Defined as indicated in the *Status Bar* area. Select the **Sketch** icon on the *Sketch* toolbar to exit the Sketch option.

### Create the Swept Feature

1.  Press the **[Esc]** key to ensure that no objects are selected.

2.  In the *Features* toolbar, left-click on the **arrow** next to the **Extruded Cut** icon and select the **Swept Cut** command from pop-up menu. This will execute the **Cut-Sweep** command.

3.  Select the new sketch from the *design tree* as the profile for the swept feature.

4.  Highlight the *Path* selection box in the *Cut-Sweep PropertyManager* by clicking once with the **left-mouse-button**.

5.  Move the cursor over the outer edge of the half-cylinder as shown and click once with the **right-mouse-button** to open the pop-up option menu. (NOTE: Do not select the edge – i.e., do not click the left mouse button.)

6. Select the **Selection-Manager** option from the pop-up menu.

➤ The *SelectionManager* toolbar appears in the graphics area. The *SolidWorks* **SelectionManager** enhances the selection of edges or guide curves for the creation of lofted or swept features. On your own, use the *SolidWorks* Help option to view a description of the *SelectionManager* tools. We will use the **Select Group** tool.

7. Select the **Select Group** icon on the *SelectionManger* as shown.

➤ Notice a preview of the cut-sweep path appears along the selected edge. A *Tangent* callout appears, indicating the next edges in the potential group are tangent.

8. Move the cursor over the *Tangent* callout and click once with the **left-mouse-button**. Notice the chain extends to select all tangent edges and the *Tangent* callout changes color to indicate it is selected.

Tangent callout

9. Select the **OK** icon on the *SelectionManager*.

10. The **Open Group** appears in the *Path* selection window in the *Cut-Sweep PropertyManager*. Click **OK** in the *PropertyManager* to accept the settings and create the swept feature.

11. On your own, save the part with the filename **Dryer_Housing**.

## Questions:

1. Keeping the *Design Tree* in mind, what is the difference between *cut with a pattern* and *cut each one individually*?

2. What is the difference between Sweep and Extrude?

3. What are the advantages and disadvantages of creating fillets using the 3D Fillets command and creating fillets in the 2D profiles?

4. Describe the steps used to create the *Shell* feature in the lesson.

5. How do we modify the *Rectangular Pattern* parameters after the model is built?

6. Describe the elements required in creating a *Swept* feature.

7. Create sketches showing the steps you plan to use to create the model shown on the next page:

# Exercises:

1. Dimensions are in inches.

2.  Dimensions are in inches.

3.  Dimensions are in inches.

**NOTES:**

# Chapter 12
# Assembly Modeling – Putting It All Together

## Learning Objectives

- ♦ **Understand the Assembly Modeling Methodology**
- ♦ **Understand and Control Degrees of Freedom for Assembly Components**
- ♦ **Understand and Utilize SolidWorks Assembly Mates**
- ♦ **Place parts using SolidWorks SmartMates**
- ♦ **Create Exploded Assemblies**
- ♦ **Create Assembly Drawings**
- ♦ **Create and Edit a Bill of Materials**

## Certified SolidWorks Associate Exam Objectives Coverage

**Certified Associate Reference Guide**

### Fillets and Chamfers

Objectives: Creating Fillets and Chamfer Features.

### Materials

Objectives: Applying Material Selection to Parts.

### Inserting Components

Objectives: Inserting Components into an Assembly.

### Standard Mates – Coincident, Parallel, Perpendicular, Tangent, Concentric, Distance, Angle

Objectives: Applying Standard Mates to Constrain Assemblies.

### Drawing Sheets and Views

Objectives: Creating and Setting Properties for Drawing Sheets; Inserting and Editing Standard Views.

### Annotations

Objectives: Creating Annotations.

# Introduction

In the previous lessons, we have gone over the fundamentals of creating basic parts and drawings. In this lesson, we will examine the assembly modeling functionality of *SolidWorks*. We will start with a demonstration on how to create and modify assembly models. The main task in creating an assembly is establishing the assembly relationships between parts. It is a good practice to assemble parts based on the way they would be assembled in the actual manufacturing process. We should also consider breaking down the assembly into smaller subassemblies, which helps the management of parts. In *SolidWorks*, a subassembly is treated the same way as a single part during assembling. Many parallels exist between assembly modeling and part modeling in parametric modeling software such as *SolidWorks*.

*SolidWorks* provides full associative functionality in all design modules, including assemblies. When we change a part model, *SolidWorks* will automatically reflect the changes in all assemblies that use the part. We can also modify a part in an assembly. Bi-directional full associative functionality is the main feature of parametric solid modeling software that allows us to increase productivity by reducing design cycle time.

# Assembly Modeling Methodology

The *SolidWorks* assembly modeler provides tools and functions that allow us to create 3D parametric assembly models. An assembly model is a 3D model with any combination of multiple part models. *SolidWorks* Mate Relations can be used to control relationships between parts in an assembly model.

*SolidWorks* can work with any of the assembly modeling methodologies:

### The Bottom Up approach
    The first step in the *bottom up* assembly modeling approach is to create the individual parts. The parts are then pulled together into an assembly. This approach is typically used for smaller projects with very few team members.

### The Top Down approach
    The first step in the *top down* assembly modeling approach is to create the assembly model of the project. Initially, individual parts are represented by names or symbolically. The details of the individual parts are added as the project gets further along. This approach is typically used for larger projects or during the conceptual design stage. Members of the project team can then concentrate on the particular section of the project to which he/she is assigned.

### The Middle Out approach
    The *middle out* assembly modeling approach is a mixture of the bottom-up and top-down methods. This type of assembly model is usually constructed with most of the parts already created and additional parts are designed and created using the assembly for construction information. Some requirements are known and some

standard components are used, but new designs must also be produced to meet specific objectives. This combined strategy is a very flexible approach for creating assembly models.

The different assembly modeling approaches described above can be used as guidelines to manage design projects. Keep in mind that we can start modeling our assembly using one approach and then switch to a different approach without any problems.

## The Shaft Support Assembly

In this lesson, the *bottom up* assembly modeling approach is illustrated through the creation of the shaft support assembly shown in the figure. All of the parts (components) required to form the assembly are created first. *SolidWorks'* assembly modeling tools allow us to create complex assemblies by using components that are created in part files or are created in assembly files. A component can be a subassembly or a single part, where features and parts can be modified at any time.

## Parts

- Four parts are required for the assembly: (1) **Collar**, (2) **Bearing**, (3) **Base-Plate** and (4) **Cap-Screw**. Create the four parts as shown below, then save the models as separate part files: *Collar*, *Bearing*, *Base-Plate*, and *Cap-Screw*. (Close all part files or exit *SolidWorks* after you have created the parts.)

## Creating the Collar using the Chamfer Command

(1) **Collar**

Chamfers: 45°X1/16

1. On your own, start a new part file using your **Part_IPS_ANSI** template and create the basic *Collar* without the chamfers, as shown below.

2. In the *Features* toolbar, left-click on the **arrow** next to the **Fillet** icon and select the **Chamfer** command from pop-up menu.

3. In the *Chamfer Parameters* panel of the *Chamfer PropertyManager,* select the **Angle distance** option.

4. Set the *Distance* to **1/16 in** (or 0.0625in).

5. Set the *Angle* to **45°**.

6. Select the two circular edges shown in the figures below.

7. Select **OK** in the *Chamfer PropertyManager* to create the chamfers.

8. Save the part with the filename ***Collar***.

## Creating the Bearing and Base-Plate

➤ On your own, create and save the *Bearing* and *Base-Plate* part files based on the drawings below. Align the base of each part with the **Top Plane**.

(2) *Bearing* (Construct the part with the datum origin aligned to the bottom center.)

**NOTE:** Fillets and Rounds R 1/8″

(3) *Base-Plate* (Construct the part with the datum origin aligned to the bottom center.)

**NOTE:** You can ignore the threads and simply create 3/8″ diameter holes.

## Creating the Cap-Screw

➢ On your own, create and save the *Cap-Screw* part file based on the drawings below.
**NOTE:** Threads are not necessary.

### (4) *Cap-Screw*

- *SolidWorks* provides two options for creating threads: **CosmeticThread** and **Helix**.
The **Cosmetic Thread** command does not create true 3D threads; a pre-defined
thread image is applied on the selected surface, as shown in the figure. The **Helix**
command can be used to create true threads, which contain complex three-
dimensional curves and surfaces. You are encouraged to experiment with the **Helix**
command and/or the **Cosmetic Thread** command to create threads.
- To represent threads on a part using the **Cosmetic Thread** option, first make sure
the shading option for Cosmetic Thread is turned on. Click Tools, Options. On the
Document Properties tab, select Detailing. Make sure the Shaded cosmetic
threads option is checked.  Also (1) check that the All Annotations button is
selected under the *View* pulldown menu and (2) right click on *Annotations* in the
*FeatureManager Design Tree* and make sure Display Annotations is selected.  To
apply a cosmetic thread, click Insert, then Annotations, then Cosmetic Thread.
Set the properties in the *PropertyManager* and select OK.

- **HINT:** First create the
profile shown here.   Then
create a revolved feature.
Use the *Selected Contours*
panel to select the upper
half of the sketch to revolve.

## Starting *SolidWorks*

1. Select the **SolidWorks** option on the *Start* menu or select the **SolidWorks** icon on the desktop to start *SolidWorks*. The *SolidWorks* main window will appear on the screen.

2. Select the **New** icon with a single click of the left-mouse-button on the *Menu Bar*. The *New SolidWorks Document* dialog box appears.

3. Select the **Templates** tab and select the **Assembly** icon as shown.

4. Click **OK** to open the new **Assembly** file.

❖ *SolidWorks* opens an assembly file, and automatically opens the *Begin Assembly PropertyManager*. The message "*Select a part or assembly to insert ...*" appears in the *PropertyManager*. *SolidWorks* expects you to insert the first component. We will first set the document properties to match those of the previously created parts.

5. Cancel the **Begin Assembly** command by clicking once with the left-mouse-button on the **Cancel** icon in the *PropertyManager* as shown.

## Document Properties

1. Select the **Options** icon from the *Menu Bar* to open the *Options* dialog box.

2. Select the **Document Properties** tab.

3. Select **ANSI** in the pull-down selection window under the *Overall drafting standard* panel as shown.

| Document Properties - Drafting Standard | |
|---|---|
| System Options    Document Properties | |
| Drafting Standard | Overall drafting standard |
|   ⊞ Annotations | ANSI ▼ |
|   ⊞ Dimensions | |
|   ⋯ Virtual Sharps | |
|   ⊞ Tables | |
| Detailing | |

4. Click **Units**, select the **IPS (inch, pound, second)** unit system, and select **.123** in the *Decimals* spin box for the *Length units* as shown.

Document Properties - Units

| System Options | Document Properties |

Drafting Standard
  Annotations
  Dimensions
  Virtual Sharps
  Tables
Detailing
Grid/Snap
Units
Colors
Image Quality
Plane Display

Unit system
- MKS (meter, kilogram, second)
- CGS (centimeter, gram, second)
- MMGS (millimeter, gram, second)
- IPS (inch, pound, second)
- Custom

| Type | Unit | Decimals | Fractions | More |
|------|------|----------|-----------|------|
| **Basic Units** | | | | |
| Length | inches | .123 | | ... |
| Dual Dimension Length | inches | .12 | | ... |
| Angle | degrees | .1234 | | |

5. Click **OK** in the *Document Properties* window to accept the settings.

## Inserting the First Component

- The first component inserted in an assembly should be a fundamental part or subassembly. The first component in an assembly file sets the orientation of all subsequent parts and subassemblies. The origin of the first component is aligned to the origin of the assembly coordinates and the part is grounded (all degrees of freedom are removed). The rest of the assembly is built on the first component, the **base component**. In most cases, this *base component* should be one that is **not likely to be removed** and **preferably a non-moving part** in the design. Note that there is no distinction in an assembly between components; the first component we place is usually considered as the *base component* because it is usually a fundamental component to which others are constrained. We can change the base component if desired. For our project, we will use the **Base-Plate** as the base component in the assembly.

1. Right-click on the *Menu Bar* and open the *Assembly* toolbar (if necessary).

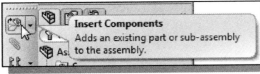

**Insert Components**
Adds an existing part or sub-assembly to the assembly.

2. In the *Assembly* toolbar, select the **Insert Component** command by left-mouse-clicking the icon.

**Part/Assembly to Insert**
Open documents:

Browse...

3. Click on the **Browse** button in the *Part/Assembly to Insert* panel in the *PropertyManager*.

4. Use the browser to locate and select the **Base-Plate** part file: **Base-Plate.sldprt**.

5.  Click on the **Open** button to retrieve the model.

6.  Click **OK** in the *PropertyManager* to place the *Base-Plate* at the origin.

## Inserting the Second Component

➢   We will retrieve the *Bearing* part as the second component of the assembly model.

1.  In the *Assembly* toolbar, select the **Insert Component** command by left-mouse-clicking the icon.

2.  Select the ***Bearing*** design (part file: **Bearing.sldprt**) in the browser. And click on the **Open** button to retrieve the model.

3.  Place the *Bearing* toward the upper right corner of the graphics window, as shown in the figure.  Click once with the **left-mouse-button** to place the component.  (**NOTE:** Your *Bearing* may initially be oriented differently.  We will apply assembly mates to orient the *Bearing*. Proceed with the instructions and the alignment of your *Bearing* will match those in the illustrations after applying the second assembly mate.)

- Inside the *FeatureManager Design Tree*, the retrieved parts are listed in their corresponding order. The **(f)** in front of the *Base-Plate* filename signifies the part is fixed and all *six degrees of freedom* are restricted. The number behind the filename is used to identify the number of copies of the same component in the assembly model.

## Degrees of Freedom

- Each component in an assembly has six **degrees of freedom (DOF)**, or ways in which rigid 3D bodies can move: movement along the X, Y, and Z axes (translational freedom), plus rotation around the X, Y, and Z axes (rotational freedom). *Translational DOFs* allow the part to move in the direction of the specified vector. *Rotational DOFs* allow the part to turn about the specified axis.

➢ It is usually a good idea to fully constrain components so that their behavior is predictable as changes are made to the assembly. Leaving some degrees of freedom open can sometimes help retain design flexibility. As a general rule, we should use only enough assembly mate relations to ensure predictable assembly behavior and avoid unnecessary complexity.

## Assembly Mates

- We are now ready to assemble the components together. We will start by placing assembly constraints on the **Bearing** and the **Base-Plate** using *SolidWorks* assembly **Mates**. Mates create geometric relationships between assembly components. Mates define the allowable directions of linear or rotational motion of the components, limiting the degrees of freedom. A component can be moved within its degrees of freedom, visualizing the assembly's behavior.

To assemble components into an assembly, we need to establish the assembly relationships between components. It is a good practice to assemble components the way they would be assembled in the actual manufacturing process. **Assembly Mates** create a parent/child relationship that allows us to capture the design intent of the assembly. Because the component that we are placing actually becomes a child to the already assembled components, we must use caution when choosing mate types and references to make sure they reflect the intent.

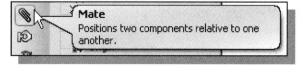

1. In the *Assembly* toolbar, select the **Mate** command by left-mouse-clicking once on the icon.

- The *Mate PropertyManager* appears on the screen.

- Assembly models are created by applying proper *assembly relations* to the individual components. The **Mate** relations are used to restrict the movement between parts. **Mate** relations eliminate rigid body degrees of freedom (**DOF**). A 3D part has *six degrees of freedom* since the part can rotate and translate relative to the three coordinate axes. Each time we add a **Mate** relation between two parts, one or more DOF is eliminated. The movement of a fully constrained part is restricted in all directions.

- Seven basic types of assembly mates, called **Standard Mates**, are available in *SolidWorks*: **Coincident, Parallel, Perpendicular, Tangent, Concentric, Distance, and Angle**. Each type of mate removes different combinations of rigid body degrees of freedom. Note that it is possible to apply different constraints and achieve the same results.

- Advanced **Mates** including **Gear** and **Cam Mates** are also available.

The **Standard Mates** are described below:

➢ **Coincident** – positions selected faces, edges, and planes (in combination with each other or combined with a single vertex) so they share the same infinite line. Positions two vertices so they touch

➢ **Parallel** – places the selected items so they lie in the same direction and remain a constant distance apart from each other

➢ **Perpendicular** – places the selected items at a 90 degree angle to each other

➢ **Tangent** – places the selected items in a tangent mate (at least one selection must be a cylindrical, conical, or spherical face)

➢ **Concentric** – places the selections so that they share the same center point

➢ **Distance** – places the selected items with the specified distance between them

➢ **Angle** – places the selected items at the specified angle to each other

## Apply the First Assembly Mate

1. Note that the *Mate Selections* panel in the *Mate PropertyManager* is highlighted. Select the **top horizontal surface** of the *Base-Plate* part as the first part for the **Mate** command.

2. On your own, rotate the displayed model to view the bottom of the *Bearing* part, as shown in the figure below. (**HINT:** Use the up arrow [↑] on the keyboard.)

3. Click on the bottom face of the *Bearing* part as the second part selection to apply the relation. The *Bearing* moves to automatically apply the default **Coincident** mate.

> Notice the two faces selected appear in the *Mate Selections* panel of the *PropertyManager*.

> Notice the **Tangent** and **Concentric** options are not available. All the mate types are always shown in the *PropertyManager*, but only the mates that are applicable to the current selections are available.

> Notice the **Coincident** mate is selected. This is the relation we want to apply.

> For the **Coincident** mate there are two options for *Mate alignment* – **Aligned** and **Anti-Aligned**. These are displayed at the bottom of the *Standard Mates* panel.

4. On your own, select the **Aligned** option at the bottom of the *Standard Mates* panel and observe the effect on the assembly.

5. Select the **Anti-Aligned** option.

6. Select the **Isometric View** to adjust the display of the assembly model.

7. Click the **OK** button in the *PropertyManager* to accept the settings and create the **Anti-Aligned Coincident** mate.

## Apply a Second Mate

❖ The Mate command can also be used to align axes of cylindrical features.

1. On your own, turn *ON* the visibility of the **Temporary Axes**. (**HINT:** Use the *Hide/Show* pull-down menu on the *Heads-up View* toolbar.)

2. Note that the *Mate Selections* panel in the *Mate PropertyManager* is highlighted. Select the **axis** of the counter bore hole of the *Bearing* part.

3.  Select the **axis** of the small hole on the *Base-Plate* part, as shown. The *Bearing* moves to automatically apply the default Coincident mate.

4.  Click **OK** in the *PropertyManager* to create the Coincident Mate.

5.  In the *PropertyManager*, click on the **Close** button (the red **X** icon), or press the [Esc] key, to exit the Mate command.

❖  The *Bearing* part appears to be placed in the correct position. But the DOF for the *Bearing* are not fully restricted; the *Bearing* part can still rotate about the displayed vertical axis.

## Constrained Move

❖  To see how well a component is constrained, we can perform a constrained move. A constrained move is done by dragging the component in the graphics window with the left-mouse-button. A constrained move will honor previously applied assembly mates. That is, the selected component and parts mated to the component move together in their constrained positions. A fixed component remains fixed during the move.

1.  Inside the graphics window, move the cursor on top of the top surface of the *Bearing* part as shown in the figure.

2.  Press and hold down the left-mouse-button and drag the *Bearing* part downward.

❖  The *Bearing* part can freely rotate about the mated axis.

3.  On your own, use the rotation commands to view the alignment of the *Bearing* part.

4.  Rotate the *Bearing* part and adjust the display as shown in the figure.

## Apply a Third Mate

•  Besides selecting the surfaces of solid models to apply constraints, we can also select the established planes to apply the assembly mates. This is an additional advantage of using the *BORN technique* in creating part models. For the *Bearing* part, we will apply a Mate to two of the planes and eliminate the last rotational DOF.

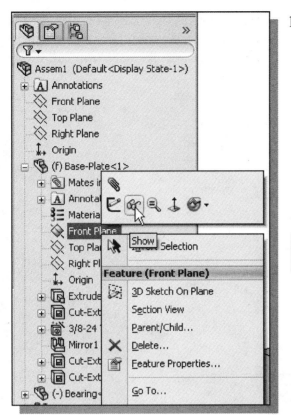

1. On your own, inside the *FeatureManager Design Tree* use the **Show** option to toggle *ON* the visibility for the planes that can be used for alignment of the *Base-Plate* and the *Bearing* parts. (**HINT:** Make sure the visibility of *Planes* is toggled *ON* in the *Hide/Show* pull-down menu.)

2. In the *Assembly* toolbar, select the **Mate** command by left-mouse-clicking once on the icon.

3. Select the *plane* of the *Base-Plate* part as the first part for the **Mate** command.

4. Select the *plane* of the *Bearing* part as the second part for the **Mate** command.

❖ The Coincident mate is executed by default and makes two planes coplanar with the **Aligned** option automatically selected. (**NOTE:** If you did not create the base plate with the front plane aligned with the middle of the plate, you will use the Parallel mate.)

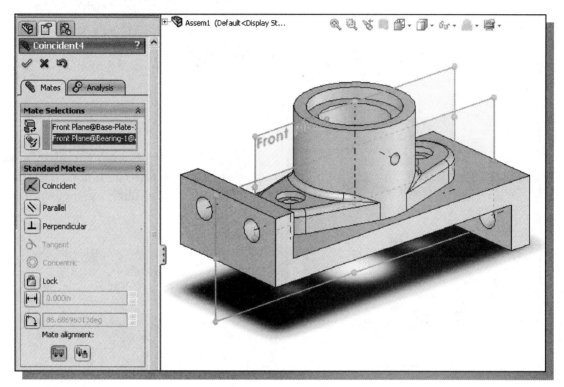

5. On your own, select the **Anti-aligned** option at the bottom of the *Standard Mates* panel and observe the effect on the assembly.

6. Select the **Aligned** option.

7. Click the **OK** button in the *PropertyManager* to accept the settings and create the **Aligned Coincident** mate.

8. In the *PropertyManager*, click on the **Close** button (or press the [**Esc**] key) to exit the Mate command.

❖ Note the assembly is fully defined.

## Inserting the Third Component

➢ We will retrieve the *Collar* part as the third component of the assembly model.

1. In the *Assembly* toolbar, select the **Insert Component** command by left-mouse-clicking the icon.

2. Select the *Collar* design (part file: **Collar.sldprt**) in the browser and click on the **Open** button to retrieve the model.

3. Insert the *Collar* part toward the lower left corner of the graphics window, as shown in the figure.

## Applying Concentric and Coincident Mates

1. In the *Assembly* toolbar, select the **Mate** command by left-mouse-clicking once on the icon.

2. Select the external cylindrical surface of the *Collar* part as shown in the figure as the first part for the Mate command. (**HINT:** Use the **arrow** keys on the keyboard to rotate the view, if necessary.)

3. Select the internal cylindrical surface of the *Bearing* part as shown in the figure as the second part for the Mate command.

4.  Notice in the *Mate PropertyManager* that the Concentric and Anti-Aligned options are automatically selected. On your own, select the correct alignment (Aligned or Anti-Aligned) for your assembly. Click the **OK** button in the *PropertyManager* to accept the settings and create the **Concentric** mate.

5.  On your own, move the ***Collar*** part to a position like that in the figure. Notice that the move is constrained to maintain the concentric relationship.

6.  Select the top circular surface of the *Bearing* part as shown in the figure as the first part for a new **Mate** command.

7.  Select the circular surface of the *Collar* part as shown in the figure as the second part for a new **Mate** command.

8.  Notice in the *Mate PropertyManager* that the **Coincident** and **Anti-Aligned** options are automatically selected. Click the **OK** button in the *PropertyManager* to accept the settings and create the **Anti-Aligned Coincident** mate.

9.  In the *PropertyManager*, click on the **Close** button (or press the [Esc] key) to exit the **Mate** command.

10. On your own, change the view to **Isometric**.

11. Note that the *Collar* part is not fully constrained. One rotational degree of freedom remains open; the *Collar* part can still freely rotate about the vertical axis. Click on the *Collar* and drag with the **left-mouse-button** to observe this constrained motion.

## Assemble the Cap-Screws using SmartMates

❖ We will place two *Cap-Screw* parts to complete the assembly model. We will use *SolidWorks* **SmartMates** to apply the geometric relations. The SmartMates function allows us to create commonly-used mates without using the *Mate PropertyManager*. Application of a SmartMate involves dragging one part to a mating position with another. In most cases, one mate is created. The type of SmartMate created depends on the geometry used to drag the component, and the type of geometry onto which you drop the component.

❖ The SmartMates functionality creates multiple mates under certain conditions. If the application finds circular edges to mate, a **Peg-In-Hole** SmartMate will be applied. Two mates are applied: a Concentric mate between cylindrical or conical faces, and a Coincident mate between the planar faces that are adjacent to the conical faces. This is the type of SmartMate we will apply when inserting the *Cap-Screw* parts.

- **Applying a SmartMate when two components are already in the assembly**

1. On your own, insert a **Cap-Screw** part into the assembly as shown.

2. Select the circular edge of the *Cap-Screw* head as shown. Press and hold down the left-mouse-button.

Revolve1 of Cap-Screw<1>

3. Press down and hold the **[Alt]** key. While holding the **[Alt]** key, drag the circular edge of the *Cap-Screw* onto the circular face of the counter sink in the *Bearing* part as shown. Notice the **Peg-In-Hole** mate icon appears. Release the left-mouse-button and the **[Alt]** key to apply the SmartMate.

• **Applying a SmartMate to a new component while adding it to the assembly**

4. Click once with the **left-mouse-button** on the **Open** icon on the *Menu Bar*.

5. Select the ***Cap-Screw*** design (part file: **Cap-Screw.sldprt**) in the browser. And click on the **Open** button to retrieve the model.

6. Select the **Tile Horizontally** option from the *Window* pull-down menu.

7.  In the *Cap-Screw* window, rotate and zoom so that the circular edge of the screw head is visible as shown in the figure.

8.  In the *Assembly* window, **Pan**, **Rotate**, and **Zoom** so that the counter bore of the *Bearing* appears as shown in the figure.

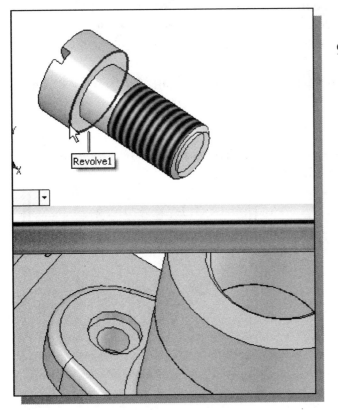

9.  Using the left-mouse-button, click and drag the circular edge of the head of the *Cap-Screw* part into the assembly window. Release the mouse-button when the cursor is over the circular surface of the counter bore, applying the **Peg-In-Hole SmartMate**.

10. Close the *Cap-Screw* window.

11. Maximize the *Assem1* window.

12. On your own, change the view to **Isometric**.

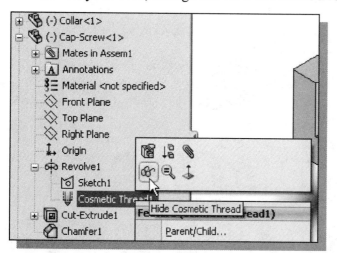

13. Notice isocircles representing the bottom the Cosmetic Threads on the screws are visible. In the *FeatureManager Design Tree*, **right-click** on the **Cosmetic Thread1** icon under **Cap-Screw(1)** and select **Hide**.

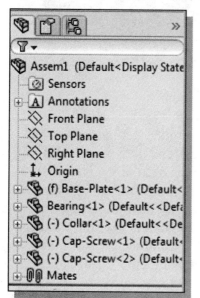

- Inside the *FeatureManager Design Tree*, the retrieved parts are listed in the order they are placed. The number behind the part name is used to identify the number of copies of the same part in the assembly model. Move the cursor to the last part name and notice the corresponding part is highlighted in the graphics window.

- The **(f)** symbol indicates the part is fixed. The **(-)** symbol indicates the part has at least one degree of freedom. The *Collar* and the two *Cap Screws* each have one rotational degree of freedom. Click and drag on each of them to observe the rotational freedom.

## Exploded View of the Assembly

- Exploded assemblies are often used in design presentations, catalogs, sales literature, and in the shop to show all of the parts of an assembly and how they fit together. In *SolidWorks*, exploded views are created by selecting and dragging parts in the graphics area.

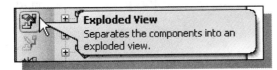

1. In the *Assembly* toolbar, select the **Exploded View** command by left-mouse-clicking once on the icon.

2. The message *"Select component(s) ..."* appears in the *Explode PropertyManager*. Select the *Collar* part by clicking on it with the left-mouse-button.

3. Notice a manipulator appears in the graphics area. Move the pointer over the manipulator handle that points in the upward direction and drag the manipulator handle to the location shown in the figure.

- ❖ The exploded view component movements can be made along the major axis directions by dragging the manipulator handle that points in the corresponding direction. Dragging the yellow sphere in the center of the manipulator will move the manipulator to a different location. The manipulator can be dropped on an edge or face and an axis of the manipulator will align with the edge or face.

4.  On your own, repeat the above steps and create an exploded assembly by repositioning the components as shown in the figure.

5.  Click **OK** in the *PropertyManager* to close the **Exploded View** command.

6.  Select the **ConfigurationManager** tab.

7.  In the *ConfigurationManager*, expand the tree to reveal the **Exploded View** icon labeled ExpView1. **Double-click** on the **ExpView1** icon to collapse the exploded view.

❖ Note that the components are reset back to their assembled positions, based on the applied assembly mates.

8.  **Double-click** on the **ExpView1** icon again to return to the exploded view.

9.  On your own, return to the collapsed view.

10. Select the **FeatureManager Design Tree** tab to return to the *Design Tree*.

## Save the Assembly Model

1. Select the **Save As** option from the *File* pull-down menu.

2. In the *Save As* pop-up window, enter **Support_Assembly.SLDASM** for the *File name* and **Shaft-Support Assembly** for the *Description*.

3. Click **Save** to save the file.

4. If the *SolidWorks* window appears, click **Save All**.

## Editing the Components

- The associative functionality of *SolidWorks* allows us to change the design at any level, and the system reflects the changes at all levels automatically.

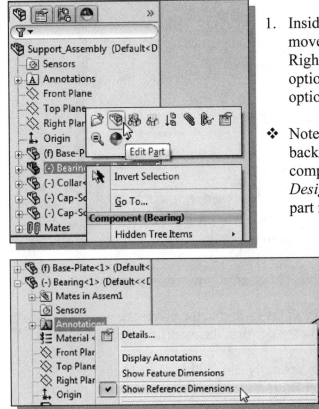

1. Inside the *FeatureManager Design Tree*, move the cursor on top of the **Bearing** part. Right-mouse-click once to bring up the option menu and select **Edit Part** in the option list.

❖ Note that we are automatically switched back to *Part Editing* mode. The Bearing component portion of the *FeatureManager Design Tree* appears blue to denote that the part model is active.

2. Expand the Bearing portion of the *Design Tree*. Move the cursor over the **Annotations** icon under the Bearing. Click once with the right-mouse-button to open the pop-up option menu. Select the **Show Feature Dimensions** option.

3. On your own, adjust the diameter of the small *Drill Hole* to **0.25** as shown.

4. Click on the **Rebuild** button in the *Menu Bar* to proceed with updating the model.

5. On your own, turn *OFF* the visibility of the feature dimensions.

6. Inside the graphics window, click once with the right-mouse-button to display the option menu.

7. Select **Edit Assembly:Support_Assembly** in the popup menu to exit *Part Editing* mode and return to *Assembly* mode.

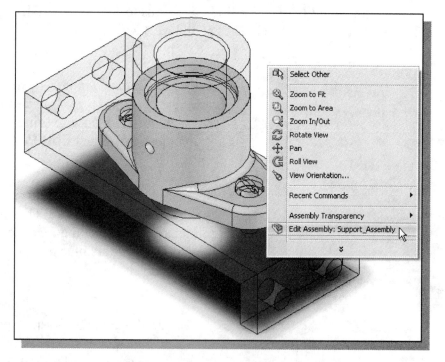

➤ *SolidWorks* has updated the part in all levels and in the current *Assembly* mode. On your own, open the *Bearing* part to confirm the modification is performed.

8. On your own, save the Support_Assembly file. If the *Save Modified Documents* window appears, select **Save All**.

## Setup a Drawing of the Assembly Model

1.  Click on the **arrow** next to the **New** icon on the *Menu Bar* and select **Make Drawing from Part/Assembly** in the pull-down menu.

2.  In the *New SolidWorks Document* window, select the **Tutorial_Templates** tab.

3.  Select the **ANSI-B-Inch** template file icon. This is the custom drawing template you created in Chapter 8.

4.  Select **OK** in the *New SolidWorks Document* window to open the new drawing file.

➢  The new drawing file opens using the **ANSI-B-Inch.SLDDRW** template. The B-size drawing sheet appears.

5.  The *View Palette* appears in the *task pane*. Views can be dragged from the *View Palette* onto the drawing sheet to create a base drawing view. Click on the **Isometric** view in the *View Palette* as shown.

6.  Hold the **left-mouse-button** down and drag to place the **isometric view** as shown.

7.  In the *Projected View PropertyManager*, select the **Hidden Lines Removed** option for the *Display Style*.

8. Left-click on the **OK** icon in the *Drawing View PropertyManager* to accept the view.

9. In the *FeatureManager Design Tree*, **right-click** on the **Sheet** icon to open the pop-up option menu and select **Properties**.

10. In the Sheet Properties window, set the scale to **1:1** and click **OK**.

## Creating a Bill of Materials

A *Bill of Materials (BOM)*, or parts list, can be automatically inserted into a drawing using *SolidWorks*. A Bill of Materials is an example of a *SolidWorks Annotation Table*. A *SolidWorks* Annotation Table can be located in the drawing by clicking in the graphics area or by using a Table Anchor.

1. Under the **Insert** pull-down menu, select **Tables**, then **Bill of Materials**.

2.  The message *"Select a drawing view to specify the model for creating the Bill of Materials"* appears in the *Bill of Materials PropertyManager*. Select on the shaft-support assembly view in the graphics area by clicking on it once with the **left-mouse-button**.

3.  Click on **OK** in the *Bill of Materials PropertyManager* to insert the BOM. Locate the BOM so that it is aligned with the right border and the top of the title block as shown. Click the left-mouse-button to insert the BOM.

| ITEM NO. | PART NUMBER | DESCRIPTION | QTY. |
|----------|-------------|-------------|------|
| 1 | Base-Plate | | 1 |
| 2 | Bearing | | 1 |
| 3 | Collar | | 1 |
| 4 | Cap-Screw | | 2 |

University of New Orleans

TITLE:

Shaft-Support Assembly

SEE DWG. NO.                    REV

B Support_Assembly

SCALE: 1:1  WEIGHT:    SHEET 1 OF 1

❖ The default *SolidWorks* BOM appears. It includes four columns. The **ITEM NO.** column lists the individual parts inserted into the assembly. The **PART NUMBER** column includes **Property Links** to the part *filenames*. The **DESCRIPTION** column contains **Property Links** to the *description* entered in each part file (currently blank because no description was entered.) The **QTY.** column automatically lists the quantity of each part included in the assembly.

## Editing the Bill of Materials

There are many ways in which the BOM table can be modified. We will change the Description column to a Material column. This could be done simply by entering text. However we will use *SolidWorks* Property Links. We will first set the material for each part in the part files. Then we will place the appropriate Property Links in the BOM.

1. Click once with the **left-mouse-button** on the **Open** icon on the *Menu Bar*.

2. Select the ***Base-Plate*** design (part file: **Base-Plate.sldprt**) in the browser. And click on the **Open** button to retrieve the model.

3. In the *FeatureManager Design Tree* for the part, right click on the **Material** icon, then select **Edit Material**.

4. In the *Material* pop-up window, expand the **Steel** folder of the selection tree, and select **Alloy Steel**.

5. Click **Apply** in the *Material* pop-up window to accept the setting and select **Close** to close the window.

❖ The material has been selected for the *Base-Plate*, and is defined as a *SolidWorks* user-defined custom property.

6. Select **Properties** from the *File* pull-down menu.

❖ The *Summary Information* window appears with the table of *Custom Properties* blank.

7. Click in the box under *Property Name* and enter **Material**.

| | Property Name |
|---|---|
| 1 | Material |

8. Click in the box under *Value/Text Expression* and use the pull-down option list to select **Material**.

| Value / Text Expression |
|---|
| Material |
| Mass |
| Density |

❖ Notice the **Material** custom property appears and the **Evaluated Value** in the table automatically becomes **Alloy Steel**, the material selected for the part.

| | Property Name | Type | Value / Text Expression | Evaluated Value |
|---|---|---|---|---|
| 1 | Material | Text | "SW-Material@Base-Plate.SLDPRT" | Alloy Steel |
| 2 | | | | |

9. Click **OK** in the *Summary Information* window to accept the settings.

10. On your own, save and close the *Base-Plate* part file. If the *SolidWorks* window appears, select **Yes**.

11. On your own, repeat the steps above to set the **Material** and the **Material Custom Property** for the *Bearing*, *Collar*, and *Cap-Screw* parts. Use the following: *Bearing* – Grey Cast Iron; *Collar* – Tin Bearing Bronze; *Cap-Screw* – Alloy Steel.

❖ The *SolidWorks* custom property **Material** for each part is now available for use in Property Links. We will not use the **Property Links** in the BOM.

12. Move the cursor over the top of the third column in the BOM. When the **Column** icon appears, left-click to select the column.

| | A | B | C | D |
|---|---|---|---|---|
| 1 | ITEM NO. | PART NUMBER | DESCRIPTION | QTY. |
| 2 | 1 | Base-Plate | | 1 |
| 3 | 2 | Bearing | | 1 |
| 4 | 3 | Collar | Column Icon | 1 |
| 5 | 4 | Cap-Screw | | 2 |

13. The pop-up *Column* toolbar appears.  Select the **Column Property** icon.

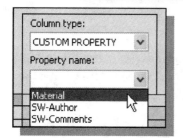

14. Select **CUSTOM PROPERTY** from the selection list under *Column type* and **Material** from the selection list under the *Property name* option in the *Column Property* panel.

15. Click on the sheet, away from the *Column Property* panel to accept the settings.

➢ Notice the corresponding material appears for each part due to the property link.

16. **Double-click** on the note entry Material in the new BOM.

17. Type over the word in all caps.

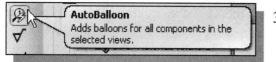

18. Press [**Esc**] to accept the change.

## Completing the Assembly Drawing

1. Press the [**F**] key to fit the drawing to the graphics area.

2. Right-click on the *Menu Bar* and open the *Annotation* toolbar (if necessary).

3. In the *Annotation* toolbar, click on the **AutoBalloon** button.

4. In the *AutoBalloon Property-Manager*, the message "*Select drawing sheet/view(s) to insert Auto Balloon*" is displayed.  Click on the assembly view in the graphics area.

5. Select **1 Character** for the *Size* option on the *Balloon Setting* panel in the *PropertyManager*.

6. Click **OK** in the *PropertyManager* to create the balloons.

7. Move the cursor over the balloon labeling the *Collar* part. Click and drag with the **left-mouse-button** to move the balloon to the new location shown in the figure.

8. Click and drag to move the arrow head to the new location shown in the figure.

9. On your own, repeat the above steps to reposition the balloons as shown.

10. On your own, use the Save As command and save the drawing with the filename **MET 317-04.SLDDRW**. Notice the new filename appears in the title block.

11. If the *SolidWorks* window appears, select **Save All**.

12. Move the cursor into the graphics area and **right-click** to open the pop-up option menu.

13. Select **Edit Sheet Format** from the pop-up option menu to change to *Edit Sheet Format* mode.

14. On your own, edit the title block to appear as shown in the figure.

| UNLESS OTHERWISE SPECIFIED: | | NAME | DATE | University of New Orleans | | |
|---|---|---|---|---|---|---|
| DIMENSIONS ARE IN INCHES | DRAWN | A. Smith | 01/08/11 | | | |
| TOLERANCES: ANGULAR: MACH± 0.1° TWO PLACE DECIMAL ±0.01 THREE PLACE DECIMAL ±0.003 | CHECKED | | | TITLE: | | A |
| | ENG APPR. | | | Shaft-Support Assembly | | |
| | MFG APPR. | | | | | |
| INTERPRET GEOMETRIC TOLERANCING PER: | Q.A. | | | | | |
| MATERIAL | COMMENTS: | | | SIZE **B** | DWG. NO. MET 317-04 | REV |
| FINISH | | | | | | |
| DO NOT SCALE DRAWING | | | | SCALE: 1:1 | WEIGHT: | SHEET 1 OF 1 |
| 3 | | 2 | | | 1 | |

15. On your own, return to *Edit Sheet* mode.

## Exporting the Bill of Materials

❖ The bill of materials can be exported as an *Excel* file.

1. Click the bill of materials on the drawing sheet.

| | A | B | C | D |
|---|---|---|---|---|
| 1 | ITEM NO. | PART NUMBER | MATERIAL | QTY. |
| 2 | 1 | Base-Plate | Alloy Steel | 1 |
| 3 | 2 | Bearing | Gray Cast Iron | 1 |
| 4 | 3 | Collar | Tin Bearing Bronze | 1 |
| 5 | 4 | Cap-Screw | Alloy Steel | 2 |

*University of New Orleans*

2. Select **Save As** from the *File* pull-down menu.

3. Select **CSV** or another appropriate Excel file type for the *Save as type:* option.

4. Enter a *File name* and click **Save**.

| File name: | bom.csv |
|---|---|
| Save as type: | CSV (*.csv) |

5. On your own, open the file using *Microsoft Excel* and examine the BOM.

## Questions:

1.  What is the purpose of using *assembly mates*?

2.  List three of the commonly used *assembly mates*.

3.  Describe the difference between the **Aligned** option and the **Anti-aligned** option.

4.  In an assembly, can we place more than one copy of a part? How is it done?

5.  How should we determine the assembly order of different parts in an assembly model?

6.  How do we adjust the information listed in the **Bill of Materials** of an assembly drawing?

7.  Create sketches showing the steps you plan to use to create the four parts required for the assembly shown on the next page:

# Exercises:

**Wheel Assembly** (Create a set of detail and assembly drawings. All dimensions are in mm.)

**NOTES:**

# Chapter 13
# Design Library and Basic Motion Study

## Learning Objectives

- ◆ **Apply and Use Mate References**
- ◆ **Use the SolidWorks Toolbox Libraries**
- ◆ **Use the Collision Detection Tool**
- ◆ **Use the Basic Motion Tool to Create a Basic Motion Study**
- ◆ **Output the Associated Simulation Video File**

| Certified SolidWorks Associate Exam Objectives Coverage |
| --- |

## Inserting Components

Objectives: Inserting Components into an Assembly.

## Standard Mates – Coincident, Parallel, Perpendicular, Tangent, Concentric, Distance, Angle

Objectives: Applying Standard Mates to Constrain Assemblies.

## Reference Geometry – Planes, Axis, Mate References

Objectives: Creating Reference Planes, Axes and Mate References.

# Introduction

In this lesson, we will examine some of the procedures that are available in *SolidWorks* to reuse existing 2D data and 3D parts. We will also build an assembly model and resolve any interference problems by performing a basic motion analysis.

In *SolidWorks*, we also have the option of using the standard parts library through what is known as the ***Design Library***. The *Design Library* consists of multiple libraries of reusable elements such as parts, assemblies and sketches. It is accessed through the *Task Pane* at the right of the *SolidWorks* work area. Significant amounts of time can be saved by using these parts. Note that we can also create and publish our libraries so that others can reuse our parts. The Design Library Task Pane divides the library into four major sections:

- **Design Library** – Contains subfolders populated by *SolidWorks* with reusable items such as parts, blocks, and annotations. Additional folders and content can be added by the user.
- **Toolbox** – Contains multiple libraries of standard parts that have been created based on industry standards. To access the content, install and add in the *SolidWorks Toolbox* browser.
- **3D ContentCentral** – Accesses 3D models from component suppliers and individuals via the internet. It includes *Supplier Content* (links to supplier web sites with certified 3D models) and *User Library* (links to models from individuals using 3D PartStream.NET).
- **SolidWorks Content** – Contains additional *SolidWorks* content for blocks, routing, and weldments in downloadable .zip files.

In the lesson, we will insert a part from the *SolidWorks Toolbox*. The reader is encouraged to explore the other options in the *Design Library*.

One main advantage of using parametric parts and assemblies is the ability to check for potential problems without actually creating a physical prototype. In *SolidWorks*, ***interference analysis*** can be performed in several different ways. The **Collision Detection** tool is a quick and easy option to examine interference between assembled components.

A ***Motion Study*** can be performed to visually confirm the proper assembly of the designs, and to check for any interference between mating parts and any other potential problems. In *SolidWorks*, several tools are available to perform motion analysis, including the **Animation**, **Basic Motion**, and **Motion Analysis** tools. The Motion Analysis tool can be used to perform a very in-depth motion analysis, while the Basic Motion tool provides a relatively simple motion analysis that can be done in matter of seconds.

In this chapter, the concepts and procedures of creating assemblies using the *Design Library* for standard parts are illustrated. The procedure for basic motion analysis of an assembly is also illustrated using the Basic Motion tool.

## The *Crank-Slider* Assembly

## Creating the Required Parts

*   Six parts are required for this assembly: (1) **Base**, (2) **Crank**, (3) **Connecting Rod**, (4) **Slider**, (5) **Main Pin**, and (6) **Pin**. On your own, create the five parts shown below. Save the models as separate part files: *CS-Base, CS-Crank, CS-Connecting Rod, CS-Slider*, and *CS-Main Pin*. Units are in inches. (Note the location of the parts relative to the datum planes and close all part files or exit *SolidWorks* after you have created the parts.) We will use a standard *Pin* that is available in the *Toolbox*.

(1) **CS-Base** (**NOTE:** Thickness = 0.250 in.)

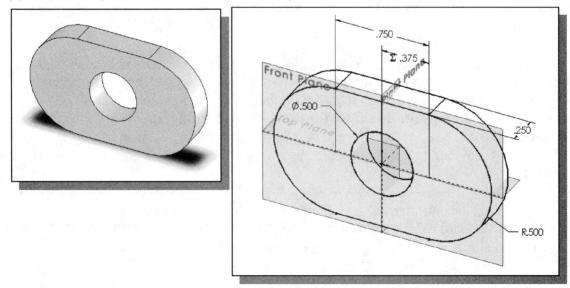

(2) **CS-Crank** (Construct the part with the datum origin aligned to the center of the part.
NOTE:  Thickness is 0.250 in.)

R.500

$\Sigma$ 2.750

5.500

Ø.500

.125

Ø.501

(3) **CS-Connecting Rod** (Construct the part with the datum origin aligned to the center
of the part.          NOTE:  Thickness is 0.250 in.)

R.500

$\Sigma$ 4.500

9.000

Ø.501

Ø.501

(4) **CS-Slider** (Construct the part with the datum planes aligned as shown. **NOTE:** Overall size is ⌀ 5.000 in. x 4.000 in.)

(5) **CS-Main Pin** (Construct the part with the datum planes aligned as shown. **NOTE:** Overall size is ⌀ 5.000 in. x 1.000 in.)

# Mate References

- *SolidWorks Mate References* specify one or more entities of a component to use for automatic mating. When a component with a mate reference is dragged into an assembly, *SolidWorks* looks for other combinations of the same mate reference name and mate type. If the mate name and type match, the mate can be added automatically.

1.  Open the **CS-Crank** part file you created and saved in the last section.

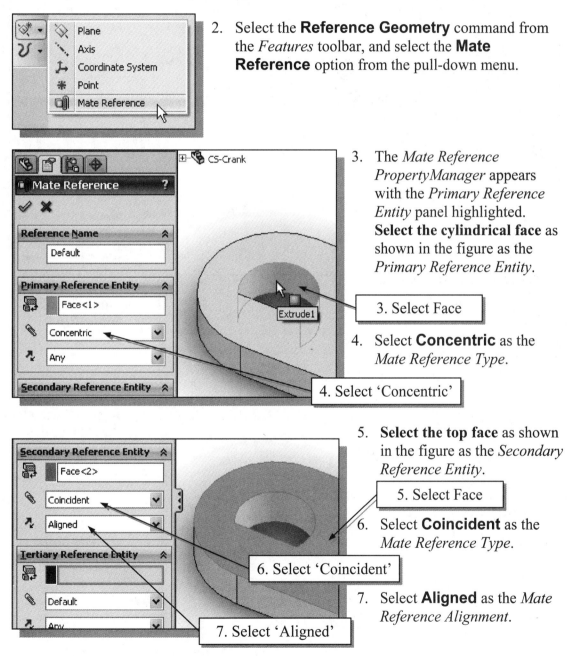

2.  Select the **Reference Geometry** command from the *Features* toolbar, and select the **Mate Reference** option from the pull-down menu.

3.  The *Mate Reference PropertyManager* appears with the *Primary Reference Entity* panel highlighted. **Select the cylindrical face** as shown in the figure as the *Primary Reference Entity*.

    3. Select Face

4.  Select **Concentric** as the *Mate Reference Type*.

    4. Select 'Concentric'

5.  **Select the top face** as shown in the figure as the *Secondary Reference Entity*.

    5. Select Face

6.  Select **Coincident** as the *Mate Reference Type*.

    6. Select 'Coincident'

7.  Select **Aligned** as the *Mate Reference Alignment*.

    7. Select 'Aligned'

**Tertiary Reference Entity**

Face<3>

Parallel

Anti-Aligned

8. Rotate the view and **select** the flat face as shown in the figure as the *Tertiary Reference Entity*.

9. Select **Parallel** as the *Mate Reference Type*.

10. Select **Anti-Aligned** as the *Mate Reference Alignment*.

**Mate Reference**   ?

**Reference Name**

Main

11. Enter **Main** as the *Reference Name*.

12. Select **OK** in the *Mate Reference PropertyManager* to accept the settings.

Material <not specified>
Front Plane
Top Plane
Right Plane
Origin
MateReferences
Main-<1>
Extrude1

13. Notice the *MateReferences* folder appears in the *FeatureManager Design Tree*. **Expand** the folder and notice the only mate reference is *Main*.

14. **Save** and **close** the *CS-Crank* part file.

CS-Main Pin

**Mate Reference**   ?

**Reference Name**

Main

**Primary Reference Entity**

Face<1>

Concentric

Any

**Secondary Reference Entity**

Face<2>

Coincident

Aligned

**Tertiary Reference Entity**

Face<3>

Parallel

Anti-Aligned

Primary

Tertiary

Secondary

15. Open the **CS-Main Pin** part file.

16. On your own, create a *Mate Reference* named **Main** with the settings shown in the figure.

17. **Save** and **close** the **CS-Main Pin** part file.

## Starting *SolidWorks*

1. Select the **SolidWorks** option on the *Start* menu or select the **SolidWorks** icon on the desktop to start *SolidWorks*. The *SolidWorks* main window will appear on the screen.

2. Select the **New** icon with a single click of the left-mouse-button on the *Menu Bar*. The *New SolidWorks Document* dialog box appears.

3. Select the **Templates** tab and select the **Assembly** icon as shown.

4. Click **OK** to open the new Assembly file.

❖ *SolidWorks* opens an assembly file, and automatically opens the *Begin Assembly PropertyManager*. The message "*Select a part or assembly to insert ...*" appears in the *PropertyManager*. *SolidWorks* expects you to insert the first component. We will first set the document properties to match those of the previously created parts.

5. Cancel the **Begin Assembly** command by clicking once with the left-mouse-button on the **Cancel** icon in the *PropertyManager* as shown.

## Document Properties

1. Select the **Options** icon from the *Menu Bar* to open the *Options* dialog box.

2. Select the **Document Properties** tab.

3. Select **ANSI** in the pull-down selection window under the *Overall drafting standard* panel as shown.

Document Properties - Drafting Standard

| System Options | Document Properties |
|---|---|

Drafting Standard
  ⊞ Annotations
  ⊞ Dimensions
  ┊ Virtual Sharps
  ⊞ Tables
Detailing

Overall drafting standard
ANSI

4.  Click **Units**, select the **IPS (inch, pound, second)** unit system, and select **.123** in the *Decimals* spin box for the *Length units* as shown.

Document Properties - Units

System Options | Document Properties

Drafting Standard
  ⊞ Annotations
  ⊞ Dimensions
  ─ Virtual Sharps
  ⊞ Tables
Detailing
Grid/Snap
Units
Colors
Image Quality
Plane Display

Unit system
  ◯ MKS (meter, kilogram, second)
  ◯ CGS (centimeter, gram, second)
  ◯ MMGS (millimeter, gram, second)
  ⦿ IPS (inch, pound, second)
  ◯ Custom

| Type | Unit | Decimals | Fractions | More |
|------|------|----------|-----------|------|
| **Basic Units** | | | | |
| Length | inches | .123 | | ... |
| Dual Dimension Length | inches | .12 / .123 | | ... |
| Angle | degrees | .1234 | | |

5.  Click **OK** in the *Document Properties* window to accept the settings.

## Inserting the First Component

*   The first component in an assembly file sets the orientation of all subsequent parts and subassemblies and therefore should be one that is **not likely to be removed** and **preferably a non-moving part** in the design. For our project, we will use the ***CS-Base*** as the base component in the assembly.

1.  Right-click on the *Menu Bar* and open the *Assembly* toolbar (if necessary).

**Insert Components**
Adds an existing part or sub-assembly
to the assembly.

2.  In the *Assembly* toolbar, select the **Insert Component** command by left-mouse-clicking the icon.

Part/Assembly to Insert
Open documents:

Browse...

3.  Click on the **Browse** button in the *Part/Assembly to Insert* panel in the *PropertyManager*.

4.  Use the browser to locate and select the ***CS-Base*** part file: **CS-Base.sldprt**.

5. Click on the **Open** button to retrieve the model.

6. By default, the component is automatically aligned to the origin of the assembly coordinates. Click **OK** in the *PropertyManager* to place the *CS-Base* at the origin.

## Inserting the Second Component

➤ We will retrieve the *CS-Crank* part as the second component of the assembly model.

1. In the *Assembly* toolbar, select the **Insert Component** command by left-mouse-clicking the icon.

2. Select the ***CS-Crank*** design in the browser. Click on the **Open** button to retrieve the model.

3. Place the *CS-Crank* toward the front side of the CS-Base part, as shown in the figure. Click once with the **left-mouse-button** to place the component.

- Inside the *FeatureManager Design Tree*, the retrieved parts are listed in their corresponding order. The **(f)** in front of the *CS-Base* filename signifies the part is fixed and all *six degrees of freedom* are restricted. The number behind the filename is used to identify the number of copies of the same component in the assembly model.

## Apply Assembly Mates

- We are now ready to assemble the *CS-Crank* component to the *CS-Base* part.

1. In the *Assembly* toolbar, select the **Mate** command by left-mouse-clicking once on the icon.

2. Note that the *Mate Selections* panel in the *Mate PropertyManager* is highlighted. Select the **bottom** horizontal surface of the *CS-Crank* part as the first part for the Mate command, as shown.

3. Click on the **front face** of the *CS-Base* part as the second part selection to apply the Mate. The *CS-Crank* moves to automatically apply the default Coincident mate.

4. Check that the Anti-Aligned option is selected as the Mate alignment.

5. Click the **OK** button in the *PropertyManager* to accept the settings and create the **Anti-Aligned Coincident** mate.

## Apply a Second Mate

❖ The Mate command can also be used to align axes of cylindrical features.

1. On your own, turn *ON* the visibility of the **Temporary Axes**. (**HINT:** Use the *View* pull-down menu.)

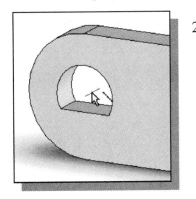

2. Move the cursor over the temporary axis of the left side hole of the *CS-Crank* part. Select the **axis** when it is highlighted as shown.

3. Move the cursor over the temporary axis of the small hole on the *CS-Base* part. Select the **axis** when it is highlighted as shown.

4. The *CS-Crank* moves to automatically apply the default Coincident mate. Click **OK** in the *PropertyManager* to create the Coincident Mate.

5. In the *PropertyManager*, click on the **Close** button (the red **X** icon), or press the [**Esc**] key, to exit the Mate command.

❖ The *CS-Crank* part is placed in the correct position; but the DOF for the *CS-Crank* are not fully restricted; the *CS-Crank* part can still rotate about the mated axis.

## Constrained Move

❖ A constrained move is done by dragging the component in the graphics window with the left-mouse-button. A constrained move will honor previously applied assembly mates. That is, the selected component and parts mated to the component move together in their constrained positions. A fixed component remains fixed during the move.

1. Press and hold down the left-mouse-button and drag the *CS-Crank* part and notice the *CS-Crank* part can freely rotate about the mated axis.

## Placing the Third Component using a Mate Reference

➢ We will next use the **Mate Reference** we named ***Main*** to automatically apply mates upon inserting the *CS-Main Pin* as the third component of the assembly model.

1. In the *Assembly* toolbar, select the **Insert Component** command by left-mouse-clicking the icon.

2. Select the ***CS-Main Pin*** design in the browser. Click on the **Open** button to retrieve the model.

3. Move the cursor over the *CS-Crank* part in the graphics window. Notice the **Mate Reference** icon appears and the *CS-Main Pin* is automatically located using the reference mates you created and named *Main*. Click once with the **left-mouse-button** to insert the *CS-Main Pin* and apply the mates.

4. Press and hold down the left-mouse-button and drag the *CS-Crank* part and notice the *CS-Crank* part still freely rotates about the axis, and that the *CS-Main Pin* rotates with it.

## Assemble the CS-Rod Part

❖ Next we will place the *CS-Connecting Rod* part in the assembly model.

1. In the *Assembly* toolbar, select the **Insert Component** command by left-mouse-clicking the icon.

2. Select the **CS-Connecting Rod** design in the browser. Click on the **Open** button to retrieve the model.

3. Place the part toward the right side of the assembly as shown in the figure.

4. On your own apply mates to constrain the *CS-Connecting Rod* as shown in the figure below. Place (1) an anti-aligned **Coincident** mate between faces of the *CS-Connecting Rod* and the *CS-Crank* parts and (2) a **Coincident** mate between the axes of the holes on the same two parts.

## Inserting a Pin from the SolidWorks Toolbox

➢ The *SolidWorks Toolbox* includes a library of standard parts. To access the content, the toolbox library must be installed and the *SolidWorks Toolbox Browser* must be activated as an **add-in** application.  **NOTE**:  If the *SolidWorks Toolbox Browser* is not available, proceed to the next section.

➢ We will add a *Pin* to our assembly from the *SolidWorks Toolbox*.  If you do not have the *SolidWorks Toolbox* library installed, simply create the *Pin* (∅0.5 in. x 0.5 in.) as a new part and insert it instead.

1.  Select the **Add-Ins** option from the *Tools* pull-down menu.

2.  Select the **SolidWorks Toolbox Browser** in the *Add-Ins* pop-up window and click **OK** to activate the *Toolbox* application.

3.  Left-click on the **Design Library** icon at the right of the graphics area to display the *Design Library Task Pane*.

4.  Select **Toolbox**.

5.  Double-click on the **ANSI Inch** folder from the *Toolbox* directory displayed in the task pane.

6.  Scroll down to find the Pins folder.  Double-click on the **Pins** folder.  Then double-click on the **All Pins** folder.

7. Move the cursor over the **Dowel Pin** icon. Press and hold down the left mouse button. Hold the left mouse button down and **drag** the *Dowel Pin* into the graphics area.

8. **Release** the mouse button to insert the *Dowel Pin*. Notice the *Dowel Pin* is inserted and the *Dowel Pin PropertyManager* appears.

9. Select **1/2** for the Size and **0.5** for the length in the *Properties* panel of the *Dowel Pin PropertyManager*.

➤ Notice the actual diameter of the 1/2″ nominal size *Dowel Pin* is 0.5002 inches (displayed in the *Properties* panel). The diameters of the holes in the *CS-Crank* and *CS-Connecting Rod* parts were defined at 0.501 in. to avoid interference.

10. Click **OK** in the *Dowel Pin PropertyManager* to accept the settings.

11. Notice the *Insert Components PropertyManager* appears, giving the opportunity to insert additional copies of this part. Click **Cancel** in the *PropertyManager* or hit the [**Esc**] key to exit the Insert Component command.

12. On your own, apply mates to constrain the *Dowel Pin* as shown in the figure below.

13. On your own, drag the different components in the graphics window with the left-mouse-button and confirm the parts are properly constrained.

## Assemble the CS-Slider Part

❖ We will insert the *CS-Slider* part to complete the assembly model.

1.  In the *Assembly* toolbar, select the **Insert Component** command by left-mouse-clicking the icon.

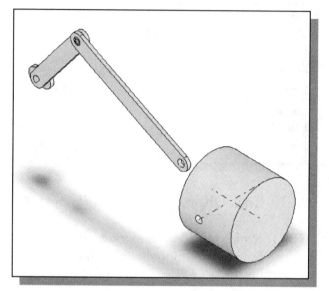

2.  Select the ***CS-Slider*** design in the browser. Click on the **Open** button to retrieve the model.

3.  Place the *CS-Slider* part on the right side of the assembly as shown in the figure.

4.  Expand the *CS-Slider* part in the *FeatureManager Design Tree*, right click on the Front Plane, and select **Show**. (**NOTE:** It may be necessary to also turn *ON* the visibility by selecting the **Planes** option in the *View* pull-down menu.)

5.  In the *Assembly* toolbar, select the **Mate** command by left-mouse-clicking once on the icon.

6.  Select the Front Plane of the *CS-Slider* as the first surface for the Mate as shown.

7. Select the back side of the *CS-Connecting Rod* part as the second surface of the Mate as shown.

8. Check that the Anti-Aligned option is selected as the mate alignment.

9. Click the **OK** button in the *PropertyManager* to accept the settings and create the **Anti-Aligned Coincident** mate.

10. On your own, apply another **Mate** constraint to align the center axes of the *CS-Rod* and the *CS-Slider* as shown.

❖ The *CS-Slider* is not fully constrained; we will next restrict the motion of the slider to the horizontal direction only.

11. On your own, turn *ON* the visibility for the Top Plane of the *Assembly* ("Assem1" at the top of the *Design Tree*) and the Top Plane of the *CS-Slider* part.

 12. On your own, create a **Coincident** mate between these two planes.

13. On your own, move the *CS-Slider* part and confirm the slider is properly constrained.

## Adding an Angle Mate

❖ The *Crank* is the driver of the assembly, and its position can be controlled by adding an Angle mate.

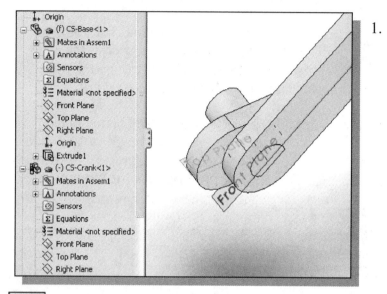

1. In the *FeatureManager Design Tree*, turn *ON* the visibility of the two datum planes that are in the length directions of the *CS-Base* and *CS-Crank* parts as shown in the figure. (These will be the Top Plane of the *CS-Base* part and the Front Plane of the *CS-Crank* is the parts were created as shown in the figures on pages 13-4 and 13-5.)

2. In the *Assembly* toolbar, select the **Mate** command by left-mouse-clicking once on the icon.

3. Select the **two planes** shown is Step 1 above as the *Mate Selections*.

4. Select the **Angle** option in the *Standard Mates* panel of the *PropertyManager* and enter **45** degrees for the angle value.

5. Select the **Anti-Aligned** option under Mate alignment in the *Standard Mates* panel of the *PropertyManager*.

6. **If necessary** to produce the orientation in the figure, check the **Flip dimension** box in the *Standard Mates* panel of the *PropertyManager*.

7. Click **OK** to create the Angle mate.

8. In the *PropertyManager*, click on the **Close** button (the red **X** icon), or press the [**Esc**] key, to exit the Mate command.

9. In the *FeatureManager Design Tree* window, right click on the **Annotations** folder directly below the Assem1 icon and select the **Show Feature Dimensions** option.

➢ Be sure to select the *Annotations* folder for the assembly and not one of the individual part *Annotations* folders. The Angle mate dimension should be the only feature dimension shown.

10. Make sure the **All Annotations** option is selected under the *View* pull-down menu.

11. Notice the 45 deg angle dimension from the Angle mate appears in the graphics area. (It may be necessary to move the cursor over the dimension location, or to change to wireframe display, to see the dimension.) **Double-click** on the dimension.

12. Change the dimension to **70.00 deg** and select **OK**.

13. Click on the **Rebuild** icon in the *Menu Bar* and the *Crank* position is adjusted accordingly.

14. On your own, adjust the angle to other values by repeating the above steps. Also confirm the *Crank, Connecting Rod* and *Slider* parts are properly constrained.

15. Change the angle to **15.00 deg** before continuing to the next section.

## Collision Detection

- *SolidWorks* allows us to perform *Collision Detection* analysis based on the current assembled positions of the assembled parts. Collisions with other components can be detected when moving or rotating a component. The software can detect collisions with the entire assembly or a selected group of components. You can set the tool to detect collisions for all of the components that move as a result of mates or for a selected group of components.

➢ We will first suppress the Angle Mate and allow the *CS-Crank* to rotate.

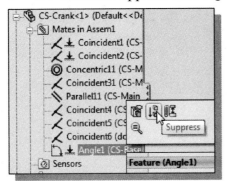

1. In the *FeatureManager Design Tree*, expand the Mates folder under the *CS-Crank* part.

2. **Right click** on the Angle mate.

3. Select the **Suppress** option from the pop-up toolbar.

4. In the *Assembly* toolbar, select the **Move Component** command by left-mouse-clicking the icon.

5. In the *Move Component PropertyManager*, select **Collision Detection**, **All components**, and **Stop at collision** on the *Options* panel, and **Highlight faces** on the *Advanced Options* panel.

6. Move the cursor over the *CS-Crank* part in the graphics area. Slowly **click-and-drag** the *CS-Crank* in the counter-clockwise direction.

➤ Notice the motion stops at the position shown and the *CS-Connecting Rod* is highlighted.

7. Use the arrow keys to **rotate** the assembly. Notice the face of the *CS-Slider* is also highlighted. This is where the collision was detected.

8. Click **OK** in the *PropertyManager* to exit the Move Component command.

## Editing the CS-Slider Part in the Assembly

1. Move the cursor over the face on the interior of the slot in the *CS-Slider* part as shown.

2. Enter the *Edit* mode by **double-clicking** on the face.

3. Notice the face is highlighted and the feature dimensions appear. **Double-click** on the 2.500 dimension of the rectangle.

4. Change the dimension to **3.75 in**.

5. Click **OK** to accept the new dimension.

6. Click on the **Rebuild** icon in the *Menu Bar* and the part and assembly are adjusted accordingly.

7. On your own, perform a **Collision Detection** analysis on the new assembly. (**HINT:** Repeat the steps in the Collision Detection section beginning on page 13-23.)

➢ The problem has been resolved and no collision occurs.

## Basic Motion Analysis

- *SolidWorks'* **Motion Study** tool allows us to perform basic motion analysis by creating simulations of assemblies with moving parts.

    1. On your own, turn *OFF* the visibility of the **Temporary Axes** using the *View* pull-down menu.

2. Select the **View Orientation** button on the *Heads-up View* toolbar and select the **Trimetric** view icon.

3. Select the **Motion Study** tab at the bottom of the *SolidWorks* window.

❖ The *SolidWorks MotionManager* appears. The *MotionManager* is a timeline-based interface with motion study tools located on the toolbar shown below.

4. Select **Basic Motion** in the *Type of Study* selection window on the left end of the *MotionManager* toolbar.

5. Move the cursor over the **Motor** command on the *MotionManager* toolbar and click once with the left mouse button to create a motor to drive the motion for the study.

6. In the *Motor PropertyManager*, select **Rotary Motor** as the *Motor Type*, select the flat face of the **CS-Crank** as the *Motor Location* in the *Component/Direction* panel. Select the **Constant speed** option on the *Motion* panel and enter **20 RPM** for the speed.

7. Click **OK** in the *PropertyManager* to accept the setting and create the motor.

8. Move the cursor over the **Calculate** command on the *MotionManager* toolbar and click once with the left-mouse-button to calculate the *Motion Study*.

➢ Once it has been calculated, the *Motion Study* can be viewed using the **Play from Start**, **Play**, and **Stop** buttons on the *MotionManager* toolbar

9. On your own, experiment with the **Play from Start**, **Play**, and **Stop** tools.

10. On your own, start the simulation and dynamically rotate the display (e.g., using the arrow keys) while the simulation is running.

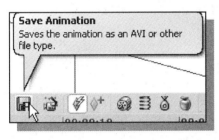

11. The simulation can also be saved as an AVI or other format file. Click the **Save Animation** button on the *MotionManager* toolbar as shown.

12. Enter **CS-Assembly** as the *File name* and click **Save** to accept the filename.

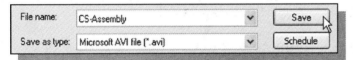

13. Select the *Video Compression* setting to set the quality and speed of the file and click **OK** to proceed.

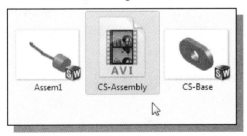

14. On your own, view the recorded video file.

15. Select the **Model** tab at the bottom of the *SolidWorks* window to return to the *Assembly Editing* mode.

16. On your own, save the assembly with the filename **CS-Assembly.SLDASM**.

17. If the *Save Modified Documents* window appears, select the **Do not save read-only documents** option and select **Save All**.

## Questions:

1.  What is included in the **SolidWorks Design Library**?

2.  What is the usage of a **Mate Reference**?

3.  How do you save the *SolidWorks* motion study as an AVI movie?

4.  How do you access the **Motor** command?

5.  How do we enter the *Edit* mode in an assembly model?

6.  Can we access the 2D sketch of a feature of a part in an assembly?

7.  How do we end the *Edit* mode and return to the assembly model in *SolidWorks*?

8.  List and describe two methods to edit the angle of an **Angle** mate.

9.  Describe the procedure to perform a *Collision Detection* in an assembly.

10. How do you control the speed of the simulation in *SolidWorks*?

## Exercises:  Leveling Assembly
(Create a set of detail and assembly drawings. All dimensions are in mm.)

(a) **Base Plate**

(b) **Sliding Block** (Rounds & Fillets: R3)

(c) **Lifting Block** (Rounds & Fillets: R3)

(d) **Adjusting Screw** (M10 × 1.5) (Use the **Threads** or **Coil** command to create the threads)

**Basic Motion Analysis**: Create a linear motor in between the **Sliding Block** and the **Base Plate** parts.

**NOTES:**

# Chapter 14
# Design Analysis with SimulationXpress

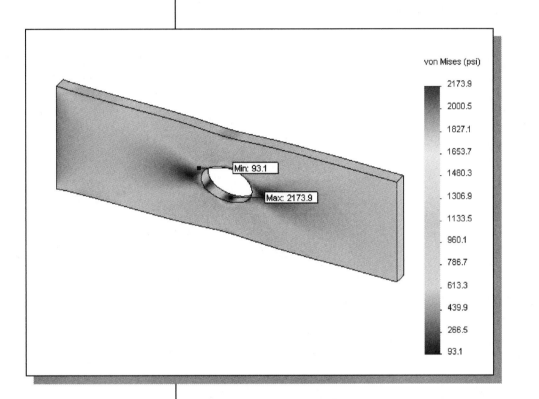

von Mises (psi)

2173.9
2000.5
1827.1
1653.7
1480.3
1306.9
1133.5
960.1
786.7
613.3
439.9
266.5
93.1

Min: 93.1

Max: 2173.9

## Learning Objectives

- ◆ **Create SimulationXpress Study**
- ◆ **Apply Fixtures and Loads**
- ◆ **Perform Basic Stress Analysis**
- ◆ **View Results**
- ◆ **Assess Accuracy of Results**
- ◆ **Output the Associated Simulation Video File**

## Certified SolidWorks Associate Exam Objectives Coverage

### Materials

Objectives:  Applying Material Selection to Parts.

Certified Associate Reference Guide

## Introduction

In this chapter we will explore basic design analysis using *SolidWorks SimulationXpress*. *SimulationXpress* provides a tool for basic stress analysis, allowing the user to examine the effects of applied forces on a design. Displacements, strains, and stresses in a part are calculated based on material properties, fixtures, and applied loads. Stress results can be compared to material properties (e.g., yield strength) to perform failure analysis. The results can also be used to identify critical areas, calculate safety factors at various regions, and simulate deformation. *SimulationXpress* provides an easy-to-use method within the SolidWorks environment to perform an initial stress analysis. The results can be used to improve the design.

In *SimulationXpress*, stresses are calculated using linear static analysis based on the *finite element method*. In linear static analysis, it is assumed that: 1) a linear relationship exists between the applied loads and the response, 2) the stress-strain relationship is linear, 3) no plastic deformation occurs, and 4) no suddenly applied loads are involved. The *finite element method (FEM)* is a numerical method for finding approximate solutions to partial differential equations. The technique is widely used for the solution of complex problems in engineering mechanics. Analysis using the method is called *finite element analysis (FEA)*.

In the finite element method, a complex body (e.g., a part created in *SolidWorks*) is modeled as an equivalent system of smaller bodies of simple shape, or *elements*, which are interconnected at common points called *nodes*. This process is called *discretization*. (An example is shown in the figures below.) Equations (e.g., for structural analysis) are formulated for each finite element and the resulting system of equations is solved simultaneously to obtain an approximate solution for the entire body. In general, a better approximation is obtained by increasing the number of elements (i.e., creating a finer mesh), but more computing time and resources are required.

*SimulationXpress* utilizes ten-node tetrahedral elements for which the edges and faces can be curvilinear, facilitating the modeling of curved surfaces (as seen in the figure above). The behavior of these elements is analyzed using linear static analysis and the appropriate material properties to relate local coordinate nodal displacements to local forces. The motion of each node is described by displacements in the X, Y, and Z directions, called *degrees of freedom* (DOFs). The equations describing the behavior of each element are assembled into a global system of equations, incorporating compatibility requirements based on connectivity among elements. Using the known material properties, fixtures, and loads, *SimulationXpress* solves the system of equations for the unknown displacements at each node. These displacements are used in the results stage to calculate strains and stresses.

While *SimulationXpress* is a powerful and easy-to-use tool, it is important to appreciate that it is the designer's responsibility to properly assess the accuracy of the results. As stated above, a better FEA approximation is generally obtained by increasing the number of elements. An assessment must be made regarding whether the mesh used to discretize the model is adequate. There are other important factors affecting the accuracy of the results. The material properties used in the analysis must accurately characterize the behavior of the material. The fixtures and loads must be applied in a manner which accurately reflects the actual conditions. Proper meshing and application of boundary conditions often requires significant experience in FEA and may require tools and capabilities not available in *SimulationXpress*. *SimulationXpress* is an easy-to-use tool for a first-pass stress analysis. More advanced capabilities are available in the *SolidWorks Simulation* design analysis application.

## The SimulationXpress Wizard Interface

The wizard interface of *SimulationXpress* appears to the right of the graphics area when *SimulationXpress* is activated from the *Tools* pull-down menu. The wizard guides the user through a six step process to perform an analysis:

(1) **Fixtures** – identify entities to be fixed in place during the analysis;
(2) **Loads** – apply loads;
(3) **Material** – specify material;
(4) **Run** – assemble equations and solve for the unknown degrees of freedom;
(5) **Results** – to view results, e.g., stress distribution; and
(6) **Optimize** – an optional step to find the optimal value for a parameter, e.g., a fillet radius, based on a selected criterion.

## Problem Statement

Determine the maximum normal stress that loading produces in the Aluminum 1060 Alloy plate.

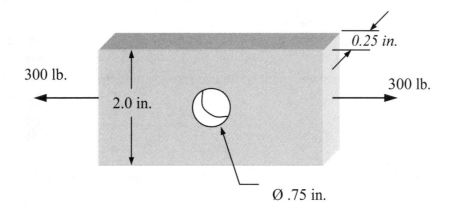

## Preliminary Analysis

- **Maximum Normal Stress**

The nominal normal stress developed at the smallest cross section (through the center of the hole) in the plate is

$$\sigma_{nominal} = \frac{P}{A} = \frac{300}{(2 - 0.75) \times .25} = 960 \text{ psi.}$$

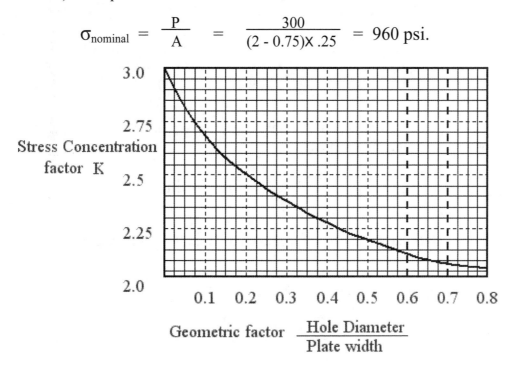

**Geometric factor = .75/2 = 0.375**

Stress concentration factor K is obtained from the graph, **K = 2.27**

$$\sigma_{MAX} = K \sigma_{nominal} = 2.27 \times 960 = 2180 \text{ psi.}$$

- **Maximum Displacement**

We will also estimate the displacement under the loading condition. For a statically determinant system, the stress results depend mainly on the geometry. The material properties can be in error and still the FEA analysis comes up with the same stresses. However, the displacements always depend on the material properties. Thus, it is necessary to always estimate both the stress and displacement prior to a computer FEA analysis.

The classic one-dimensional displacement can be used to estimate the displacement of the problem:

$$\delta = \frac{PL}{EA}$$

Where P=force, L=length, A=area, E= elastic modulus, and δ = deflection.

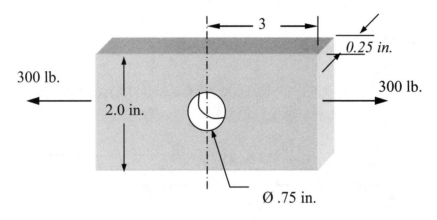

A lower bound of the displacement of the right edge, measured from the center of the plate, is obtained by using the full area:

$$\delta_{lower} = \frac{PL}{EA} = \frac{300 \times 3}{10E6 \times (2 \times 0.25)} = 1.8\text{E-4 in.}$$

and an upper bound of the displacement would come from the reduced section:

$$\delta_{upper} = \frac{PL}{EA} = \frac{300 \times 3}{10E6 \times (1.25 \times 0.25)} = 2.88\text{E-4 in.}$$

but the best estimate is a sum from the two regions:

$$\delta_{average} = \frac{PL}{EA} = \frac{300 \times 0.375}{10E6 \times (1.25 \times 0.25)} + \frac{300 \times 2.625}{10E6 \times (2.0 \times 0.25)}$$

$$= 3.6\text{E-5} + 1.58\text{E-4} = 1.94\text{E-4 in.}$$

## SolidWorks SimulationXpress Study of the Flat Plate

In this lesson we will perform a stress analysis on the flat plat with a circular hole under axial tension using *SimulationXpress*. The *SimulationXpress* results will include values for maximum stress and maximum displacement calculated using finite element analysis. These results will be compared to the values for maximum stress and displacement calculated in the previous section.

This tutorial is performed using *SolidWorks* **SimulationXpress**. S*imulationXpress* uses the same analysis methodology as *SolidWorks Simulation* to perform stress analysis, but has abbreviated capabilities and uses a different interface – the wizard described in the previous section. It is therefore necessary to ensure that the *SolidWorks Simulation* add-in (if available) is de-activated in order to follow the instructions. If *SolidWorks Simulation* is activated, the user will be presented with a different interface.

### Getting Started – Create the *SolidWorks* Part

1.  On your own, start a new part file using the **Part_IPS_ANSI** template in the Tutorial_Templates folder. (You created this template in Chapter 4.)

2.  Select the **Add-Ins** option from the *Tools* pull-down menu.

3.  In the *Add-Ins* pop-up window, make sure that the *SolidWorks Simulation* application is **not** selected and click **OK**.

4.  On your own, **create the sketch** shown below using the **Front Plane** as the sketch plane.

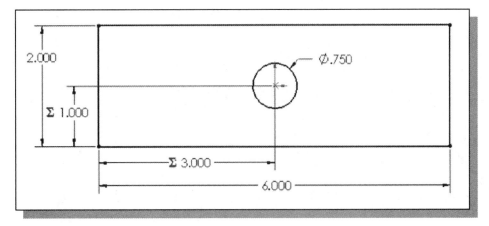

5.  On your own, create an **Extruded Boss** feature with a thickness of **0.25 in**.

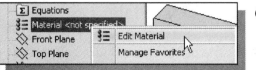

6.  Right-click on the **Material** icon in the *FeatureManger Design Tree* and select **Edit Material** from the pop-up menu.

7.  In the *Material* pop-up window, select **1060 Alloy** (in the *Aluminum Alloys* folder) as the material type. Notice the material properties (Young's modulus, etc.) listed. These properties will be used in the *SimulationXpress* analysis.

8.  Click **Apply** to select the material and **Close** the *Material* window.

9.  Save the part with the filename ***Aluminum_Plate***.

## Create a *SimulationXpress* Study

1. Select the **SimulationXpress** command from the *Tools* pull-down menu.

➢ The *SimulationXpress* wizard appears at the right of the window.

2. Select the **Options** button on the *Welcome* screen of the *SimulationXpress* wizard.

3. Select **English (IPS)** in the *System of units:* option box.

4. **Check the Show annotation for maximum and minimum in the results plots** box.

5. On the *Results location* option line, click the **Browse** button and select the folder in which you want to save the simulation results.

6. Select **OK** to accept the options and close the *SimulationXpress Options* window.

7. Click the **Next** button in the *SimulationXpress* wizard to move on to the Fixtures step.

➢ The major steps in the *SimulationXpress* process appear, with the **Fixtures** step active. The check next to the **Material** step indicates that the material we applied to the part is recognized by the *SimulationXpress* wizard. An introduction to the **Fixtures** step is displayed.

8.  Click the **Add a fixture** command in the task pane.

9.  The *Fixture PropertyManager* appears with the *Faces for Fixture* window highlighted.  Rotate the part and select the **left vertical face** as shown.

10. Click **OK** in the *PropertyManager* to accept the selection and exit the Fixture command.

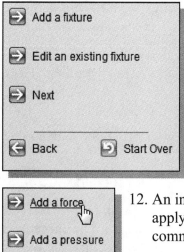

11. The Fixed-1 fixture is created and options are given to Add another fixture or Edit the existing fixture. Click the **Next** button to move on to the Loads step.

➢ Notice the fixture appears in the *SimulationXpress Study Tree* to the left of the graphics area with the default name Fixed-1, and a checkmark appears next to Fixtures in the top pane of the *SimulationXpress* wizard, showing that the step is complete.

12. An introduction to the Loads step is displayed with options to apply a Force or a Pressure load.  Click the **Add a force** command.

13. The *Force PropertyManager* appears with the *Faces for Force* window highlighted.  Rotate the part and select the **right vertical face** as shown. Select the **Normal** direction option and the **English** unit option. Enter **300 lbf** as the force value and check the **Reverse direction** option box.  Notice the direction of the force load is now outward.

14. Click **OK** in the *PropertyManager* to accept the selection and exit the Force command.

15. The Force-1 force load is created and options are given to Add another load, or Edit the existing load. Click the **Next** button to move on to the Material step.

➢ Notice the force load appears in the *SimulationXpress Study Design Tree* to the left of the graphics area with the default name Force-1. A checkmark appears next to Loads in the top pane of the *SimulationXpress* wizard, showing that the step is complete.

16. An introduction to the Material step is displayed. Notice the material we applied to the part is recognized by the *SimulationXpress* wizard. An option to change the material is given, but we will use the 1060 Alloy material properties. Click the **Next** button to move on to the Run step.

The material assigned to this part is:

**1060 Alloy**

Young's Modulus:
6.9e+010N/m^2

Yield Strength:
2.75742e+007N/m^2

➔ Change material

➔ Next

You can solve with the default settings or adjust them to better suit your needs.

→ Change settings

→ Run Simulation

17. An introduction to the Run step is displayed with options to change the analysis settings or to run the analysis with the default settings. We will use the default settings. Click the **Run simulation** command.

**SimulationXpress Study**

Solving:

Memory Usage: 27,856K
Elapsed Time: 1s
☑ Always show solver status when you run analysis

Current Task: Iteration

**88%**

Study

Degrees of Freedom: 36,885
Number of Nodes: 12,440
Number of Elements: 7,140

Solver
Type: Iterative

Warnings:

[ Convergence Plot ]    [ Solver Parameter ]

[ Continue ]    [ Cancel ]    [ Less<< ]

➢ While the solver is running, the *SimulationXpress Study* pop-up window appears briefly. This window can be used to display the number of Nodes, number of Elements, and number of degrees of freedom – D.O.F. – in the current discretization. For this analysis, there are 36,885 D.O.F., 12,440 nodes, and 7,140 elements. Your model may be slightly different. (**NOTE:** To see this view, click **Pause** and **More** in the pop-up window. It is not necessary to do this; simply continue to the Results step.)

## Viewing *SimulationXpress* Results

➢ When the analysis is complete, the wizard moves on to the Results step and displays an animation of the part's response to the Fixtures and Loads entered in the previous steps. We will move on to view the stress results.

1. Verify that the deformation in the animation matches that in the figure shown above.

2. Click the **Stop animation** command in the *SimulationXpress* wizard.

3. Below the question *"Does the part deform as you expected?"* click **Yes, continue**.

➢ We will now view the stress results.

4. The wizard moves to the next Results screen. Click the **Show von Mises stress** command to display the stress distribution in the model.

➢ A plot of equivalent stress (von Mises stress) is generated and displayed in the graphics area.

➢ The stresses are plotted on the deformed shape of the part. **NOTE:** The actual deformation is very small. The deformation is exaggerated in the plot to better illustrate how the part deforms.

➢ A color-coded scale is used with the associated scale bar displayed at the right. Red represents the regions of highest stress.

➢ The maximum stress is 2113.2 psi (your result may be slightly different), well below the yield strength of the material (3999.3 psi), and is located at the stress concentration points at the upper and lower quadrants of the hole. (**NOTE:** The trimetric view is used for the display shown here.)

5.  In the *SimulationXpress Study Tree*, **right-click** on the Fixed-1 fixture and select **Hide** from the pop-up menu.

➢   Notice the arrows representing the fixture in the graphics area are no longer visible.

6.  On your own, hide the arrows representing the force load Force-1.

➢   We will now view the displacement results.

Show displacement

7.  In the *SimulationXpress* wizard, click the **Show displacement** command to display the displacement distribution in the model.

➢   A plot of the displacement in the model is displayed.   **NOTE:** The actual deformation is very small.   The deformation is exaggerated in the plot to better illustrate how the part deforms.
➢   A color-coded scale is used with the associated scale bar displayed at the right.   Red represents the regions of highest displacement.
➢   The maximum displacement is $4.040(10^{-4})$ in.
    (**NOTE:** The trimetric view is used for the display shown here.)

➢ We will now use the factor of safety result display option.

➢ The wizard indicates the lowest factor of safety (FOS) in the model, i.e., the FOS associated with the maximum stress.

➢ An option is given to select a FOS value and have *SimulationXpress* display regions which do not meet this criterion.

8. Enter **2.5** for the factor of safety and click the **Show FOS** button.

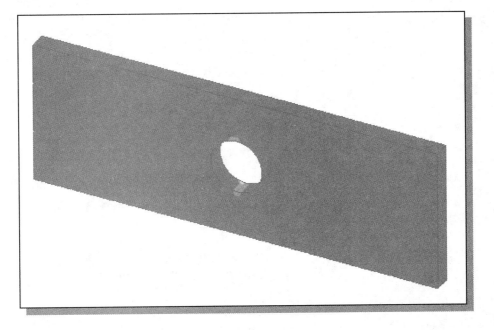

➢ For the factor of safety of 2.5, the plot displays the safe and unsafe regions in blue and red, respectively.

➢ We have used the *SimulationXpress* wizard to view the stress, displacement, and factor of safety results. An alternate method is to right-click on the desired view in the *SimulationXpress Study Design Tree* and select **Show**.

9. In the *SimulationXpress Study Tree*, **right-click** on the **Stress** view and select **Show** on the pop-up menu.

10. Notice the stress distribution is displayed. In the *SimulationXpress Study Tree*, **right-click** on the **Stress** view and select **Animate** on the pop-up menu.

11. The *Animation PropertyManager* appears and an animation of the exaggerated deformation and associated stresses is active in the graphics area. Select the **Stop** button to stop the animation.

12. In the *Basics* panel of the *Animation PropertyManager* enter **20** for the *frames* option, move the slider to select the **minimum** *speed* option, and select the **Reciprocate** option.

13. Select the **Play** button to view the animation with the new settings.

14. Select the **Stop** button to stop the animation.

15. We will save this animation as an .AVI file. Check the **Save as AVI file** option box.

16. Select the **Browse** button to select the folder location.

17. In the *Save as* pop-up dialog box, select the folder location, enter the *File name* **Plate_Animation_1**, and select the **Save** button.

| File name: | Plate_Animation_1 | ▼ | Save |
| Save as type: | Movie clip (*.AVI) | ▼ | Cancel |

18. Select the **Play** button to view the animation and save the .AVI file.

19. On your own, view the animation by playing the .AVI file using an appropriate media playing application.

20. Select the **Cancel** button on the *PropertyManager* to exit the Animation command.

21. Click on the **Done viewing results** command.

## Creating a Report and an eDrawings File

*SimulationXpress* includes options to create a report in Microsoft Word format which contains data related to the simulation and an *eDrawings* file for viewing the results. These options appear in the *SimulationXpress* wizard when the Done viewing results command is executed.

1.  Select the **Generate report** option.

2.  In the Report Settings window, enter text in the fields as desired (description of problem, your name, etc.) for inclusion in the report.

3.  Click the **Generate** button to create the report file.

➤ *SimulationXpress* will create a document file and automatically open it in Microsoft Word. The file is saved in the folder selected earlier as the *Results location* for the *SimulationXpress* study.

4.  On your own, read through the report. Notice that all the relevant data are recorded. From the report, we can see that for this simulation the number of elements is ~**7,150** and the maximum stress is ~**2120 psi**. We will use this data in the next section.

5.  On your own, close the report document.

6.  Select the **Generate eDrawings file** option.

7.  In the *Save as* pop-up dialog box, select the **Save** button to save the file with the default name and location. (If the *Graphics Performance Check* window appears, select **OK**.)

➤ *SimulationXpress* will create the *eDrawings* file and open the *eDrawings* viewer. The equivalent stress plot is displayed by default, but the displacement, deformation, and factor of safety plots can also be viewed.

8.  On your own, experiment with the *eDrawings* viewing options.

9.  On your own, close the *eDrawings* window.

## Accuracy of Results

The accuracy of the *SimulationXpress* results for this problem can be checked by comparing them to the analytical results presented earlier.   In the Preliminary Analysis section (pages 14-5 – 14-6), we calculated the maximum stress using a stress concentration factor and obtained a value of **2180 psi**.  The maximum stress obtained by finite element analysis using *SimulationXpress* (page 14-13) was **2113.2 psi**.  The *SimulationXpress* result thus differs from the analytical result by 3.1%.  (**NOTE:** The von Mises stress reported in the *SimulationXpress* result is the same as the axial stress for the uniaxial loading condition in this example.)  In the Preliminary Analysis section, we estimated the maximum displacement to be 1.94E-4 inches, measured from the center of the hole to one end of the plate.  The total displacement from one end of the plate to the other would therefore be **3.88E-4 inches**.  The maximum displacement obtained by finite element analysis using *SimulationXpress* (page 14-14) was **4.051E-4 inches**.  The *SimulationXpress* result thus differs from the analytical result by 4.4%.  The agreement between the analytical results and those from *SimulationXpress* demonstrate the potential of *SimulationXpress* as a tool to perform an initial stress analysis within the *SolidWorks* environment.

In general, FEA is applied to problems for which there is no readily available analytical solution.  It is therefore necessary to assess the accuracy of the results independently.  A standard method is to perform a ***convergence test***.

1. Click the **Back** button until the initial *Run* panel is displayed as shown below.  (Alternately, click on Run in the top pane of the wizard.)

2. The message "*You can solve with the default settings or adjust them to better suit your needs*" appears.  Select the **Change settings** command.

➢ An introduction to the mesh density is displayed with the option to change the mesh density settings or to continue with the default settings.

3. Click the **Change mesh density** command.

4. A pop-up window appears with the message "*Remeshing will delete the results for study*" appears. Click **OK**.

SolidWorks SimulationXpress

⚠ Remeshing will delete the results for study: SimulationXpress Study.

OK    Cancel

5. The *Mesh PropertyManager* appears and presents the option to adjust the fineness/coarseness of the mesh (i.e., adjust the size/number of elements used). **Move the slider** to the left-most position (this selects the coarsest mesh, i.e., the largest element size).

6. Click the **OK** button to remesh the model and exit the Mesh command. Notice a coarse mesh is displayed on the model in the graphics area.

7. Click **Next** in the *SimulationXpress* wizard to continue.

8. Click **Run Simulation** to run the analysis with the new mesh.

➢ When the analysis is complete, the wizard moves on to the Results step.

9. On your own, display the **stress distribution** results (**NOTE:** This can be done either using the *SimulationXpress* wizard or the *SimulationXpress Study Tree*.)

➢ Notice the maximum stress is lower (~1,940 psi). The coarser mesh produced a less accurate approximation, as would be expected. To perform a convergence test, we refine the mesh in steps until the parameter of interest converges to an accurate value.

10. On your own, select **Done viewing results** and **Generate report**, and record the number of elements and maximum stress values in the report (e.g., Number of elements = 1,344; Maximum stress = 1,937.79).

11. On your own, go back to the Run panel, choose Change settings, and set the mesh to the **finest** setting as shown.

12. On your own, **Run** the analysis.

13. On your own, view the **Stress Distribution** and note the maximum stress.

14. On your own, generate the HTML report and record the number of elements and maximum stress values in the report (e.g., Number of elements = 55,072; Maximum stress = 2,180.26).

➢ We now have run three analyses with different levels of refinement. We will plot these to observe the effect of refinement on the result. The number of elements will be used as a parameter to describe the fineness of the mesh. The results of the three analyses are shown in tabular and graphical form below. One additional analysis was performed and included. (The numbers you obtain may vary.)  The value for maximum stress can be seen to converge to the analytical result.

| Elements | $\sigma_{max}$ (psi) |
|----------|----------------------|
| 1344 | 1938 |
| 7140 | 2113 |
| 30086 | 2177 |
| 55072 | 2180 |

➢ When further refinement produces no significant change in the result, the solution is considered to have reached a 'converged' solution.

## Closing SimulationXpress and Saving Results

1. Click on the **Close** button on the *SimulationXpress* wizard to exit the application.

2. A pop-up window appears with the question "... *save SolidWorks SimulationXpress data?*" Select **Yes** to save the data.

➢ The data is saved and, when you return to the *SimulationXpress* application, the restraints, loads, results, etc. will be loaded automatically.

3. On our own, **Save** and **Close** the *Aluminum_Plate* part file.

## Questions:

1. What analysis method is used by *SolidWorks SimulationXpress*?

2. Describe the steps in performing a stress analysis using *SimulationXpress*.

3. Describe two ways the material properties can be defined or edited.

4. How do we open the *SimulationXpress* wizard interface and create a *SimulationXpress* study?

5. What is meant by the term *Fixture* in *SimulationXpress*?

6. How do we control whether a load applied to a face is in the *outward* or *inward* direction?

7. Can we return to a previous step in the *SimulationXpress* study and make changes? If so, how?

8. Define degrees of freedom (DOF). How can you obtain the number of DOFs for a *SimulationXpress* analysis. How can you change the number of DOFs?

9. How is the 'lowest factor of safety' found?

10. How do we end the *SimulationXpress* study and return to the model in *SolidWorks*?

## Exercises:

1. The shaft shown below is fixed at the large end and a 50 kN force is applied to the small end. Find the maximum stress and maximum deflection in the shaft. The material is AISI 1020. (Dimensions in mm).

2. For the hanging bracket, the top face is fixed and a 100 psi pressure load is applied to the horizontal surface as shown. Find the maximum stress and maximum deflection in the bracket. The material is Alloy Steel. (Dimensions in inches).

# Chapter 15
# CSWA Exam Preparation

## Learning Objectives

- **Control Part Orientation**
- **Create a New View Orientation**
- **Use the SolidWorks Mass Properties Tool**
- **Obtain the Mass and Center of Mass of a Part**
- **Obtain the Mass and Center of Mass of an Assembly**
- **Use Distance and Angle Mates**
- **Create and Use Reference Axes**

Certified Associate Reference Guide

## Certified SolidWorks Associate Exam Objectives Coverage

### Mass Properties

Objectives: Obtaining Mass Properties for Parts and Assemblies.

### Standard Mates – Coincident, Parallel, Perpendicular, Tangent, Concentric, Distance, Angle

Objectives: Applying Standard Mates to Constrain Assemblies.

### Reference Geometry – Planes, Axis, Mate References

Objectives: Creating Reference Planes, Axes, and Mate References.

## Tips about Taking the Certified SolidWorks Associate (CSWA) Examination

1. **Study:** The first step to maximize your potential on an exam is to sufficiently prepare for it. You need to be familiar with the *SolidWorks* package, and this can only be achieved by doing designs and exploring the different commands available. The Certified SolidWorks Associate (CSWA) exam is designed to measure your familiarity with the *SolidWorks* software. You must be able to perform the given task and answer the exam questions correctly and quickly.

2. **Make Notes**: Take notes of what you learn either while attending classroom sessions or going through study material. Use these notes as a review guide before taking the actual test.

3. **Time Management**: The examination has a time limit. Manage the time you spent on each question. Always remember you do not need to score 100% to pass the exam. Also keep in mind that some questions are weighed more heavily and may take more time to answer. You can flip back and forth to view different problems during the test time by using the arrow buttons. If you encounter a question you cannot answer in a reasonable amount of time, use the *Save As* feature in *SolidWorks* to save a copy of the file, and move on to the next question. You can return to any question and enter or change the answer as long as you do not hit the [**I am done**] button.

4. **Use the *SolidWords Help System***: If you get confused and can't think of the answer, remember the *SolidWorks Help System* is a great tool to confirm your considerations. In preparing for the exam, familiarize yourself with the help utility organization (e.g., Contents, Index, Search options).

5. **Use Internet Search**: Use of an internet search utility is allowed during the test. If a test question requires general knowledge, for example definitions of engineering or drafting concepts (stress, yield strength, auxiliary view, etc.), remember the internet is available as a tool to assist in your considerations.

6. **Use Common Sense**: If you are unable to get the correct answer and unable to eliminate all distracters, then you need to select the best answer from the remaining selections. This may be a task of selecting the best answer from amongst several correct answers, or it may be selecting the least incorrect answer from amongst several poor answers.

7. **Be Cautious and Don't Act in Haste:** Devote some time to ponder and think of the correct answer. Ensure that you interpret all the options correctly before selecting from available choices. Don't go into panic mode while taking a test. Use the *Arrow Buttons* to review each question. When you are confident that you have answered all questions, end the examination using the [**I am done**] button to submit your answers for scoring. You will receive a score report once you have submitted your answers.

8. **Relax before exam:** In order to avoid last minute stress, make sure that you arrive 10 to15 minutes early and relax before taking the exam.

Certified User Reference Guide

## Introduction

In this lesson, we will create and examine part and assembly files in a manner consistent with the format of the CSWA exam. This is a multiple choice exam. You are asked to build complex models and assemblies and your work is assessed in a multiple choice format by asking the value of parameters such as the mass or center of mass. These can be retrieved using the *SolidWorks* **Mass Properties** tool. In answering questions related to the location of the center of mass, it is important to ensure that the origin and coordinate system axes are consistent between your model and the exam problem as posed.

We will first create a part based on a dimensioned drawing with the origin and coordinate axes annotated. We will create the part, apply the correct material properties, and retrieve the mass and center of mass data. In building the model, we will ensure that it is oriented relative to the default coordinate system in the manner indicated in the problem. While the part is relatively simple, the procedure – taking care to locate the part, applying material properties, retrieving mass properties – is the same as should be followed for many CSWA exam questions. The part requires the creation of an inclined **Reference Plane** to use in creating a sketch.

We will then create an assembly using multiple copies of two mating parts. The assembly will require the use of **Distance** and **Angle** mates, based on the dimensions given in the problem. In this case, we will not orient the parts or assembly based on the problem definition. Instead, after the assembly has been completed, we will create **Reference Axes** to match those in the problem statement and use these reference axes when retrieving the center of mass.

## The Part Problem

We will model the part shown below and use the **Mass Properties** tool to determine the mass and center of mass of the part.  The problem is presented below in a manner similar to that encountered on the CSWA exam.

Build the part shown below.
Unit system:  MMGS (millimeter, gram, second)
Part origin:  As shown.
Part material:  Ductile iron    Density:  0.0071 g/mm$^3$

What is the overall mass of the part in grams?
What is the center of mass of the part?

Before starting to build the model, it is important to select a strategy for controlling the origin and orientation of the X, Y, and Z axes since the center of mass must be defined relative to a known reference system.   In this case the axis directions are defined in the drawing.  We can either (1) build the part aligned to the default or global coordinate system as specified in the figure, or (2) build the part independent of this constraint and, after the part is complete, create a reference coordinate system with axes aligned with the part as shown in the figure. We will use the first strategy for the part problem. The second strategy will be used in the assembly problem to be done later in the chapter.

## Strategy for Aligning the Part to the Default Axis System

The first feature to be created will be the base feature of the part. We must determine which plane to use to define the first sketch in order to align the part correctly. In the dimensioned drawing defining the part, we can see that the base rests on the X-Z plane (i.e., the **Top Plane**) with the positive X-axis aligned with the long dimension and the positive Z-axis aligned with the short dimension. We therefore want to create the base feature as shown below, with the origin located at the * and the X and Z axes aligned as shown.

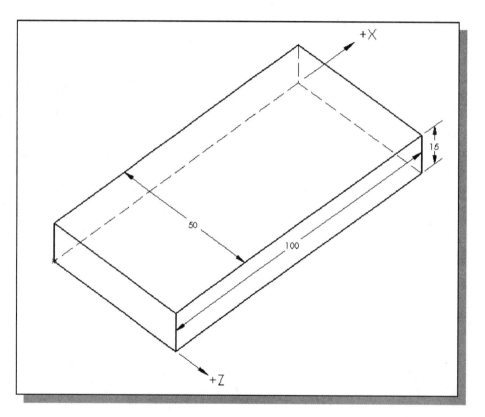

## Creating the Base Feature

1. On your own, start a new part file using the default **Part** template in the *SolidWorks* Templates folder.

2. Select the **Options** icon from the *Menu Bar* to open the *Options* dialog box. Select the **Document Properties** tab.

3. Select **ANSI** in the pull-down selection window under the *Overall drafting standard* panel as shown.

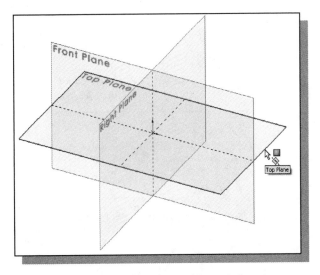

4. Click on the **Units** option. We will use the default **MMGS (millimeter, gram, second)** unit system as instructed in the problem definition.

5. Select **.123** in the *Decimals* spin box for the *Length units* as shown to define the degree of accuracy with which the units will be displayed to 3 decimal places.

 6. Select the **Sketch** button on the *Sketch* toolbar to create a new sketch.

7. Select the **Top** (XZ) **Plane** as the sketch plane for the new sketch.

8. On your own, draw a **rectangle** with one corner coincident with the origin, the long edge aligned with the positive X-axis, and the short edge aligned with the positive Z-axis as shown below.

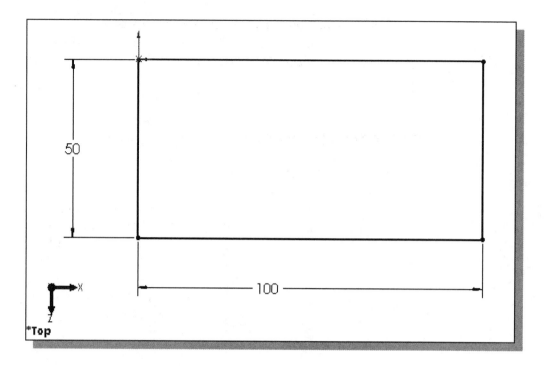

9. Apply the **Smart Dimensions** as shown above.

10. On your own, exit the sketch and create a **Boss Extrude** feature with a height of **15 mm**.

## Creating a New View Orientation

1. Left-click on the **View Orientation** icon on the *Heads-up View* toolbar to reveal the *View Orientation* pull-down menu. Select the **Isometric** command.

2. If necessary, use the *Hide/Show* pull-down menu on the *Heads-up View* toolbar to turn *ON* the origin's visibility.

➢ Notice the axes are aligned correctly relative to the part, but the default isometric view does not correspond to the view orientation used in defining the problem. We will create a new view orientation which better matches the view used in defining the problem (page 15-5).

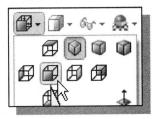

3. Left-click on the **View Orientation** icon on the *Heads-up View* toolbar to reveal the *View Orientation* pull-down menu. Select the **Front** command.

4. Click the right arrow button [→] three times to rotate the view 45°.

5. Click the down arrow button [↓] three times to rotate the view 45°.

➢ The view should appear as shown here. This view orientation corresponds to the one in the problem definition. We will want to return to this view as we continue working on the part. *SolidWorks* allows the user to define a new view orientation for this purpose.

6. Select **Modify** under the *View* pull-down menu and then select **Orientation**. This opens the *Orientation Dialog Box*.

7. In the *Orientation Dialog Box*, select the **New View** button.

8. Enter **Custom** as the name for the new view and click **OK**.

9. Click anywhere in the graphics area to close the *Orientation Dialog Box*.

10. Left-click on the **View Orientation** icon on the *Heads-up View* toolbar to reveal the *View Orientation* pull-down menu. Notice the *Custom* view we created now appears as an option.

## Completing the Part

1.  On your own, create the second extruded boss and the fillet feature as shown below.

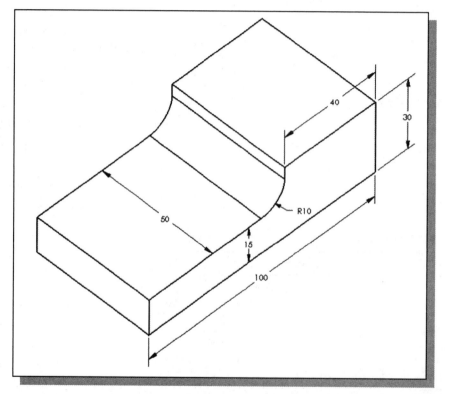

➢  We will now create the reference geometry needed to create the inclined feature. To create an inclined reference plane, we must select an existing plane and an axis of rotation. The strategy we will use for creating the inclined reference plane involves three steps: (1) create a vertical reference plane offset from the left face by 30 mm; (2) create a reference axis at the intersection of the offset plane and the top face of the base feature; and (3) create the inclined reference plane by rotating the top face of the base feature about the reference axis.

2.  Select the **Reference Geometry** command from the *Features* toolbar, and select the **Plane** option from the pull-down menu.

3. Move the cursor over the left face of the base feature as shown below. Click once with the **left-mouse-button** to select the face.

4. Notice the face, called **Face<1>**, appears in the *First Reference* panel of the *Plane PropertyManager*, and the **Offset Distance** option is automatically selected.

5. Enter **30 mm** as the offset distance.

6. Check the **Flip** option box.

7. Click **OK** in the *ProperyManager* to accept the settings and create the new reference plane.

8. Press the **[Esc]** key to unselect the new plane.

9. In the *Features* toolbar, select the **Reference Geometry** command by left-clicking the icon.

10. In the pull-down option menu of the **Reference Geometry** command, select the **Axis** option.

11. In the *Selections* panel of the *Axis PropertyManager*, select the **Two Planes** option. (We will define the reference axis as the intersection of the offset reference plane and top face of the base feature.)

12. Select the offset reference plane **Plane1** in the *Design Tree* (expand the *Design Tree* in the graphics area if necessary) and the **top face of the base feature** in the graphics area.

13. Click **OK** in the *PropertyManager* to create the new reference axis.

14. Press the [**Esc**] key to ensure no features are selected.

15. Select the **Reference Geometry** command from the *Features* toolbar, and select the **Plane** option from the pull-down menu.

16. Select **Axis1** (the reference axis created above) as the *First Reference* and the **top face of the base feature** as the *Second Reference*.

17. In the *Second Reference* panel of the *Plane PropertyManager*, select the **At Angle** option button.

18. Enter **45 deg** as the angle in the *PropertyManager*. The preview of the new plane should appear as in the figure below.

19. Click **OK** in the *PropertyManager* to create the new reference plane.

➤ We now have the correct inclined reference plane on which to sketch the inclined feature.

20. On your own, create the sketch shown using the inclined reference plane **Plane2** as the sketch plane. (**NOTE:** Use the **Normal to** view orientation to view the sketch plane as shown.)

21. Left-click on the **View Orientation** icon on the *Heads-up View* toolbar to reveal the *View Orientation* pull-down menu. Select the **Custom** view that we created earlier.

22. On your own, create an **Extruded Boss** feature as shown below. (**NOTE:** Use the **Reverse Direction** option if necessary. Use the **Up To Next** option for the *end condition*.)

23. On your own, create a sketch as shown using the inclined face as the sketch plane.

24. Create the 10 mm **Extruded Boss** feature as shown below.

25. On your own, create the extruded cut features necessary to complete the part. (See page 15-5 for dimensions.)

26. On your own, save the part with the filename **Problem1.SLDPRT**.

## Selecting the Material and Viewing the Mass Properties

1. Right-click on the **Material** icon in the *FeatureManger Design Tree* and select **Edit Material** from the pop-up menu.

2. In the *Material* pop-up window, select **Ductile Iron** (in the Iron folder) as the material type. Notice the density listed in the *Material Property* table is 0.0071 $g/mm^3$, as required in the problem statement.

**Material**

- ☐ ⋮ SolidWorks DIN Materials
- ☐ ⋮ SolidWorks Materials
  - ☐ ⋮ Steel
  - ☐ ⋮ Iron
    - ⋮ **Ductile Iron**
    - ⋮ Ductile Iron (SN)
    - ⋮ Gray Cast Iron
    - ⋮ Gray Cast Iron (SN)
    - ⋮ Malleable Cast Iron
  - ☐ ⋮ Aluminium Alloys
  - ☐ ⋮ Copper Alloys
  - ☐ ⋮ Titanium Alloys
  - ☐ ⋮ Zinc Alloys
  - ☐ ⋮ Other Alloys
  - ☐ ⋮ Plastics
  - ☐ ⋮ Other Metals
  - ☐ ⋮ Other Non-metals
  - ☐ ⋮ Generic Glass Fibers
  - ☐ ⋮ Carbon Fibers
  - ☐ ⋮ Silicons
  - ☐ ⋮ Rubber
  - ☐ ⋮ Woods

| Properties | Appearance | CrossHatch | Custom | Application Data | Favorites |

Material properties

Materials in the default library can not be edited. You must first copy the material to a custom library to edit it.

| Model Type: | Linear Elastic Isotropic |
| Units: | SI - N/m^2 (Pa) |
| Category: | Iron |
| Name: | Ductile Iron |
| Description: | |
| Source: | |

| Property | Value | Units |
|---|---|---|
| Elastic Modulus | 1.2e+011 | N/m^2 |
| Poissons Ratio | 0.31 | N/A |
| Shear Modulus | 7.7e+010 | N/m^2 |
| Density | 7100 | kg/m^3 |
| Tensile Strength | 861695000 | N/m^2 |
| Compressive Strength in X | | N/m^2 |

3. Click **Apply** to select the material and **Close** the *Material* window.

4. Select the **Mass Properties** option on the *Tools* pull-down menu.

| Tools | Window | Help |

- DrawCompare...
- SolidWorks Explorer...
- DriveWorksXpress...
- DFMXpress...
- SimulationXpress...
- FloXpress...
- Format Painter...
- Invert Selection
- Sketch Entities ▶
- Sketch Tools ▶
- Sketch Settings ▶
- Blocks ▶
- Spline Tools ▶
- Dimensions ▶
- Relations ▶
- Measure...
- Mass Properties...
- Section Properties

➢ The *Mass Properties* window is displayed.  Notice the *Output coordinate system* is the default system.

**Mass Properties**

| Print... | Copy | Close | Options... | Recalculate |

Output coordinate system: -- default --

Selected items:  Problem1.SLDPRT

☑ Include hidden bodies/components

☑ Show output coordinate system in corner of window

☐ Assigned mass properties

Mass properties of Problem1 ( Part Configuration - Default )

Output  coordinate System: -- default --

Density = 0.01 grams per  cubic millimeter

Mass = 822.82 grams

Volume = 115889.63  cubic millimeters

Surface area = 19824.98  square millimeters

Center of mass: ( millimeters )
    X = 56.85
    Y = 14.54
    Z = 25.00

Principal axes of inertia and principal moments of inertia: ( grams *  square millimeters )
Taken at the center of mass.
    Ix = (0.99, 0.10, 0.00)      Px = 225478.37
    Iy = (0.00, 0.00, -1.00)      Py = 637997.01
    Iz = (-0.10, 0.99, 0.00)      Pz = 709605.50

Moments of inertia: ( grams *  square millimeters )
Taken at the center of mass and aligned with the output coordinate system.
    Lxx = 230326.28        Lxy = 48202.71        Lxz = 0.05
    Lyx = 48202.71         Lyy = 704757.60       Lyz = 0.01
    Lzx = 0.05             Lzy = 0.01            Lzz = 637997.01

Moments of inertia: ( grams *  square millimeters )
Taken at the output coordinate system.
    Ixx = 918641.86        Ixy = 728492.82       Ixz = 1169343.44
    Iyx = 728492.82        Iyy = 3877912.53      Iyz = 299181.76
    Izx = 1169343.44       Izy = 299181.76       Izz = 3470946.90

➢ Notice the *Mass* is **822.82 grams**.

➢ Notice the *Center of mass* is:
   **X = 56.85 mm**
   **Y = 14.53 mm**
   **Z = 25.00 mm**

➢ Look again at the problem on page 15-5.  Note that the *Center of mass* coordinates above are based on the correct origin and along the correct X, Y, Z directions.

➢ Notice that *Moments of Inertia* are also reported.

➢ Look at the part in the graphics area. (Minimize the *Mass Properties* window if necessary.)

➢ Notice the center of mass and the principal axes are displayed. On your own, view the part from different directions and observe the location of the center of mass.

➢ Also displayed are the origin and coordinate axes used as the basis for the calculated properties. Verify that we have successfully created our part in the correct orientation based on the problem statement. The values for the center of mass in the *Mass Properties* dialog box therefore represent the correct values for the problem as stated.

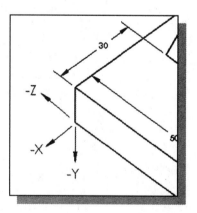

5.  **Close** the *Mass Properties* window.

6.  On your own, save the part with the filename ***Problem1.SLDPRT***.

➢ We have successfully completed the problem. The part was created using the coordinate axes defined in the problem statement and the mass and center of mass were obtained. The *SolidWorks* **Mass Properties** tool provides an efficient method to obtain properties of parts and/or assemblies with complex shapes.

# The Assembly Problem

We will model the assembly shown below and use the **Mass Properties** tool to determine the mass and center of mass of the assembly.  The problem is presented below in a manner similar to that encountered on the CSWA exam.

Build the assembly shown.

It contains two **Brackets** and two **Rods**.

Unit system:  MMGS (millimeter, gram, second)

Assembly origin:  as shown.

**Brackets**:  A dimensioned figure appears to the right (holes through all).  The 1 mm radius notch is semicircular and located with its center 25 mm from the bottom edge of the bracket. Material:  1060 Alloy; Density = 0.0027 g/mm$^3$.

**Rods**:  10 mm in diameter and 150 mm long, with 1mm x 45° chamfers at each end. Material:  201 Annealed Stainless Steel (SS); Density = 0.00786 g/mm$^3$.

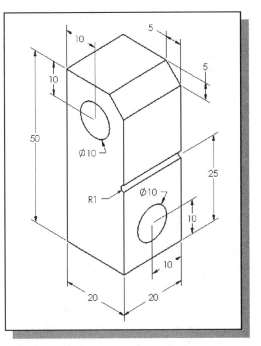

What is the overall mass of the assembly in grams?

What is the center of mass of the assembly?

➢ Before starting to build the model, it is important to select a strategy for controlling the origin and orientation of the X, Y, and Z axes since the center of mass must be defined relative to a known reference system.   The axis directions are defined in the drawing.  We will build the part independent of this constraint and, after the part is complete, create a **reference coordinate system** aligned with the part as shown in the figure.

## Creating the Parts

1. On your own, start a new part file using the default **Part** template in the *SolidWorks* Templates folder.

2. Select the **Options** icon from the *Menu Bar* to open the *Options* dialog box.   Select the **Document Properties** tab.

3. On your own, set the *Overall drafting standard* to **ANSI** and the *Units* to the default **MMGS (millimeter, gram, second)** unit system as instructed in the problem definition.

4. On your own, create the *Bracket* using the dimensions shown in the figure in the previous section.  Build the part so that the isometric view appears as shown.

➢ The axis alignment is not the same as in the problem definition.  We will address this later using the Reference Coordinate System tool.

5. Right-click on the **Material** icon in the *FeatureManger Design Tree* and select **Edit Material** from the pop-up menu.

6. In the *Material* pop-up window, select **1060 Alloy** (in the Aluminum Alloys folder) as the material type.

7. Save the part with the filename ***Bracket.SLDPRT***.

8. On your own, start a new part file using the default **Part** template in the *SolidWorks* Templates folder, set the *Overall drafting standard* to **ANSI** and the *Units* to the default **MMGS (millimeter, gram, second)** unit system.

9. On your own, create the *Rod* using the description in the previous section. Build the part so that the isometric view appears as shown. (**HINT:** Draw a circle on the Front Plane and extrude.)

10. On your own, set the material to **201 Annealed Stainless Steel (SS)** (in the Steel folder).

11. Save the part with the filename ***Rod.SLDPRT***.

## Creating the Assembly

1. Select the **New** icon with a single click of the left-mouse-button on the *Menu Bar*. The *New SolidWorks Document* dialog box appears.

2. Select the **Templates** tab and select the **Assembly** icon as shown.

3. Click **OK** to open the new Assembly file.

➢ *SolidWorks* opens an assembly file, and automatically opens the *Begin Assembly PropertyManager*. The message "*Select a part or assembly to insert ...*" appears in the *PropertyManager*. *SolidWorks* expects you to insert the first component.

➢ The *Part/Assembly to Insert* panel displays *Open documents*, including the *Bracket* and *Rod* parts.

4. Select the *Bracket* part as the base part for the assembly by clicking on **Bracket** in the *Part/Assembly to Insert* panel. (**NOTE:** If you have closed the *Bracket* part, it will not appear. In that case, click the Browse button and use the browser to open the *Bracket* part file.)

5.  By default, the component is automatically aligned to the origin of the assembly coordinates. Click **OK** in the *PropertyManager* to place the *Bracket* at the origin.

6.  On your own, set the *Overall drafting standard* to **ANSI** and the *Units* to the default **MMGS (millimeter, gram, second)** unit system.
    (**HINT**: Select Tools → Option → Document Properties.)

7.  In the *Assembly* toolbar, select the **Insert Component** command by left-mouse-clicking the icon.

8.  Select the **Rod** part in the *Part/Assembly to Insert* panel. (**NOTE:** If you have closed the *Rod* part, it will not appear. In that case, click the **Browse** button and use the browser to open the *Rod* part file.)

9.  Place the *Rod* in the graphics area as shown in the figure. Click once with the **left-mouse-button** to place the component.

10. In the *Assembly* toolbar, select the **Mate** command by left-mouse-clicking once on the icon.

11. Select the **external cylindrical face** of the *Rod* as the first surface for the Mate, and the **interior cylindrical race** of the *Bracket* as the second face for the Mate, as shown.

12. A Concentric mate is applied by default. Click the **OK** button in the *PropertyManager* to accept the settings and create the **Concentric** mate.

❖ We will now add a **Distance** mate to define the position of the *Rod* relative to the *Bracket* as defined in the problem statement.

13. Rotate the view (e.g., using the arrow keys) to display the reverse side of the *Rod* and *Bracket* as shown below.

14. Select the **edge face** of the ***Rod*** and the **side face** of the ***Bracket*** as shown below.

➢ *SolidWorks* will apply a **Coincident** mate by default. We want to apply a mate which is offset by a specific distance (30 mm as defined by the problem statement).

15. Select the *Distance* option by clicking the **Distance** button in the *Standard Mates* panel of the *PropertyManager*.

16. Enter **30 mm** as the distance.

17. Click the **OK** button in the *PropertyManager* to accept the settings and create the **Distance** mate.

18. Click **OK** again (or hit the **[Esc]** key) to exit the Mate command.

19. On your own, return to the **Isometric** view.

20. In the *Assembly* toolbar, select the **Insert Component** command by left-mouse-clicking the icon.

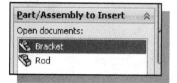

21. Select the *Bracket* part as the base part for the assembly by clicking on **Bracket** in the *Part/Assembly to Insert* panel.

22. Place the *Bracket* in the graphics area as shown in the figure. Click once with the **left-mouse-button** to place the component.

23. In the *Assembly* toolbar, select the **Mate** command by left-mouse-clicking once on the icon.

24. Select the **external cylindrical face** of the ***Rod*** as the first surface for the Mate, and the **interior cylindrical race** of ***Bracket<2>*** as the second face for the Mate, as shown.

25. An Anti-Aligned Concentric mate is applied by default. On your own, select the **Aligned** option at the bottom of the *Standard Mates* panel and observe the effect on the assembly.

26. Select the **Anti-Aligned** option. Look at the drawing in the problem statement to verify that it is the Anti-Aligned option that is required.

27. Click the **OK** button in the *PropertyManager* to accept the settings and create the **Anti-Aligned Concentric** mate.

❖ We will now add a Distance mate to define the position of *Bracket<2>* relative to *Bracket<1>* as defined in the problem statement.

28. Select the **face** of *Bracket<1>* as shown.

29. Rotate the view and select the **face** of *Bracket<2>* as shown.

30. Select the *Distance* option by clicking the **Distance** button in the *Standard Mates* panel of the *PropertyManager*.

31. Enter **50 mm** as the distance.

32. Click the **OK** button in the *PropertyManager* to accept the settings and create the **Distance** mate.

❖ We will now add an Angle mate to define the angular orientation of *Bracket<2>* relative to *Bracket<1>* as defined in the problem statement.

33. Select the **face** of *Bracket<1>* and the **face** of *Bracket<2>* as shown below.

34. Select the *Angle* option by clicking the **Angle** button in the *Standard Mates* panel of the *PropertyManager*.

35. Enter **60°** as the angle.

36. Check the **Flip diminsion** box **if necessary** to set the angle as shown in the figure below.

37. Click the **OK** button in the *PropertyManager* to accept the settings and create the **Angle** mate as shown.

38. Click **OK** again (or hit the [**Esc**] key) to exit the Mate command.

39. On your own, use the **Insert Component** command to insert a second *Rod* part.

40. On your own, create a **Concentric** mate to align the *Rod* to *Bracket<2>*.

41. On your own, create a **Distance** mate to define the position of *Rod<2>* relative to *Bracket<2>* as defined in the problem statement.

42. Compare the assembly to the drawing in the problem statement. Note that the locations and orientations of the brackets (particularly the locations of the chamfers and notches) and rods are correct.

43. On your own, save the assembly with the filename *Problem2.SLDASM*.

# Creating a Reference Coordinate System

We have created the assembly without aligning it with the origin and coordinate axes defined in the problem statement. In order to calculate the center of mass relative to the correct origin and coordinate axes we will create a Reference Coordinate System.

➤ The Reference Coordinate System will be defined to be aligned with the edges of the base bracket (*Bracket<1>* in our assembly) as shown in the figure defining the problem.

1. In the *Assembly* toolbar (or the *Features* toolbar), select the **Reference Geometry** command by left-clicking the icon.

2. In the pull-down option menu of the Reference Geometry command, select the **Coordinate System** option.

3. The *Coordinate System PropertyManager* opens with the *Origin* selection window active. Select the **lower right corner** of *Bracket<1>* as the origin, as shown.

➤ The origin selection appears in the *Property-Manager* as **Vertex<1>@Bracket-1**.

4. The *X-axis* selection window is now active. We want to align the X-axis with the **bottom edge on the right face** of *Bracket<1>*. Move the cursor over the edge and click once with the left-mouse-button to **select** it.

➢ The X-axis selection appears in the *PropertyManager* as Edge<1>@Bracket-1. Look at the coordinate icon which is now attached to the newly defined reference origin. Notice the X-axis in the figure is aligned with the correct edge, but the positive X-axis points in the wrong direction.

5. In the *PropertyManager*, select the **Reverse X Axis Direction** option by clicking once with the left-mouse-button on the toggle button located to the left of the *X axis* selection window (if necessary).

6. Verify that the X-axis is now aligned with the correct edge and points in the correct direction.

7. The *Y-axis* selection window is now active. We want to align the Y-axis with the **right edge of the right face** of ***Bracket<1>***. Move the cursor over the edge and click once with the left-mouse-button to **select** it.

8. The Y-axis selection appears in the *PropertyManager* as Edge<2>@Bracket-1. Verify that the Y-axis is aligned with the correct edge, and the positive Y-axis points in the correct direction. (If the positive Y-axis points in the wrong direction, use the **Reverse Y Axis Direction** option to correct it.)

9. The origin and coordinate axes are now aligned as defined in the problem statement. Click **OK** in the *PropertyManager* to accept the setting and create the **Reference Coordinate System**.

➤ Notice the **Reference Coordinate System** appears in the *FeatureManager Design Tree* as **Coordinate System1**, and that the reference axes correspond to the axes defined in the problem statement. We are now ready to calculate the *mass properties*.

## View the Mass Properties

1. Select the **Mass Properties** option on the *Tools* pull-down menu.

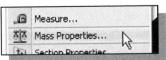

2. The *Mass Properties* window is displayed. Notice the *Output coordinate system* is the default system.

➤ In the graphics area, the default coordinate system in shown. The values appearing in the *Mass Properties* window were calculated relative to this coordinate system. These are **not** the results we need for the solution to the problem.

➤ We must change the *Output coordinate system* to the **Reference Coordinate System** we created.

3.  Inside the *Mass Property* window, **left-click** on the arrow at the right end of the *Output coordinate system:* selection window, and select **Coordinate System1** from the selection list.

➢ Coordinate System1 is now the basis for the mass property calculations. Notice the calculated values for the center of mass (and other properties) change to those for the new coordinate system.

➢ Notice the coordinate system displayed in the graphics area is the correct system for the problem.

**Mass Properties**

Print...    Copy    Close    Options...    Recalculate

Output coordinate system:    Coordinate System1

Selected items:    Problem2.SLDASM

☑ Include hidden bodies/components

☑ Show output coordinate system in corner of window

☐ Assigned mass properties

Mass properties of Problem2 ( Assembly Configuration - Default )

Output coordinate System: Coordinate System1

Mass = 274.25 grams

Volume = 56657.28 cubic millimeters

Surface area = 21017.30 square millimeters

Center of mass: ( millimeters )
    X = -56.76
    Y = 53.95
    Z = -14.95

Principal axes of inertia and principal moments of inertia: ( grams * square millimeters )
Taken at the center of mass.
    Ix = (-0.79, 0.62, 0.02)    Px = 244627.83
    Iy = (-0.58, -0.73, -0.37)                    Py = 503768.67
    Iz = (-0.22, -0.30, 0.93)    Pz = 675431.89

➢ Notice the *Mass* is

**274.25 grams**

➢ Notice the *Center of mass* is:

**X = -56.76 mm**
**Y = 53.95 mm**
**Z = -14.95 mm**

4. **Close** the *Mass Properties* window.

5. On your own, save the part with the filename ***Problem2.SLDASM***.

➢ We have successfully completed the problem. The correct alignment of the coordinate system was accomplished through the creation of a Reference Coordinate System.

➢ The *SolidWorks* **Reference Coordinate System** and **Mass Properties** tools can be used in combination to obtain mass properties of complex parts and assemblies relative to a specific coordinate system.

## Questions:

1. How do we save a new *View Orientation* for future use?

2. Describe the effect of using the *Up to Next* end condition for an extruded boss feature.

3. How can we view the mass of a part or assembly?

4. Describe the steps in creating a **Reference Coordinate System**.

5. What mass properties are dependent on the selection of the output coordinate system?

6. What mass properties are independent of the selection of the output coordinate system?

7. How do we control the output coordinate system used in calculating mass properties?

8. How can we apply an assembly mate establishing an offset distance between two planes or faces?

## Exercises:

1. Build the part shown below.
   Unit system: IPS (inch, pound, second)
   Part origin: As shown.
   Part material: AISI 1020
   Density: 0.285406 lb/in$^3$

What is the overall mass of the part in pounds?

What is the center of mass of the part?


Answer:

Mass:
   18.58 pounds

Center of mass:
   X = -6.07 inches
   Y = 1.91 inches
   Z = -1.98 inches

2.  Build the assembly in *SolidWorks*.  The assembly includes 8 components – 1 base, 1 jaw, 2 keys, 1 screw, 1 handle rod, 2 handle knobs.
    Use the IPS (inch, pound, second) unit system.

**Base:** A dimensioned figure appears to the right.  The 1.5 inch wide and 1.25 inch wide slots are cut through the entire base.
Material:  Gray Cast Iron
Density = 0.260116 lb/in$^3$

**Jaw:** A dimensioned figure appears to the right. The shoulder of the jaw rests on the flat surface of the base and the jaw opening is set to 1.5 inches.
Material: Gray Cast Iron
Density = 0.260116 lb/in$^3$

**Key:** 0.1875 inch H x 0.375 inch W x 1.75 inch L. The keys fit into the slots on the jaw with the edge faces flush as shown in the sub-assembly to the right.
Material: Alloy Steel
Density = 0.27818 lb/in$^3$.

**Screw:** A dimensioned figure appears to the right. There is one chamfered edge (0.0625 inch x 45°). The flat ⌀ 0.75″ edge of the screw is flush with the corresponding recessed ⌀ 0.75 face on the jaw.
Material: Alloy Steel
Density = 0.27818 lb/in$^3$

**Handle Rod:** ∅ 0.375″ x 5.0″ L. The handle rod passes through the hole in the screw and is rotated to an angle of 30° with the horizontal as shown in the assembly view. The flat ∅ 0.375″ edges of the handle rod are flush with the corresponding recessed ∅ 0.735 faces on the handle knobs.
Material: Alloy Steel
Density = 0.27818 lb/in$^3$.

**Handle Knob:** A dimensioned figure appears to the right. There are two chamfered edges (0.0625 inch x 45°).The handle knobs are attached to each end of the handle rod. The resulting overall length of the handle with knobs is 5.50″. The handle is aligned with the screw so that the outer edge of the upper knob is 2.0″ from the central axis of the screw.
Material: Alloy Steel
Density = 0.27818 lb/in$^3$

What is the mass of the assembly?

What is the center of mass of the assembly with respect to the coordinate system illustrated in the assembly view?

Answer:

Mass:
    17.52 pounds

Center of mass:
    X = 1.74 inches
    Y = 1.75 inches
    Z = 3.98 inches

# Chapter 16
# Assembly Modeling with the LEGO®
# MINDSTORMS® NXT Set

## Learning Objectives

♦ **Using the SolidWorks CommandManager
   User Interface**

♦ **Creating an Assembly using parts from the
   LEGO® MINDSTORMS® NXT Set**

♦ **Understand and Perform proper
   constraints in Assembly**

♦ **Adjust Components' Orientations**

♦ **Using Subassemblies in Assemblies**

## Introduction

The rapid development in computer hardware technology, during the past few decades, has brought many changes in the practice of engineering in general. Many areas that were traditionally identified as electrical engineering or mechanical engineering are now multidisciplinary, integrating digital electronics, kinematics analysis, and computing together. Additionally, the use of microcontrollers and embedded systems has become inevitable in almost every engineering field. Given these developments, engineering education has also witnessed significant changes, such as adapting to project-oriented courses that emphasize real world applications, and the use of new educational tools such as robot kits.

The use of robot kits provides many benefits through assembling, building, and following instructions which help develop fine motor skills and hand-eye coordination. Students are exposed to multiple subjects such as mechanics, electronics, and programming. By working together to create robots that perform exciting challenges, students also gain valuable critical thinking, problem-solving and team-building skills. Students can also participate in several national/world robot competitions held annually, which can provide a strong sense of accomplishment.

In this lesson, we will create a *WaddleBot* assembly model using the **LEGO**® **MINDSTORMS**® **NXT Set**. This design was created by *Steve Nelson* and further improved by *Devin Hunter* of **Oregon Robotics and Outreach Program**. (Note that additional information and resources can be found at the website **www.ortop.org**.) The modeling process can be used as part of a design process, to simulate and confirm a design, prior to the actual construction of the project. All of the required parts and subassemblies have been modeled in SolidWorks, and can be downloaded from the SDC Publications website: **www.SDCpublications.com/downloads/978-1-58503-633-2.zip**.

## The *WaddleBot* Assembly (Design used with special permission from **Oregon Robotics and Outreach Program**).

## Modeling Strategy

## Creating the NXT Motor Assembly

1. Select the **SolidWorks** option on the *Start* menu or select the **SolidWorks** icon on the desktop to start *SolidWorks*. The *SolidWorks* main window will appear on the screen.

- We are now ready to assemble the components. We will start by assembling the **NXT Motor** parts into a **Motor** subassembly. A subassembly is a unit assembled separately but designed to fit with other units in a manufactured product. Subassemblies are commonly used to help manage complex designs and when the same configurations are used multiple times in a design. Note that a subassembly behaves just the same as a part within an assembly; i.e., a subassembly possesses only six degrees of freedom, just like a regular part, and any moving parts within a subassembly become fully locked inside the main assembly.

2. Select the **New** icon on the *Menu Bar* with a single click of the left-mouse-button as shown.

3. Select the **Templates** tab and select the **Assembly** icon as shown. (If the *New SolidWorks Document* window is in *Novice* mode, simply select the **Assembly** icon.)

4. Click **OK** to open the new **Assembly** file.

**IMPORTANT NOTE:** The Solidworks *CommandManager* provides an alternate method for displaying the most commonly used toolbars (see page 1-13 for a more complete description). We will use the *CommandManager* in this lesson.

5. To turn **ON** the *CommandManager*, right click on any toolbar and toggle the *CommandManager ON* by selecting it at the top of the pop-up menu.

- Note that the *CommandManager* has toolbars embedded in it based on the document type. In the Assembly document, the appropriate toolbars appear with the Assembly toolbar active as shown below.

- To the left side of the graphics area, note that the *Begin Assembly PropertyManager* is displayed. *SolidWorks* expects us to insert parts and/or assemblies into the new assembly model. This option can be disabled by changing the settings in the *Options* panel near the bottom of the *PropertyManager*.

6. In the *Part/Assembly to Insert* panel of the *Begin Assembly PropertyManager*, click on the **Browse** button to open parts to be inserted into the current assembly.

7. In the *Open* dialog box, select the **NXT-Motor-Base** part as shown.

8. Click on the **Open** button to insert the selected part into the current assembly.

9. Place a copy of the **NXT-Motor-Base** part near the center of the graphics area.

- Inside the *FeatureManager Design Tree*, the retrieved parts are listed in their corresponding order. The **(f)** symbol in front of the **NXT-Motor-Base** part signifies the component is fixed and all *six degrees of freedom* are restricted. The number behind the name is used to identify the number of copies of the same component in the assembly model.

10. In the *Assembly* toolbar on the *Command-Manager* area, select the **Insert Components** command as shown.

11. In the *Part/Assembly to Insert* panel of the *Property-Manager*, click on the **Browse** button to open parts to be inserted into the current model.

12. In the *Open* dialog box, select the **NXT-Motor-Connector** model as shown.

13. Click on the **Open** button to insert the selected part into the current assembly.

14. Place a copy of the *NXT-Motor-Connector* part to the right side of the graphics area.

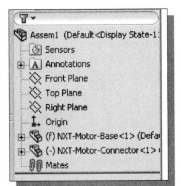

- Inside the *FeatureManager Design Tree*, the inserted parts are listed in their corresponding order. The **(-)** symbol in front of the *NXT-Motor-Connector* signifies the component is not fixed and therefore all *six degrees of freedom* are available.

## Apply Assembly Mates

1. In the *Assembly* toolbar, select the **Mate** command by left-mouse-clicking once on the icon.

2. Select the **top surface** of the *NXT-Motor-Connector* as the first surface for the mate.

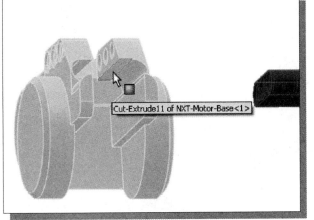

3. Click on the **inside horizontal flat surface** of the *NXT-Motor-Base* part as the second surface to apply the Mate command.

4. Click on the **Finish Mate** button on the pop-up toolbar to accept the default settings and create the Anti-Aligned, Coincident mate.

5. Click on **the inside vertical face** of the *NXT-Motor-Base* part as the first surface to apply a new mate.

6. Select the **back surface** of the *NXT-Motor-Connector* part, as the second surface for the Mate command.

7. In the *PropertyManager*, click on the **OK** button to accept the default settings and create the Anti-Aligned, Coincident mate.

- An alternate method to apply a mate is to first select the *type* of mate and then select the required features.

8. In the *Standard Mates* panel of the *Property-Manager* select **Concentric** as the mate *Type*.

9.  Select the **inside cylindrical surface** of the *NXT-Motor-Base* part, as the first item for the Concentric Mate command.

10. Click on the **inside left cylindrical surface** of the *NXT-Motor-Connector* part as the second item to apply the Mate command.

11. Click on the **Finish Mate** button to accept the selection for the Concentric mate.

❖ Next, we will assemble a copy of the *NXT-Motor-Housing* part to the assembly model.

12. In the *Assembly* toolbar on the *Command-Manager* area, select the **Insert Components** command as shown.

13. In the *Part/Assembly to Insert* panel of the *Property-Manager*, click on the **Browse** button to open parts to be inserted into the current model.

14. In the *Open* dialog box, select the **NXT-Motor-Housing** part as shown.

15. Click on the **Open** button to insert the selected model into the current assembly.

16. Place a copy of the **NXT-Motor-Housing** part to the right side of the graphics area.

17. Click on the **inside vertical face** of the *NXT-Motor-Base* part.

18. Press down the [**Ctrl**] key and select the **back surface** of the *NXT-Motor-Housing* part.

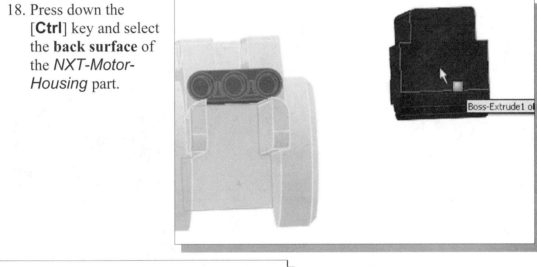

19. In the popup option list, select the **Mate** command.

• Note that *SolidWorks* provides us with a very flexible user-interface. Besides activating the **Mate** command first, it is also feasible to **pre-select** the surfaces to be mated first.

20. In the pop-up toolbar, click on the **Flip Mate Alignment** option. Note the active mate is set to **Coincident**.

21. Click on the **Finish Mate** button on the pop-up toolbar to accept the settings and create the Anti-Aligned, Coincident mate.

22. On your own, apply two more Mate constraints to fully assemble the *Motor-Housing* part as show.

## Completing the Subassembly

1.  In the *Assembly* toolbar on the *Command-Manager* area, select the **Insert Components** command as shown.

2.  In the *Part/Assembly to Insert* panel of the *Property-Manager*, click on the **Browse** button to open parts to be inserted into the current assembly.

3.  On your own, place a copy of the **NXT-Motor-Drive** part and **NXT-Motor-Jack** part next to the assembly.

4.  On your own, assemble the *NXT-Motor-Drive* and the *NXT-Motor-Jack* parts as shown.

5.  Select the **Save** icon with a single click of the left-mouse-button in the *Menu Bar* as shown.

6.  Save the assembly as **NXT-Motor.SLDASM** as shown.

## Starting the Main Assembly

1. Left-click on the arrow next to the **New** button on the *Menu Bar* to reveal additional options and select the **Make Assembly from Part/Assembly** command as shown.

2. The *New SolidWorks Document* window appears with the default Assembly template selected. Left-click the **OK** button to create the new Assembly document.

3. In the *Part/Assembly to Insert* panel of the *Property Manager*, the **NXT-Motor** assembly is displayed in the open documents list. In *SolidWorks*, opened parts and subassemblies can be quickly inserted into an assembly.

4. Place a copy of the **NXT-Motor** assembly, by clicking with the **left-mouse-button**, near the center of the screen.

- Inside the *FeatureManager Design Tree*, the retrieved parts/assemblies are listed in their corresponding order. The **(f)** symbol in front of the **NXT-Motor** assembly signifies the component is fixed and all *six degrees of freedom* are restricted.

- Note that the *NXT-Motor* assembly is currently up-side-down for the *WaddleBot* design.

## Adjusting the Orientation of a Fixed Component

- The orientation of the first component of an assembly, the fixed component, can be adjusted by applying additional mates.

1. Click once with the **right-mouse-button** on the **NXT-Motor** assembly in the *FeatureManager Design Tree* to show the option list.

2. Select **Float** to allow the component to be adjusted. Note the fixed symbol is removed in the *Design Tree*.

3. Expand the item list by clicking on the [**+**] symbol in front of the **NXT-Motor** assembly.

4. Select the **Top Plane** of the *NXT-Motor* assembly from the *Feature Manager* as shown.

5. Press down the [**Ctrl**] key and select the **Top Plane** of the current assembly (*Assem2* here) as shown.

6. Select the **Mate** command from the pop-up option list as shown.

7. Click on the **Anti-aligned** icon to flip the direction of the alignment.

8. Click **OK** to accept the applied mate.

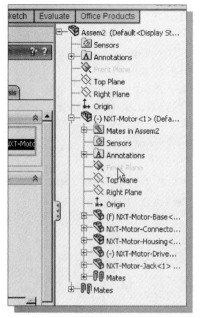

9.  In the graphics area, expand the *Design Tree* by clicking on the [**+**] symbol in front of the **Assem** assembly icon. If necessary, also expand the *NXT-Motor* assembly item list.

10. Select the **Front Plane** of the current assembly (*Assem2* here) as shown.

11. Press down the [**Ctrl**] key and select the **Front Plane** of the *NXT-Motor* assembly from the *Feature Manager* as shown.

12. Click on the **Flip Mate Alignment** icon in the pop-up *Mate* toolbar to flip the direction of the alignment.

13. In the pop-up *Mate* toolbar, click on the **Finish Mate** button as shown.

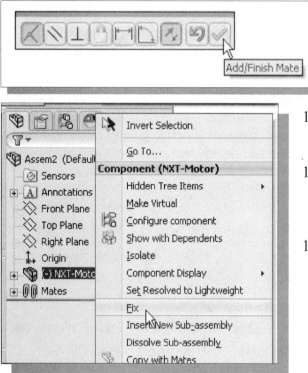

14. Exit the Mate command by clicking on the **OK** button.

15. Click once with the **right-mouse-button** on the *NXT-Motor* component to show the option list.

16. Select **Fix** to lock all DOF of the component. Note the fixed symbol re-appeared in the *Design Tree*.

*   Note that each assembly also contains a set of datum features (e.g., planes), just like a regular part. These datum features can be used to align the different components of the design.

## Adding the Next Components for the Chassis

1. In the *Assembly* toolbar, select the **Insert Components** command as shown.

2. In the *Part/Assembly to Insert* panel, click on the **Browse** button.

3. On your own, place a copy of the **beam 11-module** part and two copies of the **peg 1-module** part next to the assembly.

4. In the *Assembly* toolbar, click the **arrow** below the Move Component button to reveal additional options, and select the **Rotate Component** command by left-mouse-clicking once on the icon.

5. Select one of the **peg 1-module** parts.

6. Using the left-mouse-button, drag and drop the selected part to rotate the part until it is about parallel to the *NXT-Motor* assembly.

7. Click on the **OK** button to end the **Rotate** command.

8. In the graphics area, **pre-select** the two surfaces on the *peg 1-module* and the *NXT-Motor* (remember to use the [**Ctrl**] key), and choose the **Mate** command from the pop-up option menu as shown in the figures.

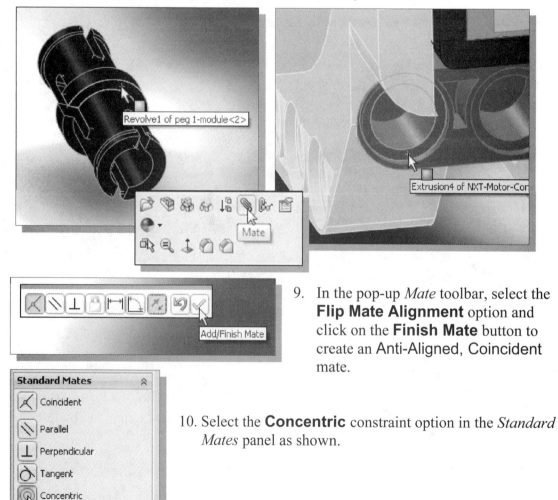

9. In the pop-up *Mate* toolbar, select the **Flip Mate Alignment** option and click on the **Finish Mate** button to create an Anti-Aligned, Coincident mate.

10. Select the **Concentric** constraint option in the *Standard Mates* panel as shown.

11. Select the corresponding **cylindrical surfaces** and assemble one copy of the *peg 1-module* part on *NXT-Motor* assembly as shown.

12. On your own, repeat the above steps and assemble the *beam 11-module* part and the other *peg 1-module* as shown in the figure below.

13. In the *Assembly* toolbar, select the **Insert Components** command as shown.

14. In the *Part/Assembly to Insert* panel, confirm that the *NXT-Motor* assembly is highlighted. If it is not highlighted, click once with the left-mouse-button to select it.

15. Place another copy of the *NXT-Motor* assembly to the left of the current assembly model as shown.

16. In the *Assembly* toolbar, select the **Rotate Component** command by left-mouse-clicking once on the icon.

17. On your own, rotate the second copy of the *NXT-Motor* assembly so that it is about in the same orientation of the first copy.

18. In the *Assembly* toolbar, select the **Mate** command by left-mouse-clicking once on the icon.

19. Select the **Coincident** mate option in the *Standard Mates* list as shown.

20. **Align** the two *NXT-Motor* assemblies by selecting the corresponding flat surfaces as shown.

21. On your own, apply two more mates to assemble the *NXT-Motor* subassembly as shown.

## Assemble the Frame and Chassis

1. In the *Assembly* toolbar, select the **Insert Components** command as shown.

2. In the *Part/Assembly to Insert* panel, click on the **Browse** button.

3. On your own, place a copy of the ***axle-8***, ***bushing***, ***bushing half, beam 3-module*** parts and two copies of the ***peg 1-module*** part next to the assembly.

4. First, assemble the two ***peg 1-module*** parts as shown.

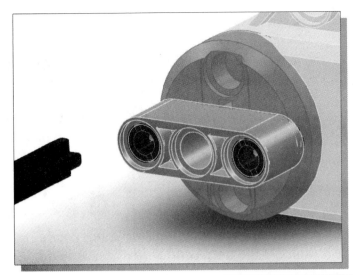

5. Assemble the **beam 3-module** part to the assembly as shown.

6. Complete the assembly of the **bushing**, **bushing half** and **axle-8** as shown.

7. On your own, repeat the above steps and assemble a second set of the axle-bushing parts to the other *NXT-Motor* subassembly as shown.

## Completing the Frame and Chassis

1. In the *Assembly* toolbar, select the **Insert Components** command as shown.

2. In the *Part/Assembly to Insert* panel, click on the **Browse** button.

3. On your own, place a copy of the **beam 15-module**, **peg half-axle**, **cross block 3-module** parts and two copies of the **peg 3-module** part next to the assembly.

4. Assemble the two copies of **peg 3-module** to the assembly as shown.

5.  Assemble the ***beam 15-module***, ***peg half-axle*** and ***cross block 3-module***
    parts to the assembly as shown.

6.  On your own, repeat the above steps and assemble a second set of the beam-peg-
    cross block parts as shown.  Then insert and assemble a ***beam 9-module*** part as
    shown.

## Assemble the Wheels and Front Legs

1. In the *CommandManager* area, select the **Insert Components** command as shown.

2. In the *Insert component* dialog box, click on the **Browse** button.

3. On your own, place one copy of the *Wheel 56X26 VR* assembly, one copy of the *Beam Angular-4x6*, *bushing, peg 1-module* parts, and two copies of the *peg half-axle* part next to the assembly. **NOTE:** You may have to select the file type (e.g., SLDASM), or select All Files, in the browser to locate a file.

4. Assemble the *Wheel 56X26 VR* assembly and the *bushing* part to the wheel axle as shown.

5. Assemble the two copies of the **peg half-axle** model to the two ends of the **Beam Angular-4x6** as shown.

6. Assemble the **peg 1-module** model to the end of the **beam 15-module** part as shown.

7. Assemble the **Beam Angular-4x6** to the assembly as shown.

8. On your own, assemble one copy of the **Beam Angular-3x5**, and **peg 1-module** to the assembly as shown.

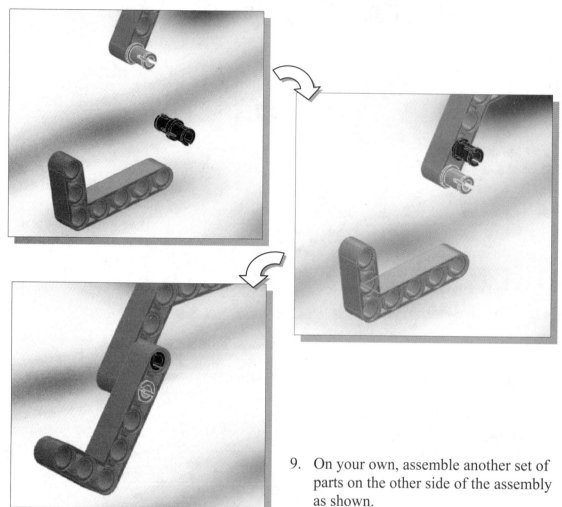

9. On your own, assemble another set of parts on the other side of the assembly as shown.

## Assemble the NXT Intelligent Brick

1. In the *Assembly* toolbar, select the **Insert Components** command as shown.

2. In the *Part/Assembly to Insert* panel, click on the **Browse** button.

3. On your own, place one copy of the **NXT-Brick** assembly and four copies of the **peg 3-module** part next to the assembly.

4. Assemble the **NXT-Brick** to the frame assembly as shown.

## Assemble the Head Subassembly

1.  In the *Assembly* toolbar, select the **Insert Components** command as shown.

2.  In the *Part/Assembly to Insert* panel, click on the **Browse** button.

3.  On your own, place one copy of the **Head** subassembly (which consists of an ultrasonic sensor and a light sensor), one copy each of the **Axle-Extender** and **peg half-axle** parts and two copies of the **bushing** part next to the assembly.

4.  First assemble the **peg half-axle** part to the frame assembly as shown.

5. Next assemble the **Axle-Extender** part to the **peg half-axle** part and the assembly as shown.

6. Now assemble the two **bushing** parts to the frame assembly as shown.

7. Next assemble the **Head** assembly to the frame assembly as shown.

## Assemble the Touch Sensors

1. In the *Assembly* toolbar, select the **Insert Components** command as shown.

2. In the *Part/Assembly to Insert* panel, click on the **Browse** button.

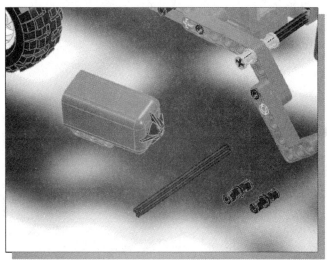

3. On your own, place one copy of the **NXT-Touch** assembly, one copy of the **axle-8** part and two copies of **peg 1-module** part next to the assembly.

4. Assemble the **NXT-Touch** assembly to the assembly as shown.

5. Repeat the above steps and complete the assembly by adding another **NXT-Touch** assembly as shown.

## Conclusion

Design includes all activities involved from the original concept to the finished product. Design is the process by which products are created and modified. For many years designers sought ways to describe and analyze three-dimensional designs without building physical models. With advancements in computer technology, the creation of parametric models on computers offers a wide range of benefits. Parametric models are easier to interpret and can be easily altered. Parametric models can be analyzed using finite element analysis software, and simulation of real-life loads can be applied to the models and the results graphically displayed.

Throughout this text, various modeling techniques have been presented. Mastering these techniques will enable you to create intelligent and flexible solid models. The goal is to make use of the tools provided by SolidWorks and to successfully capture the **DESIGN INTENT** of the product. In many instances, only a single approach to the modeling tasks was presented; you are encouraged to repeat all of the lessons and develop different ways of thinking in accomplishing the same tasks. We have only scratched the surface of SolidWorks' functionality. The more time you spend using the system, the easier it will be to perform computer aided modeling with SolidWorks.

## Questions:

1.  Is there any difference between a regular part and a subassembly when they are placed inside an assembly?

2.  How many subassemblies were used in the tutorial?

3.  Describe two ways to access the **Mate** command.

4.  What is the main difference between an **Aligned** constraint and an **Anti-Aligned** constraint?

5.  How do you control the orientation of the parts before applying constraints in a SolidWorks assembly model?

6.  What are the advantages of using subassembly in assembly modeling?

## Exercise:

Create the *Basic Car Model* as described in the LEGO® MINDSTORMS® Education NXT Set user guide.

**NOTES:**

# INDEX